THE HIDDEN
POWERS of
ANIMALS

THE HIDDEN
POWERS of
ANIMALS

Uncovering the Secrets of Nature

Dr. KARL P. N. SHUKER

Reader's
Digest

The Reader's Digest Association, Inc.
Pleasantville, New York • Montreal

To my good friend
Professor John L. Cloudsley-Thompson,
in sincere gratitude for his encouragement
and interest in all of my varied writings
down through the years.

A Reader's Digest Book
Conceived, edited, and designed by
Marshall Editions Ltd
The Orangery, 161 New Bond Street
London W1S 2UF

First published in Great Britain in 2001 by Marshall Editions Ltd.

MARSHALL EDITIONS STAFF

Editor	Ellen Dupont
Designer	Philip Letsu
Picture Editor	Frances Vargo
Proofreader	Peter Kirkham
Indexer	Helen Smith
Production Controller	Nikki Ingram
Editorial Coordinator	Gillian Thompson
Art Director	Dave Goodman
Editorial Director	Ellen Dupont

READER'S DIGEST PROJECT STAFF

Editor	Marianne Wait
Senior Designer	Judith Carmel
Editorial Manager	Christine R. Guido

READER'S DIGEST ILLUSTRATED REFERENCE BOOKS

Editor-in-Chief	Christopher Cavanaugh
Art Director	Joan Mazzeo
Director, Trade Publishing	Christopher T. Reggio
Editorial Director, Trade	Susan Randol
Senior Design Director, Trade	Elizabeth L. Tunnicliffe

Library of Congress Cataloging in Publication Data
  Shuker, Karl.
    The hidden powers of animals : uncovering the secrets of nature / Karl Shuker.
    p. cm.
    Includes bibliographical references (p.).
    ISBN 0-7621-0328-0
    I. Animal behavior. I. Title.

QL751 .S585 2001
591.5—dc21
                                    2001019689

Jacket Credits t = top; c = center;
b = bottom; l = left; r = right

Front cover photographs:
tl & tc Images Colour Library, tr Natural History
Photographic Agency / Anthony Bannister,
b Telegraph Colour Library / Gail Shumway.

Back cover photographs:
t Oxford Scientific Films / Mahipal Singh,
ct Bruce Coleman Collection / Pacific Stock,
cb BBC Natural History Unit Picture Library /
Alan James, b Oxford Scientific Film / David Tipling

Printed and bound in Germany by Möhndruck
Originated in Leeds, United Kingdom by Grasmere (Digital Imaging) Ltd

1 3 5 7 9 10 8 6 4 2

contents

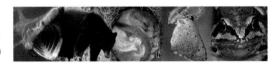

Introduction

Bees have an amazing ability to discern and employ polarized light. They use the position of the sun to navigate their way to and from the hive.

The peacock uses its fan of shimmering, iridescent "eyes" to attract a potential mate. There are many different myths and legends that purport to tell the story of how this majestic bird acquired his dazzling tail.

Since the earliest times, mankind has been fascinated by the animal kingdom, and especially by the exotic, seemingly inexplicable behavior of its members – which in many cases must have appeared decidedly alien, and sometimes even magical, to our ancestors. Consequently, a wealth of folklore and superstition was gradually woven around our fellow creatures in an attempt to reconcile the wonders we witnessed whenever we encountered species other than our own.

In modern times, science has stripped away much of this cloak of fallacy and credulity to unmask some of the mechanisms responsible for such erstwhile animal mysteries as migration, interspecies cohabitation, communication, sensory perception, hibernation, cyclical activity, and survival in extreme environmental conditions, among others. These discoveries have often proved to be even more astonishing than the myths and legends formerly associated with these activities. Moreover, even today there are numerous zoological enigmas and anomalies that still await a satisfactory scientific solution, and so remain exiled within a shadowy netherworld uneasily sandwiched between the natural and supernatural realms. But don't just take my word for it – let this book help you to see for yourself. If you have ever wondered, for example, how birds sustain themselves during their arduous overseas journeys, been fascinated by the sight of a spider weaving its intricate web, puzzled over how animals navigate their way home over long distances, or tried to imagine what your pet is dreaming of, this book will put you in the picture.

The Hidden Powers of Animals features the very latest scientific research on a wide array of topics, from psychic pets to whale strandings, fainting goats to talking apes, and homing horses to waltzing worms. Some of the stories reported here, such as the bizarre case of tadpoles being reared by ants, may seem fantastic, the stuff of science fiction. But they are simply scientific proof that fact can indeed be stranger than fiction.

This book's diverse contents are organized into eleven chapters, each

Hill mynah   **Flying squirrel**   **Blister beetle**

> "We need another and a wiser and perhaps a more mystical concept of animals. Remote from universal nature, and living by complicated artifice, man in civilization surveys the creature through the glass of his knowledge and sees thereby a feather magnified and the whole image in distortion. We patronize them for their incompleteness, for their tragic fate of having taken form so far below ourselves. And therein we err, and greatly err. For the animal shall not be measured by man. In a world older and more complete than ours they move finished and complete, gifted with extensions of the senses we have lost or never attained, living by voices we shall never hear. They are brethren, they are not underlings; they are other nations, caught with ourselves in the net of life and time, fellow prisoners of the splendour and travail of the earth."
>
> **Henry Beston -**
> **The Outermost House (1928)**

dealing with a different facet of animal behavior or a particular skill. Yet unlike many previous books devoted to these fascinating subjects, which tend to be written either for an exclusively academic readership or else take a wildly sensationalist approach, *The Hidden Powers of Animals* has been specially designed to be readily accessible to all readers. It is not intended, therefore, to be a formal work of zoological ethology, but rather a popular-format survey of animal behavior and a fascinating source of information about animal feats and phenomena and wonders of nature.

Like all of my publications, however, it is soundly based throughout in zoological fact, presenting and assessing the latest scientific discoveries and theories relevant to the cases under consideration in an objective yet thought-provoking way. Moreover, it is amply supplemented by an extensive bibliography of works that can be consulted by readers who would like to delve deeper into any of the topics documented here.

Of course, with some animals, the most intriguing stories concern their relationships with, and behavior toward, people. From famous cases of canine devotion, to inspirational tales of dolphin rescues, to extraordinary examples of cats warning of impending disaster, human interest stories are included wherever pertinent, often as features scattered throughout the main text. So too are interesting examples of traditional or ancient folklore and legends that have a bearing on current behavioral topics. And, as one would naturally expect from a Reader's Digest publication, lavish illustrations and stunning full-color photographs abound throughout, vividly bringing these remarkable cases to life.

The result is a truly unique guide to animal behavior that educates, informs and entertains in seamless continuity, and, in so doing, reveals that our fellow creatures are no less astounding and mystifying today than they were in bygone times when viewed with marveling eyes by our ancestors.

Karl Shuker

CHAPTER ONE

SUPER SENSES

*Our senses – sight,
hearing, smell, taste, and touch – enable
us to obtain an extraordinarily detailed,
multifaceted view of the world around us.
However, other animals have far more
finely tuned senses, and some even possess
exotic, additional capabilities – ranging
from thermal vision and ultrasonic hearing
to distant touch and ripple
fingerprinting – that allow them to
perceive the world around them
in ways we can hardly even
begin to comprehend.*

Extraordinary Eyes

see also:
- The Visual Spectrum, p.16
- Infrared Vision, p.17
- Ultraviolet Vision, p.20

Common sense tells us that in animals with a single pair of eyes, such as mammals, birds, and other vertebrates, the two eyes should be identical. Judging from recent research on the eyes of the European starling (*Sturnus vulgaris*), however, this may not always be the case. In 2000, a team of researchers led by biologist Dr. Nathan Hart of Queensland University in Australia revealed that the retinal cellular composition of a starling's two eyes differs.

All eyes are not created equal: Some animals have evolved eyes that give them unusual — and very useful — visual powers.

In its left eye, the retina has more single cones — photosensitive cells that respond to color. Conversely, in the retina of its right eye, double cones — which detect movement — predominate. The two eyes seem to fulfill different functions, which may well explain why starlings (as well as many other birds) tend to look at objects with either one eye or the other. So if a starling looks at an object with its left eye, it may be scrutinizing its coloration, whereas if it looks with its right eye, it may be watching for movement.

Native to Caribbean lagoons, *Anableps anableps* is commonly known as the four-eyed fish because its two eyes are split by horizontal partitions into two halves, each of which has its own iris and retina. This unique optical construction lets the fish

The starling fixes the camera with a gaze from its left eye, indicating that it is looking out for color rather than movement.

The four-eyed fish can see above and below the water at the same time as it swims along the surface, allowing it to scan the air for predators while it searches the water for prey.

swim at the surface of the water, with the upper half of each eye scanning the air for predatory fish-eating birds, and the lower half peering down below the surface, in search of small fish to feed on.

Despite each eye being partitioned, there is only one oval-shaped lens per eye. Because vision through water requires a thicker lens than vision through air, the fish's eye is ingeniously adapted to fulfill two purposes, with the lower portion of each eye's lens (through which the fish sees underwater) thicker than the upper portion (through which the fish sees in air).

Through the eyes of the chameleon

In most higher animals, the eyes have a lens for focusing incoming light onto the retina to create an image. The chameleon, however, uses the cornea for this purpose, and therefore avoids drawing attention to itself when trying to see how far away a potential prey is. Most other animals judge distances by moving their heads from side to side, causing closer objects to appear to move more quickly than distant ones. This is known as the parallax effect. But the chameleon can achieve this effect by only moving its eyes. This ability means that the chameleon does not attract the attention of predators when it looks around.

The six-eyed spookfish (*Bathylychnops exilis*) has an optical system that is unique in the animal kingdom. Unknown to scientists until as recently as 1958, and dwelling at depths of 330-3280 feet (100-1000 m), this slender pike-like fish has paired, downward-pointing, spherical organs housed within the lower half of its large eyes. These were once believed to be light-producing organs – bioluminescence is a common phenomenon among deep-sea fishes. Closer examination, however, exposed their much more extraordinary, true identity. In reality, these organs, now referred to as secondary globes, are accessory eyes. Each of

these globes possesses its own lens and retina and probably serves to increase the spookfish's sensitivity to light (photosensitivity) within its dimly lit undersea realm.

But this is not the only anomaly of its optical system. Scientists subsequently unfurled a further surprise associated with the fish's accessory eyes. Behind them is a third set of "eyes," even tinier than the secondary globes, but less sophisticated. These "eyes" lack retinae. Instead, they serve merely to direct incoming light into the spookfish's principal pair of eyes, thereby enhancing these latter organs' powers of vision.

Able to look in two directions at once, the chameleon can see all around itself.

Compound Eyes

see also:
- Extraordinary Eyes, p.12
- Exotic Senses, p.38
- Enhanced Vision, p.47

Look at the world through the eyes of an insect and you will be surprised. Movement appears slower, images are broken up into mosaiclike fragments, and even colors take on a new look.

The difference lies in the composition of the eyes. Our eyes have a single lens, which focuses light to produce a single image. Insects, however, have paired compound eyes made up of many different light-focusing lenses, known as ommatidia, clustered together on each side of the insect's head.

Ever swatted a fly and missed? That's because what looks to us like a swing so fast it's a blur appears to the fly as slow motion. Flies and other insects can detect movement up to six times more quickly than we can.

A many-faceted image

Since each ommatidium is very small, it can collect light only from a small portion of an insect's field of view. Insects therefore see the world not as a single image, but as a mosaic made up of dozens or even thousands of small images. The number of images depends on the number of ommatidia; the more ommatidia there are, the sharper the picture. Like a pixelated image on a computer screen, the resolution improves as the number of elements increases.

Not all insects are created equal as far as vision goes. Some worker ants have only around ten ommatidia in each eye, resulting in very poor vision, whereas dragonflies, which need acute vision to catch their prey on the wing, have up to 30,000.

Panoramic views

Insects have almost 360-degree vision because of the distinctive curved surface of their eyes. But they don't have shape-changing lenses, so they cannot adjust their focus between near and distant objects. To see something better, an insect must move closer to it.

Moving pictures

Although insects cannot see as sharply as we can, they compensate by being better at sensing motion. The rate at which the eye can distinguish separate static images before they fuse to create the illusion of

ANIMAL PROFILE

The Tiger Beetle

Why would the aggressive tiger beetle stop while chasing its prey, seemingly letting it get away? While studying these insects in 1998, entomologist Dr. Cole Gilbert of Cornell University discovered that the ommatidia in the compound eyes of tiger beetles cannot gather enough light to produce an image of the prey when they are running. By pausing, the beetle gives its eyes time to gather enough light to re-form an image of its prey. Far from letting prey escape, the beetle's pause helps it catch them.

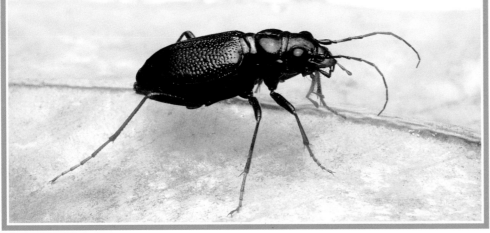

The eye of a dragonfly is unusually large and complex, with up to 30,000 ommatidia (lenses).

How a Compound Eye Works

A compound eye consists of many ommatidia. Each ommatidium contains a cornea (lens), made from a transparent portion of the head's cuticle, and a crystalline cone, which forms the light-focusing lens. A photoreceptive unit known as the retinula lies at the base. Light entering the lens passes along a rod called the rhabdom before hitting the retinula, stimulating electric pulses passing to the optic nerve.

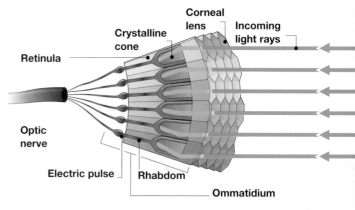

continuous movement is called the flicker-fusion frequency. Our eyes can see around 50 images per second in good light, less in dim conditions. That's why movies appear to move even though they are really a series of separate frames. With a flicker-fusion frequency six times faster than ours, dragonflies see 300 images per second, so they would see a movie for what it truly is – a slide show made up of a sequence of static images.

Motion-sensitive
What looks fast to us appears in slow motion to a dragonfly. Like many other flying insects that are active during the day, dragonflies have eyes that are incredibly responsive to movement. Flowers swaying back and forth in a breeze are therefore more visible to them than stationary plants are.

Nocturnal species of insects need time to gather light in order to form an image, and therefore have a slower flicker-fusion frequency, which means that they don't see movement as well.

THE VISUAL SPECTRUM

Electromagnetic radiation consists of the energy waves associated with electric and magnetic waves, and results from the acceleration of an electric charge. There are several types of electromagnetic radiation, including radio waves, infrared (heat), visible light, ultraviolet, x-rays, and gamma rays, which are distinguished by their wavelength and frequency bands. Frequency is inversely proportional to wavelength. The longer the wavelength of a type of electromagnetic radiation, the shorter its frequency, and vice versa. The different types can be arranged in a continuous spectrum, with the longest wavelengths at one end, and the shortest wavelengths at the other. Humans can see only one small band of wavelengths – the visible spectrum – which comprises seven colors: red, orange, yellow, green, blue, indigo, and violet. Red has the longest wavelength and violet the shortest.

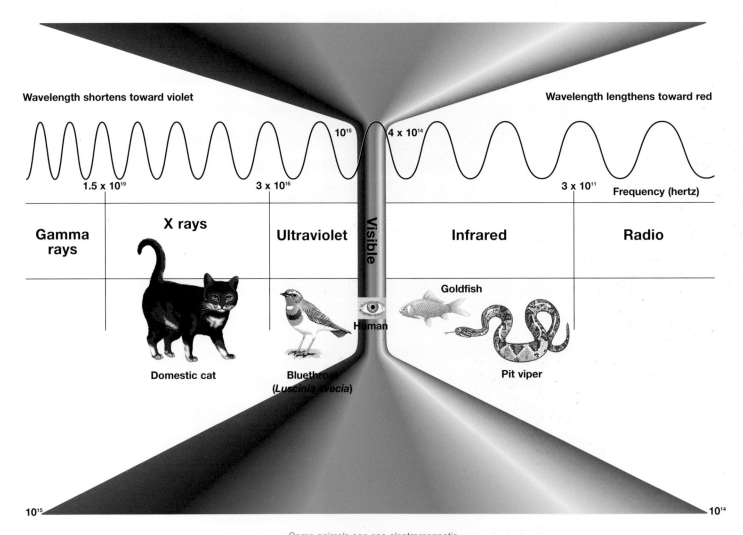

Wavelength shortens toward violet

Wavelength lengthens toward red

10^{15} 4×10^{14}

1.5×10^{19} 3×10^{16} 3×10^{11} **Frequency (hertz)**

| Gamma rays | X rays | Ultraviolet | Visible | Infrared | Radio |

Domestic cat

Bluethroat
(*Luscinia svecia*)

Human

Goldfish

Pit viper

10^{15} 10^{14}

Some animals can see electromagnetic radiation wavelengths beyond the visible spectrum. Various insects, such as bees and butterflies, and certain birds, like bluethroats, can perceive ultraviolet light. Fishes, such as the piranha and dragonfish, can detect the longest red wavelengths. Rattlesnakes, as well as goldfish, can see infrared radiation wavelengths. This enables the snakes to locate warm-blooded prey in total darkness. Cats may be able to detect x-rays, but apparently not with their eyes.

Infrared Vision

see also:
- Extraordinary Eyes, p.12
- Ultraviolet Vision, p.20
- Exotic Senses, p.38

As far back as 1892, scientists knew that rattlesnakes were attracted to lighted matches, but they assumed that the snakes were responding to the flickering flame. Now we realize that some types of snakes and other species can see the body heat of other animals.

Heat-seeking snakes

During the 1930s, scientific experiments with rattlesnakes and the closely related pit vipers (a group known collectively as crotalids) revealed that the snakes could actually *see* the heat the flame gave off. The fact that these snakes could detect the tiny amount of heat given off by the matches meant that they were able to sense radiant heat, or infrared radiation (IR), a wavelength that is invisible to the human eye.

The pit viper's ability to register heat is so sensitive that they can feel the temperature variation produced by a mouse from 6 inches

Different animals have evolved different ways of seeing in the absence of light. Some use infrared vision to see in the dark.

(15 cm) away. The heat sensors are located in the pit-shaped holes on their faces that give them their name. Positioned on each side of the snake's head between the eye and nostril, these small, shallow pits point forward, and their tiny, pinhole openings are supplied with a grid of 7,000 nerve endings from a branch of the trigeminal nerve leading to the head and face. Toward the base of this pit is a membrane, similar to the retina of the eye,

The pit viper uses heat-sensitive receptors to track rodents at night and in their dark subterranean burrows. The receptors are located in two facial pits, one of which can be seen above and to the left, below the pit viper's nostril.

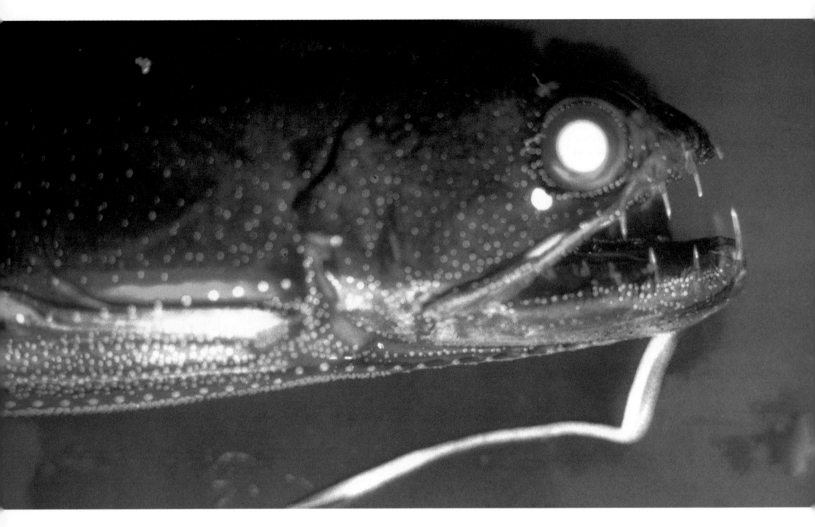

The jaws of the dragonfish are designed for catching large prey. However, the diet of this deep-sea fish is made up of small crustaceans, whose bodies contain bacteria that possess a chlorophyll pigment, enabling the dragonfish to see far-red light.

which has minuscule thermoreceptors, numbering 500–1,500 per square millimeter. Because the fields of sensitivity of the two pits overlap, a pit viper can see heat in stereo. This bifocal thermal vision provides the snake with a fiery infrared image of its prey and enables it to judge how far away it is. The pit viper's sensory awareness is coupled with quick reactions, allowing it to respond to a heat signal in under 35 milliseconds. With these abilities, it's no wonder that these snakes are feared.

Moving in for the kill

The ability to see infrared radiation gives pit vipers a tremendous advantage. They can hunt at night and pursue rodents and other warm-blooded prey into their underground burrows. Although these snakes use their highly developed sense of smell to find prey, their killing strike is always guided by the heat-sensitive pits, with help from additional thermoreceptors located inside their mouths.

Although not as well known for infrared vision as the crotalids, another group of snakes, the boas and pythons, also have heat sensors. Instead of pits,

however, these snakes have up to 13 pairs of thermoreceptors arranged around their lips.

Seeing red

The deepest parts of the ocean are dark. What light there is does not come from the sun, which cannot penetrate to these depths, but from deepsea creatures who literally glow in the dark. Like fireflies or glowworms on land, these creatures have organs or tissues that generate light.

The black, loose-jawed dragonfish (*Malacosteus niger*) is a predatory deep-sea species that normally lives in near darkness at depths of 3,000 to 6,000 feet (915 to 1,830 m). How can they hunt in the dark? By being able to see far-red light.

Light at the far-red end of the so-called visible spectrum has the longest wavelength of all, around 0.73–0.8 micrometers. Although invisible to the human eye, this type of light can be seen by some animals, including the dragonfish. Behind the dragonfish's eyes is a pair of bioluminescent organs that emit blue-green light. The majority of other bioluminescent creatures in this dark realm also emit bluish light, and have eyes that are sensitive to wavelengths within the blue portion of the visible spectrum.

A second pair of bioluminescent organs, located beneath the dragonfish's eyes, give off far-red light, which is invisible to nearly all other life in the ocean depths. These organs give the dragonfish an advantage over its competitors, since the far-red light they emit enables the dragonfish to illuminate potential prey and to communicate with others of its own species without betraying its presence.

Food to watch fish by

But how is the dragonfish able to see far-red light? In a strange case of "you are what you eat," it probably obtains this ability by feeding on tiny crustaceans known as copepods, which have in turn eaten bacteria that can absorb far-red light. As revealed in 1998 by a team of scientists in Britain, including Bristol University researcher Dr. Julian Partridge and City University researcher Dr. Ron Douglas, the retinae of the dragonfish contain modified versions of bacterial chlorophyll, pigments that can absorb far-red light.

Seeing in the dark

Thanks to far-red light, some fish can see even in water that appears black to us. The ferocious piranha, for example, swimming in the murky waters of the Amazon, perceives the water as dark red, a color that is visually penetrable, rather than black. The water looks red because the molecules of rotting vegetation in it absorb most wavelengths of visible light except far-red light, which is reflected back and can be seen by the piranha, allowing it to see the prey that it is hunting, apparently in the dark.

Like the piranha, the goldfish often inhabits murky, vegetation-choked stretches of freshwater in its natural habitat. It has therefore adapted so that it is able to detect far-red light. Indeed, its visual range exceeds

The eyes of the piranha are specially adapted for seeing far-red light. This enables it to hunt for prey in the murky rivers of South America.

that of the piranha because it can see beyond far-red light, into true infrared. So your pet goldfish can spy more than you might think – including the "invisible" infrared beams emitted by common household electronic gadgets such as television remote controls and trip beams from intruder alarm systems.

ANIMAL PROFILE

Why Goldfishes See Red

The goldfish can see far-red and infrared light due to the composition of the retinae in its eyes. Although these contain cone cells that are sensitive to different colors, the red-sensitive cones are dominant. As a result, red signals override other signals reaching the brain, shifting the goldfish's vision to the red end of the spectrum.

Ultraviolet Vision

see also:
- Extraordinary Eyes p.12
- The Visual Spectrum p.16
- Enhanced Vision p.47

Many animals across the zoological spectrum – from bees to squid, birds to horseshoe crabs – can see ultraviolet radiation, giving them a view of the world that bears no resemblance to ours.

If you could see the world in ultraviolet light as bees and birds do, it would look very different; red would be black, and solid might be striped.

Humans have color vision that is produced by three different types of retinal cone cell. Called trichromatic vision, our color vision is sensitive to three different wavelengths of light: red, green, and blue. Bees also have trichromatic vision, and three different types of retinal cone cell, but they are most sensitive to yellow, blue, and ultraviolet wavelengths of light. (Ultraviolet, or UV, light lies beyond the blue, indigo, and violet end of the visible spectrum of electromagnetic radiation.)

They therefore perceive red light, and anything reflecting red (such as poppies and other red flowers), as black.

Although hidden to our eyes, the world of ultraviolet light is visible to bees. Some plants use this fact to their own benefit. Many flowers pollinated by bees have UV-colored lines known as nectar guides. Visible only to creatures that can see UV radiation, these lines are not present on the flower petals of wind-pollinated plants or plants pollinated by animals unable to see UV light.

Butterflies can also see UV light. Some species use this ability for sexual identification. Male and female clouded yellow butterflies look as if they are the same color to our eyes, but to each other they appear totally distinct due to the differing patterns of UV markings on their wings.

To our eyes, plants such as the evening primrose appear as a uniform pale yellow (left). When photographed with UV film (above), we can see them as bees do. Far from being plain, their petals are patterned with UV-colored lines that point toward the flower's nectaries – thereby leading visiting bees straight to the nectar.

The plumage of the bluethroat (*Luscinia svecica*) has UV-reflecting feathers, which male birds use to attract a mate.

In 1999, Dr. Sarah Hunt from England's Bristol University discovered that blue tits (*Parus caeruleus*) choose mates by the extent of UV plumage they sport. Male blue tits select females whose feathers reflect the most UV light.

Ultra-attractive

In Sweden, another bird, the bluethroat, chooses a mate in much the same way. During the display season, the male of this little thrush has, as its name suggests, a bright blue throat, highlighted with either a red or white spot in the center. Other bluethroats perceive ultraviolet tones there, too, as confirmed in 1998 by a team of Scandinavian researchers, led by Dr. Trond Amundsen from the Norwegian University of Science and Sweden's Dr. Staffan Andersson of Gothenburg University. By applying sunblock to the throat feathers of male bluethroats, they prevented UV reflection without affecting the feathers' other, visible colors. They then placed some female bluethroats in the company of several males – some with sunblock-treated throat feathers, the others with normal, untreated throat feathers. The females consistently preferred those males whose throat feathers were untreated, and which were therefore reflecting ultraviolet light.

But while UV vision helps many species of insect, it can also be used to trick them. Several species of spider, for example, include UV-colored sheets of silk in their webs, which insects mistake for nectar guides or for escape routes from dense vegetation, only to be lethally snared by the web's sticky coating. Some insect-eating pitcher plants have UV lines running down into their depths, which insects unsuspectingly follow; instead of finding nectar, they find themselves captured.

Birds use ultraviolet decorations, too. The sparkling shimmer of starlings and the gaudy finery of parrots appear even more startling to eyes that see UV light. Many birds can not only discern this exotic hue but are influenced by it during mating.

ANIMAL PROFILE

X-ray-sensitive Cats

X rays have even shorter wavelengths than UV light, and are supposedly invisible not only to humans but also to other animals. In 1965, a team of biologists at the Veterans Administration Hospital in Long Beach, California, performed experiments that seemed to show that cats could detect X rays. In conditioning experiments, cats reacted to five-second exposures of X-ray radiation in order to avoid a mild rebuff. In attempting to pinpoint the body region responsible for this remarkable feat, the researchers found that the olfactory bulb behind the nasal and oral passages was the most responsive region, rather than the eyes.

Ultrasonic Hearing

see also:
● Exotic Senses, p.38
● Cetacean Communication, p.144
● Animal Rescuers, p.208

Bats can form a detailed picture of their surroundings and of the size, relative movement, and even the texture of their prey as they fly through the night sky. Many insect-eating bats can even navigate and hunt in total darkness. But how do they do it?

With their ears. Bats use a technique called echolocation, emitting ultrasonic squeaks and listening to the precise nature of the reflected echo. This highly evolved sonar (SOund Navigation And Ranging) technique uses frequencies in the ultrasonic range. These sounds have frequencies greater than around 20,000 Hz (20 kHz) and are well above the upper limit of human hearing.

The ability of bats to echolocate was first suspected in the 1790s by Italian zoologist Prof. Lazzaro Spallanzani and Swiss surgeon Charles Jurine. It was not confirmed until 1938, when Harvard student Donald Griffin and physicist George W. Pierce made the first recordings of bats' ultrasonic calls.

The little brown bat is equipped with such sharp hearing that it can catch two flying mosquitoes in half a second. This insect-eating bat, found across much of North America, can sonically detect and avoid objects no wider than a hair. Equally sophisticated, fish-eating bats can grab fish

Although humans are unable to hear ultrasonic noise, a wide range of other animals not only sense these very high-pitched sounds but can also use them as a medium for communication or to help them navigate.

The South American oilbird, which shelters in caves during the day and feeds on fruit at night, echolocates using short audible clicks.

swimming just beneath the surface of the water by meticulously detecting and identifying the ripples caused by their underwater movements.

Hunting by ear

While searching for its prey, the big brown bat squeaks about five times per second, with each call lasting 10-15 milliseconds. When the bat detects a potential victim, it instantly increases its call rate while decreasing the duration of each squeak, so that now each squeak lasts for only one millisecond and the squeaks are emitted at a rate of up to 200 per second. Most other insect-eating bats hunting in open spaces also vary the frequencies of their calls and use harmonics to help pinpoint their prey. Bats hunting in a jungle, such as the leaf-nosed bat, echolocate using a call

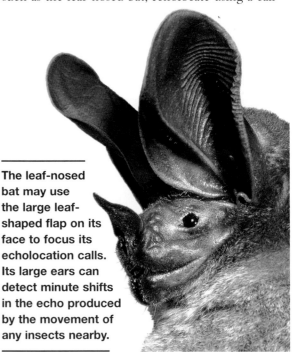

The leaf-nosed bat may use the large leaf-shaped flap on its face to focus its echolocation calls. Its large ears can detect minute shifts in the echo produced by the movement of any insects nearby.

Echolocation Calls of North American Bats

SPECIES	LOW	HIGH
Big Brown Bat (Eptesicus fuscus)	25KHZ	50KHZ
Spotted Bat (Euderma maculatum)	9KHZ	15KHZ
Little Brown Bat (Myotis lucifugus)	38KHZ	78KHZ
Eastern Long-eared Bat (Myotis septentrionalis)	38KHZ	110KHZ

How Dolphins Echolocate

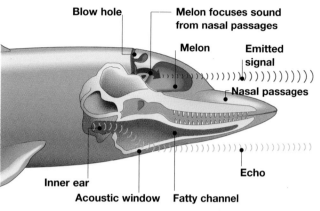

Blow hole

Melon focuses sound from nasal passages

Melon

Emitted signal

Nasal passages

Inner ear

Acoustic window

Fatty channel

Echo

Dolphins generate ultrasonic clicks in the nasal passages beneath the blow hole. These sound waves are focused into a narrow beam in a dome-shaped, fat-filled cavity called the melon. The beam is then directed at potential targets. The returning echo reaches the inner ear of the dolphin via an acoustic channel in its lower jaw, which is filled with fat.

that does not change frequency. Instead they rely on the Doppler effect – a distortion of sound produced as objects move toward or away from each other – to detect prey.

Evasion tactics

Many species of moth can hear bats coming by listening in to their ultrasonic echolocation calls. They can therefore escape before being caught. Once the bat is within approximately 20 feet (6 m), moths take abrupt evasive action, either by folding up their wings and dropping down out of the bat's flight path, or by embarking on a random, weaving flight that the bat cannot follow.

Some moths listen with their bodies through a pair of eardrum-like organs in their abdomens. Each organ consists of a thin membrane of cuticle, behind which is an airsac that enables the membrane to vibrate when it is hit by sound waves. Connected by nerves to the brain, these organs are sensitive to the frequency range of ultrasonic squeaks emitted by insect-eating bats.

Ultrasonic weapons

Whales may use ultrasonic noise like a stun gun against fish. Since 1942, researchers have known that dolphins and other toothed whales emit ultrasonic echolocation clicks, which they use to navigate and find fish in murky water. Working with captive Hawaiian spinner dolphins (*Stenella longirostris*), California University cetologist Prof. Ken Norris found that when they direct ultrasonic beams at a shoal of fish, they can stun or even kill some of them. The beams may cause the fishes' air-filled swimbladders to resonate so intensely that their body tissues also vibrate, disorienting them.

More recent, but equally intriguing, is the discovery that dolphins may use not only very high- but also low-frequency sound to stun their prey. In 2000, Dr. Vincent Janik of St. Andrews University in Scotland was studying bottlenose dolphins (*Tursiops truncatus*) in Scotland's Moray Firth. He announced that they give voice to a distinctive low-frequency braying noise almost exclusively at feeding times. Since dolphins themselves are not sensitive to low sonic frequencies, Janik speculates that the dolphins emit these particular sound waves to stun their prey.

In water the ultrasonic clicks of the spinner dolphin travel faster than they do in air and pass into the bodies of fish.

SOUND-FREQUENCY COMPARISONS

Sound is created by vibrations. Faster vibrations generate sound waves with a shorter wavelength and a higher pitch than slower vibrations, which produce sound waves with longer wavelengths and a lower pitch. The ultrasonic calls of bats are well suited to pinpointing small objects because the wavelengths are close together. These high-pitched sound waves, however, are easily absorbed by air and do not travel far. Conversely, low-frequency sound waves give poor resolution but carry much farther.

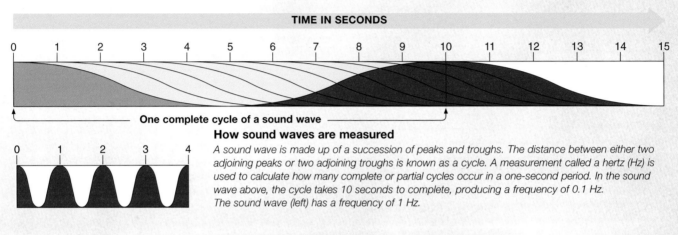

TIME IN SECONDS

0 1 2 3 4 5 6 7 8 9 10 11 12 13 14 15

One complete cycle of a sound wave

How sound waves are measured

0 1 2 3 4

A sound wave is made up of a succession of peaks and troughs. The distance between either two adjoining peaks or two adjoining troughs is known as a cycle. A measurement called a hertz (Hz) is used to calculate how many complete or partial cycles occur in a one-second period. In the sound wave above, the cycle takes 10 seconds to complete, producing a frequency of 0.1 Hz. The sound wave (left) has a frequency of 1 Hz.

COMPARATIVE HEARING RANGES MEASURED IN HERTZ (HZ)

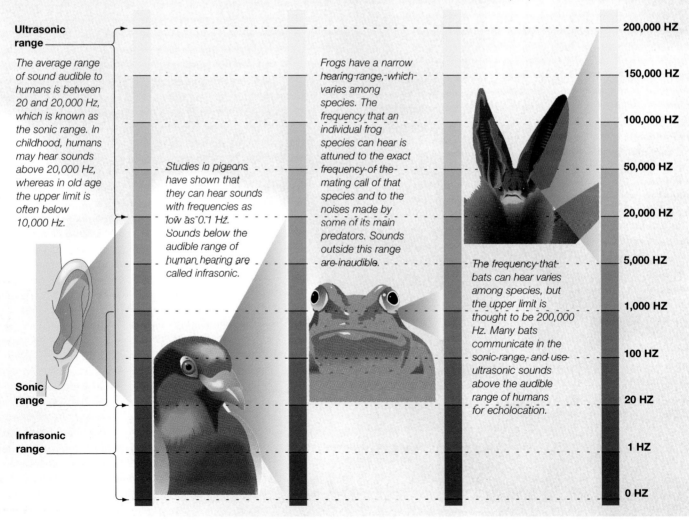

Ultrasonic range

The average range of sound audible to humans is between 20 and 20,000 Hz, which is known as the sonic range. In childhood, humans may hear sounds above 20,000 Hz, whereas in old age the upper limit is often below 10,000 Hz.

Studies in pigeons have shown that they can hear sounds with frequencies as low as 0.1 Hz. Sounds below the audible range of human hearing are called infrasonic.

Frogs have a narrow hearing range, which varies among species. The frequency that an individual frog species can hear is attuned to the exact frequency of the mating call of that species and to the noises made by some of its main predators. Sounds outside this range are inaudible.

The frequency that bats can hear varies among species, but the upper limit is thought to be 200,000 Hz. Many bats communicate in the sonic range, and use ultrasonic sounds above the audible range of humans for echolocation.

Sonic range

Infrasonic range

200,000 HZ
150,000 HZ
100,000 HZ
50,000 HZ
20,000 HZ
5,000 HZ
1,000 HZ
100 HZ
20 HZ
1 HZ
0 HZ

Infrasonic Messages

see also:
- Ultrasonic Hearing, p.22
- Exotic Senses, p.38
- Mammal Migration, p.77

According to common fallacy, the giraffe is mute. Living on open plains and having acute eyesight, giraffes can easily see one another and so seem to have no need for vocal communication. But recently, researchers have heard giraffes talking – by recording them and listening in infrasonically.

From talking giraffes to elephants that can communicate over long distances, nature is full of surprises if you listen infrasonically.

This proof followed the discovery that the okapi, a short-necked cousin of the giraffe native to the Congo's densest jungles, communicated at infrasonic frequencies. While researching the hearing of rhinoceroses at the San Diego Zoo, scientists inadvertently recorded one of the zoo's okapis vocalizing at frequencies as low as 7 Hz – below those that leopards and other predators of its Congolese domain could hear.

Low pitched

Using infrasonics, okapis can communicate over great distances through thick vegetation, free from detection by predators.

After the okapi's infrasonic abilities were established, attention turned to its relative, the giraffe. They also emit low-frequency cries below the threshold of human hearing.

Giraffes, although often believed to be mute, in fact communicate using low-frequency sounds that are inaudible to their predators.

Elephant ears

The elephant was the first land mammal shown to communicate infrasonically – a landmark discovery that came from two independent observations. In 1981, Kansas University scientists Dr. Rickye Heffner and Dr. Henry Heffner were surprised to discover that elephants could detect sound frequencies as low as 17 Hz, which were within the infrasonic range. But why should they be able to do this? What purpose does it serve?

In May 1984, animal-sounds specialist Dr. Katharine Payne from Cornell's Laboratory of Ornithology was visiting Portland's Metro Washington Park Zoo when she experienced a bizarre sensation, which she later described in a *National Geographic* article (August 1989): "While observing three Asian elephant mothers and their new calves, I repeatedly noticed a palpable throbbing in the air like distant thunder, yet all around me was silent." Later she realized

that the sensation reminded her of standing next to the largest organ pipe when she was a choir girl in Ithaca, New York, while the organ blasted out the bass line in a Bach chorale.

Suspecting that the elephants were the source of the throbbing, Payne teamed up with fellow Cornell biologists Dr. William Langbauer and Dr. Elizabeth Thomas to make recordings of the zoo's elephants. When analyzed, these recordings revealed a sizable infrasonic component. Indeed, the electronic printout showed that within one month 400 separate calls had been recorded – three times the number of calls heard by the researchers in the sonic range. Analyses showed that the elephants emitted short calls at a frequency range of 14-24 Hz, which lasted for 5-10 seconds, over a period of 10 minutes.

The team also uncovered an important visual clue to the production of these secret sounds by elephants. When an elephant is vocalizing infrasonically, the skin on its brow flutters, vibrating gently as air passes through its nasal passage.

This hitherto unsuspected talent solved an age-old behavioral mystery – how elephants could coordinate the movements of a herd spread out over a large area. Since infrasound travels over long distances, it is useful in this regard. Subsequent studies have shown that elephants in Africa can hear calls from as far away as 2½ miles (4 km) during the day, whereas in the evening this range can extend to up to 6 miles (10 km) as a result of temperature inversions in the atmosphere that make sound travel farther.

These Indian elephants are bathing with their young in a river. Since elephants live in social groups, they need to communicate with one another; they often use infrasonic sound to "talk."

Several other herd mammals in Africa are now known to communicate infrasonically, including rhinoceroses and hippopotamuses. This ability is also shared by a number of large reptiles, such as alligators and crocodiles.

The low-frequency calls of the baleen whale may travel over many hundreds of miles. These calls help whales communicate over long distances. Sound waves move through water at about five times the speed they pass through air, so these low-frequency messages carry much farther than they would on land.

To date, the species shown to be able to hear sound at the lowest frequency is the pigeon. This discovery has led some researchers to speculate that **many birds are able to detect the infrasonic sounds produced by hot air currents.**

ANIMAL PROFILE

The Capercaillie

Large grouse native to North America, such as the prairie chicken, produce loud mating calls that can be heard up to half a mile (1 km) away. It therefore seemed surprising that the call of Europe's largest grouse, the capercaillie (*Tetrao urogallus*), seemed to carry for only 650 feet (200 m). When two British researchers recorded and analyzed the call of the capercaillie, they found that much of its vocalization was infrasonic, and that its calls carried as far as those **produced by its American cousins.**

Sensitive Smell

see also:
- Exotic Senses, p.38
- Spider Attack, p.120
- Insect Language, p.148

Relatively speaking, we humans have barely developed noses; we rely on sight and sound rather than scent. Many other animals, however, depend upon their sense of smell and have therefore developed it to extraordinary levels. That's why, for centuries, humans have harnessed the powers of animals such as hunting dogs and truffle-finding pigs to sniff out odors that our noses cannot register. Clearly these animals can smell things we can't, but other animals have even more remarkable olfactory abilities.

Olfaction – the sense of smell – has been called the most mysterious sense of all. Supremely well developed in many animals, it lets them scent a mate from miles away and may even let them warn one another of danger.

The nose knows

Certain types of moth have an olfactory sensitivity that verges on the supernatural. They can detect a single molecule of the female sex hormone from miles away. Males of the saturniid, bombycid, and lasiocampid families of moth, which include luna, emperor, polyphemus, vaporer, and silk moths, have large, feathery antennae that bear the moths' hairlike olfactory receptors in great quantities (as many as 60,000 in some species). Thanks to their broad shape, the antennae come into contact with the largest possible volume of air, making them perfect scent receivers.

They are incredibly sensitive to the sex attractant chemical (pheromone) released from the posterior abdominal glands by females of their species during the breeding season. But this sensitivity remained unsuspected until exposed by German

The pig's well-developed sense of smell is exploited by truffle hunters in France and Italy, who use them to sniff out truffles that lie hidden beneath the ground.

Female moths release minute quantities of pheromones from their abdomens (left) which are picked up by the male's sensitive antennae (below).

scientist Adolf Butenandt's experiments with Europe's great peacock moth (*Saturnia pyri*).

A male saturniid moth's nose is so sensitive that he can detect one molecule of the female sex pheromone if it should land on his antennae. Tests revealed that the amount of sex pheromone produced by each female great peacock moth was so minute that the glands of approximately half a million virgin female specimens were required to produce a mere 12 mg of it. And yet it is enough to stimulate the male.

Silky scent

Working with male specimens of the domestic silk moth (*Bombyx mori*), Dr. Deitrich Schneider has shown that 1 molecule of bombykol (this species' female sex pheromone) per 10^{15} air molecules, when the air is flowing at 23 inches (60 cm) per second for just two seconds, is sufficient to incite a response from a male. Moreover, a male will begin to flap his wings excitedly when as few as 40 of his antennal olfactory receptors (out of a total of 20,000) each detect 1 molecule of bombykol.

The moth with the most developed sense of smell, however, is that of a relative, the Indian luna moth (*Actias selene*). The male of this species is so sensitive to the female's sex pheromone that he

can trace a female via her scent from as far away as 6½ miles (11 km). In experiments in which male specimens were released this distance away from caged females, 26 percent successfully located the females, while 46 percent of the males located the females if released 2½ miles (4.1 km) from them.

Scent is certainly the main attraction for a moth. Males will ignore females enclosed in glass containers since they can't detect the females' sex pheromone through glass. And they pay no attention to uncaged females that lack abdomens (and hence pheromone-secreting abdominal glands). Wing markings aren't important either; altering the wing markings of females has no influence upon their selection by male moths. The males are immune to all other potential stimulants except one: the smell of the female's sex pheromones.

ANIMAL PROFILE

Deadly Deception

In Australia, amorous male moths attracted by the fragrant scent of a female's sex pheromone sometimes find themselves literally ensnared by the remarkable bolas spider (*Dicrostichus* spp.). So called for their talent for producing a large, sticky, ball-shaped lure that is twirled around on the end of a silken rope, held by one of their eight legs, the cunning bolas spider coats the object with a special secretion that smells like the female sex pheromone of certain moths, thus attracting males of these species. When the spider detects their fluttering wing movements close by, it begins whirling its scented lure in the air. Irresistibly drawn by the deceptive odor, the male moths come closer. When they are close enough, the spider deftly hits them with the lure, trapping them on its sticky surface. When satisfied with its catch of up to eight moths in one night, the spider hauls in the lure, and wraps each moth in silk, to be eaten later.

Built-in alarm system

Not all pheromones spell sex appeal. Some sound chemical warning bells instead. They are released by animals to warn others of their kind that there is danger. Since 1938, following experiments with aquarium fish, scientists have believed that alarm pheromones are released by injured or frightened fish to warn others. In minnows, this pheromone is called Schreckstoff. In 1997, however, St. Andrews University zoologist Dr. Anne Magurran and a team of Oxford University colleagues revealed that this warning effect almost certainly happened only in the laboratory, not in the wild.

When Schreckstoff is released in an aquarium, from which there is no escape, the minnows panicked. But when this chemical was added to a river in Dorset, England containing many minnows, the fish did not display alarm or any other change of behavior. It now seems unlikely that Schreckstoff has any influence upon this species in the wild. Indeed, the scientists are now wondering whether it is even an alarm pheromone at all. Other species, however, do secrete a pheromone that acts as a warning to their fellows.

Minnows (*Phoxinus phoxinus*) in captivity react with alarm to a pheromone secreted by injured fish, whereas those in the wild ignore this scent.

Refined Taste

see also:
● Sensitive Smell, p.28
● Exotic Senses, p.38
● Multiple Senses, p.40

Although our sense of taste comes from the taste buds on our tongues, elsewhere in the animal kingdom some far more unusual and exotic gustatory systems have evolved.

Many snakes and reptiles combine the senses of smell and taste. When a snake flicks its forked tongue in and out of its mouth, it is sampling the air. The snake does not even need to open its mouth to do this. The tongue is flicked out through a small hole in the snake's lips, so its two slender forks can collect scent particles from the air or from an object such as a stone. Back inside the mouth, the tongue's forks are pressed into a pair of domed pits in the roof of the mouth, which have a moist lining that is sensitive to the chemicals it has picked up. The olfactory particles are transferred to the pits, which are well supplied with nerve endings, and are collectively known as Jacobson's organ. Although most often found in snakes, this organ is also common in other reptiles, especially terrestrial lizards.

From flies and bees that taste with their feet to fish that use their whole bodies to taste the water they swim in, the animal kingdom has come up with some novel strategies for sampling the flavors of the world around them.

Snakes use Jacobson's organ to follow trails left behind by potential prey or mates, to recognize the sex of others of their own species, and to get together before hibernation (snakes often hibernate in colonies). Lizards use this organ to find their nests in the brooding season.

Do fish smell?

Fish pose a problem for scientists – do they smell or taste the water around them? The debate starts from a theory about these two senses. Smell is usually defined as the detection

This garter snake is literally tasting the air when it flicks its tongue out of its mouth. By later pressing its tongue against pits in the roof of its mouth, the snake can analyze the chemicals present in the air.

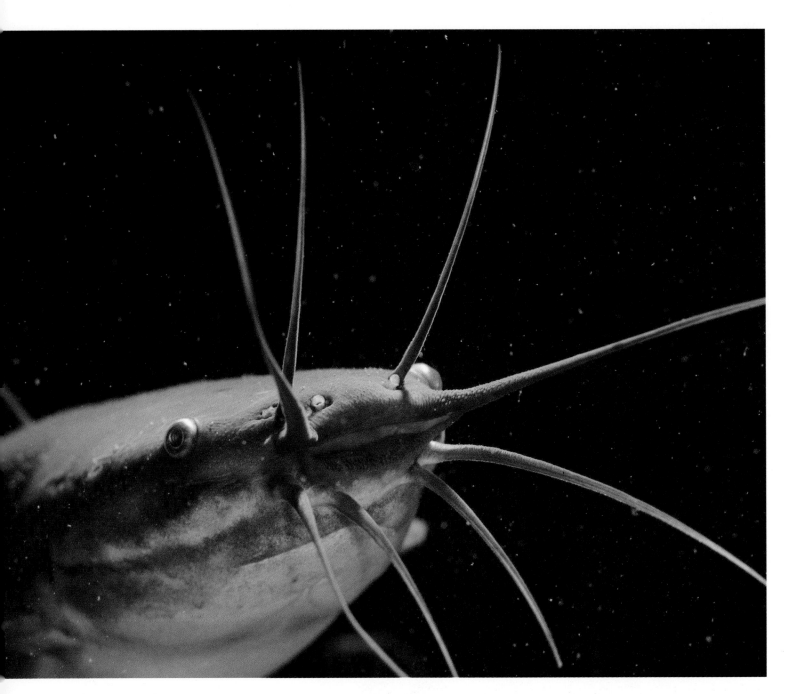

The catfish has most of its taste buds on the whiskerlike barbels around its mouth.

of chemical signals from distant sources whereas taste implies direct contact with the animal's chemoreceptors. So we smell odors when they reach our noses through the air, but taste when something touches our tongues. For fish that are surrounded by water, particles of scent and taste are both in direct physical contact with these receptors and hence "tasted," or are they smelled? The answer lies in the way a fish's brain is wired.

Studying the neurological connections of the fishes' smell and taste receptors reveals that taste is more important than smell to fishes, since there are more nerve connections to the taste buds. A fish's olfactory buds are supplied by only one nerve to the brain, whereas its taste buds are supplied by branches of three different cranial nerves.

Walking on taste buds

Whereas land vertebrates house their taste buds in their mouths, fish can have them almost anywhere. The long, slender fins of many species bear taste buds at their tips, enabling them to taste a potential food just by touching it. The pectoral fins of gurnards (*Trigla* spp.) and sea-robins (*Prionotus* spp.), for example, include several separate, fingerlike sections, which the fish uses not just for

"walking" along the sea bottom, but also for tasting – by touch – any potential food. Only if satisfied with the taste signals will the fish eat the object.

Swimming tongues

Certain fish take the distribution of taste buds to extreme limits, becoming in effect swimming tongues. Species as diverse as carp, cod, mullet, and sturgeon have taste receptors sprinkled liberally all over their bodies. The entire body of the channel catfish (*Ictalurus punctatus*) is covered in taste buds, with the densest concentration found on the whiskerlike barbels around its mouth. Investigations carried out by electrophysiologist Dr. J. Caprio have revealed that these particular taste buds are extremely sensitive and are able detect certain proteins in water at concentrations as low as 1-100 micrograms per liter.

Flavor-sensing feet

The blowfly (*Phormia regina*) has taste buds not only in the expected place – the mouthparts – but also in its feet. Moreover, those on its feet become more sensitive to sugars when the fly is hungry – 700 times more so with specimens that had been starved for 10 days.

No matter where they are on an insect's body, taste sensors normally take the form of hairlike structures called taste hairs. Each one usually has five sensory nerve cells (neurons) at its base, four of which are concerned with taste. Of these, one always responds to sugar, a second to water, and the other two to various salts.

Butterflies also have feet that can sense sweetness. When they have been starved, they can detect sugar diluted in water down to

concentrations as low as 0.003 percent using their feet. This is a sensitivity 200 times greater than that of the human tongue.

Conversely, when presented with a wide selection of tastes, insects are sometimes far less responsive than we are. In one series of tests, in which 34 different sugars and similar substances were sampled, human volunteers stated that 30 of them tasted sweet. In sharp contrast, honeybees offered this selection responded to only nine of them – all substances that occurred in their natural foodstuffs, such as nectar and honeydew. The bees were not fooled by artificial sweeteners such as saccharin. In high concentrations, these substances actively repelled the discriminating honeybees.

Best foot forward

Having taste hairs on their feet is handy for insects because they often land feet-first on a potential food. The insect can then use its feet to find out whether the object contains any nutritional substances, particularly sugar. If sugar is detected by the taste hairs on the feet, this automatically stimulates the insect to put the food in its mouth by extending its proboscis (in butterflies) or labellar lobes (in blowflies). The taste hairs on these and other mouthparts analyze whether the substance is edible or not before any of it is actually eaten.

Flies use their feet as well as their mouths to taste things they land on, such as this bread and honey.

Distant Touch

see also:
● Ultrasonic Hearing, p. 22
● Infrasonic Messages, p. 25
● Summer Hibernation, p. 104

To feel something, we humans must actually touch it. But fishes and some other animals can feel things from a distance. Our sense of touch is generally stimulated only by direct physical contact with the skin, or by very close contact (for example, being near enough to a fire to feel its heat but not to be burned by its flames). Other animals, however, possess a sense of touch that is far superior to ours, and some also have a separate yet closely related sense called distant touch, which detects vibrations from sources that are far away. This sense also interprets detailed data yielded by these vibrations.

From spiders with motion-sensitive hairs to tiny shrimplike creatures that can recognize other creatures by the ripples they leave in their wake, many animals have incredible abilities to feel the world around them without touching anything.

Fishes are well known for their ability to sense movement through their skin using their lateral line system. This system forms the basis of a sophisticated mode of navigation that uses water-borne vibrations to give the fish an accurate picture of its surroundings.

Listening with their skin

The lateral line system is a kind of underwater sonar and is very similar to the sonar-based navigation system employed by bats. But instead of listening to ultrasonic squeaks bouncing back from solid objects, the fish is able to feel the movement of water reflected back against its body from objects around it.

The lateral line system consists of a horizontal groove running along each flank and onto the head, where it splits into three shorter grooves. Within each groove is a line of tiny sense organs known as neuromasts. A neuromast consists of several minute sensory cells whose hairs are embedded together within a triangular tongue of jelly called a cupula.

As a fish swims, its movements create ripples or waves in the water that travel outward until they make contact with an object in the fish's surroundings, whereupon they bounce back toward the fish. The returning vibrations are deflected by the neuromasts' cupulae, thereby stimulating nerve connections to the brain, which give the fish sophisticated information about its surroundings. Neuromasts also cover the entire surface of a fish's skin, and can serve as normal touch receptors, responding to physical contact with objects as well as vibrations.

Underwater interference

In certain primitive fishes, such as the frilled shark (*Chlamydoselachus anguineus*), African lungfishes, and chimaeras, the grooves of the lateral lines are open instead of closed. When the grooves are open, the neuromasts are stimulated not only by reflected vibrations but also by the water movements created as the fish swims. This produces a sort of background "noise." These fishes tend to live in still water, which limits the amount of neuromast stimulation they experience from water movement alone and means that they can sense motion without being distracted. Fishes with open grooves that inhabit flowing or rough water may not be able to employ this open type of sensory detection.

The codfish gets a feel for its underwater world with its whiskerlike barbels.

The male of the Siamese fighting fish uses the movement of his large, flowing fins to warn his offspring of danger.

In more advanced fishes, or fishes that live in more turbulent waters, the grooves are closed. Each neuromast makes external contact through its own mucus-filled canal which leads to a pore on the fish's body surface. This prevents the neuromasts from being stimulated by the fish's own movements as it swims through the water, thereby ensuring that these sensory organs detect only vibrations reflected from other objects.

Swimming blind

The Mexican cave fish (*Astyanax hubbsi*) has no eyes and lives in total darkness within streams in underground caves, yet its vibration-guided navigational skills are so highly developed that it can detect objects smaller than a pinhead. These fish, and others like them, are able to build up a detailed picture of their surroundings using distant touch.

Many species that live in the lightless zones of the deep ocean also swim "blind." They possess sparse (if any) eye development, but do have hyperdeveloped lateral line systems that allow them to find their way around in the dark.

Some fishes use their sense of distant touch not just to navigate but also to communicate, vibrating their fins in specific ways to warn others of their species of danger. The male of the Siamese fighting fish (*Betta splendens*), which cares for the young, alerts its offspring to danger by vibrating its long,

These fish live in streams at the bottom of caves in Mexico, where they never see the light of day. They find their way around using distant touch rather than sight.

flowing fins. Other fishes use their powers of distant touch to synchronize their movements when swimming together in schools.

Good vibrations

Spiders can detect vibrations traveling through the air from sources far away. They can do this thanks to specialized vibration-sensitive hairs, called trichobothria, on certain segments of their limbs. These hairs are able to move in any direction, and tell the spider the direction from which an object is approaching and its size. They are so responsive to airborne vibrations that they can even detect those caused by the wings of insects in flight, alerting the spider to the approach of a potential victim as it heads toward the spider's web.

The pupa of the Australian blue butterfly (*Jalmenus evagorus*) uses vibration to attract ants, whose presence deters would-be predators. In turn, the ants drink the sweet-tasting fluid secreted by the pupa. In 2000, Harvard University researchers Dr. Mark Travassos and Dr. Naomi Pierce revealed that the pupa attracts the ants by rubbing together a series of closely aligned teeth-like projections on its body, vibrating the branch to which it is attached. Alerted by the vibrations, nearby ants run to the pupa to feast on the fluid.

Elephant ears

It has long been observed that when elephants are threatened, they sometimes stomp the ground with their feet. It was traditionally assumed that this was merely a sign of aggression. In recent years,

however, zoologists have discovered that this stomping has a far greater significance, and that it does more than raise a cloud of dust.

In reality, it is a means of communication that uses the elephant's sensitivity to vibrations. The elephant is in effect creating a groundborne telegraph system. Thus, if an elephant is alarmed or disturbed by something, it stomps the ground in order to alert others to the danger. The vibrations produced by its feet travel rapidly through the ground and are sensed through the feet of other elephants as far away as 31 miles (50 km).

The spider's hairy legs allow it to feel movements in the air, alerting it to the presence of flying prey.

ANIMAL PROFILE

A Sensitive Shellfish

One tiny crustacean, *Euchaeta rimana*, combines elements of the fish's sensitive skin and the spider's motion-sensitive hairs. The shrimp moves its mouthparts to create a smooth water current that it can detect through sensory hairs on its antennae. As creatures swim by, they create ruffles in this current, creating a ripple "fingerprint" that the little shellfish can instantly recognize as food or foe. If it is food, the passing organism will be grabbed and eaten. If the organism's ripple fingerprint betrays it as a predator, the sensitive shrimp will be able to swim away quickly.

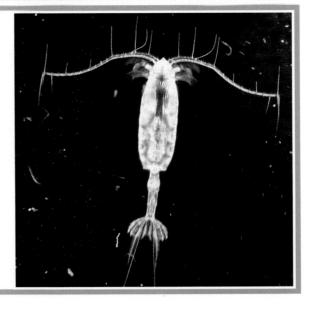

With an earth-shaking stamp of its foot, this elephant can communicate with other elephants standing miles away.

Exotic Senses

see also:
- Infrasonic Messages, p. 25
- Enhanced Vision, p. 47
- Circadian Rhythms, p. 90

Animals use a whole arsenal of exotic senses to help them track prey and survive in a hostile world.

Rhodnius bugs are large, blood-sucking insects found throughout the Americas. They live in close proximity to their victims, in nests or burrows, and detect potential victims – small, warm-blooded creatures such as mice – by sensing their body heat. A *Rhodnius* bug has its own built-in thermometers on its antennae in the form of numerous exceedingly sensitive hairlike thermoreceptors, which can detect air that has been warmed by its prey's body heat. These mini-thermometers are so sensitive that if someone places a glass jar over a starved *Rhodnius*, the bug trapped inside will press its mouthparts against those specific areas where its captor's fingers had held the outside of the jar.

From thermoreceptive hairs to third eyes, animals have some weird and wonderful senses to help them keep track of what is going on in the world around them.

To avoid being fooled by inanimate warm objects, however, this insect responds not merely to a creature's temperature but also to its scent. Thus, when offered the choice of a tube of warm water and a similar tube over which a fresh mouse skin has been stretched, the *Rhodnius* bug will initially extend its antennae toward each of the two objects in turn, detecting both the warmth and the odor of the air particles surrounding each object, before choosing the mouse-skin-covered version.

The *Rhodnius* bug can sense the presence of its warm-blooded prey by heat receptors on its antennae.

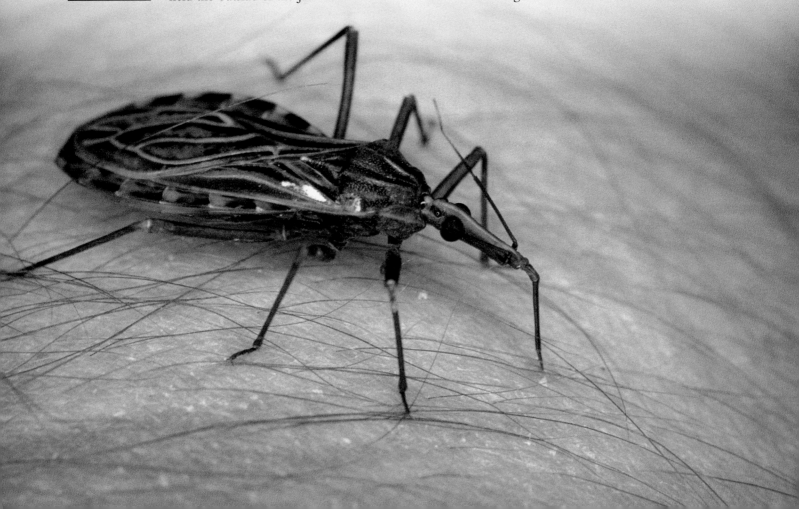

Seeing through a third eye

The superficially lizardlike tuataras (*Sphenodon punctatus* and *S. guntheri*) of New Zealand are the only modern-day representatives of an otherwise long-extinct group of reptiles known as the sphenodontids, which flourished alongside the dinosaurs. These lizards have an exceptionally well-developed pineal organ on top of their heads.

This mysterious structure is an outgrowth of the posterior portion of the forebrain and is linked to the sympathetic nervous system. It helps regulate circadian rhythms in physiological processes, secreting the hormone melatonin in response to changes in external levels of light. In higher vertebrates the structure is hidden in surrounding neural tissue, but in certain lower vertebrates, it is visible externally – in the tuatara it is distinctive enough to be called the pineal eye.

The tuatara's pineal organ sports a primitive lens and retina and connects directly to the outside world via a tiny hole in the skull immediately above it. Yet this so-called "third eye" cannot form a true image, lacks an iris, and in adult tuataras its hole is hidden by thickening skin. In fact, it derives information concerning external light levels not from the brain but directly from the tuatara's eyes. Hence the capabilities of the "third eye" remain controversial even today.

ANIMAL PROFILE

Lung-listeners

How is it possible for a land vertebrate to hear if it has neither external nor middle ears to transmit sounds from the outside world to its inner ears? One species that can do so is the fire-bellied toad (*Bombina orientalis*). It is responsive to a wide range of air-borne noises, and is also a versatile vocalist – but how can it detect sound waves? In 1999, Ohio State University researchers Dr. Erik Lindquist and Dr. Thomas Hetherington unmasked its remarkable secret.

Sound waves travel through its mouth and skin, entering its lungs, where they resonate before passing through the soft tissue around the lungs and into the inner ears. This auditory system should function when the toad is underwater, too. Indeed, since sound waves travel faster through water than air, it should be more efficient there.

Multiple Senses

see also:
- Sensitive Smell p.28
- Refined Taste p.31
- Distant Touch p.34

An animal's senses, however exotic and well developed they may be, rarely function in isolation. Instead, they usually work together as a team, giving the animal a complete picture of the world. Of all the creatures in the animal kingdom, one, the great white shark (*Carcharodon carcharias*), stands out as one of the most dramatic examples of sensory coordination on record.

The great white shark's hunting technique is more complex than the most sophisticated computer attack strategy ever devised.

Sharks have not changed much since they first swam the prehistoric seas more than 350 million years ago. Their ability to coordinate their senses to catch prey is astounding, giving them an accurate reputation as a killing machine.

The great white shark at up to 20 feet (6 m) in length is large enough to attack human beings, and for this it has become famously but unjustly feared. Great whites seem to prefer to eat seals or other large fish rather than humans. In fact, more people die from bee stings than shark attacks.

The great white shark's success as a hunter is due to its fantastic array of sensory powers. Some of its highly developed senses are wholly different from ours; others are similar but vastly superior. An intricate interplay of several different senses guides the shark unerringly through a step-by-step input of data to an injured creature that it can eat.

Step 1: Smelling

The first of the great white shark's senses to come into play when seeking prey is smell. The nasal sacs in a shark's nostrils can detect minute quantities of blood – as low as 1 part in 1,000,000,000 – seeping from an injured animal.

Step 2: Listening

Once it has detected this promising smell, the shark rapidly swims toward its source. About half a mile (1 km) away, it hears low-frequency sounds produced by a wounded, struggling animal. Although the shark has no external ear holes, it has a pair of inner ears flanking its braincase, each connected to an external pore on top of the shark's head, which detect sounds, especially low-frequency ones, traveling through the water.

Step 3: Using distant touch

When the great white is about 650 feet (200 m) away from its intended victim, the shark's "distant touch" sense is also activated. Running along the side of the shark is its lateral line system. Sensory cells within the lateral line system allow the shark to sense the presence of other creatures from the vibrations created by their movements in the water. Both splashing and swimming motions can be felt by the shark.

Step 4: Looking

Swimming even closer, the shark begins searching for the injured animal, employing sophisticated eyes that can see color. And as soon as it spies its victim, the shark circles it, taking a closer look to ensure that it is suitable as prey.

Satisfied with its choice of victim, the shark's eyes serve no further function so, when opening its jaws to bite, the great white actually rolls its eyes back out of harm's way, thereby rendering it temporarily blind.

Step 5: Exploring through electric vision

Even sightless, the shark is nevertheless still being guided toward its victim by its sensory armory – by now the shark's electrical sense is operating. Beneath the skin in its snout are numerous tiny, electrosensitive organs known as ampullae of Lorenzini, each linked to the outside world by an external pore. They detect the minute electrical fields produced by the shark's victim and permit the shark to home in on its prey, and to aim with devastating accuracy its first but generally lethal bite. After the first bite, the shark waits for the creature to die before devouring it.

Step 6: Touching

Lastly, the shark may nudge its prey, to find out more about its texture and size from the tiny touch receptors located on its snout. This final step concludes the shark's beautifully choreographed ballet of the senses.

The great white shark is a finely adapted feeding machine, which uses a formidable array of senses to find, hunt, and finally dispatch its prey.

CHAPTER TWO

ELECTRO-MAGNETIC FORCES

*Electricity and magnetism are two natural forces
that play vital but often unseen roles in the lives of
many animals. Many different creatures exhibit
a remarkable sensitivity to our planet's electromagnetic
forces, which in turn exert a significant influence
upon their lives. Some species,
including eels, can even generate their own
electric fields, and other members of the
animal kingdom are inordinately receptive to the
minute electrical signals powering the
nervous systems of others.*

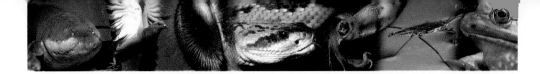

Magnetoreception

see also:
● Exotic Senses, p.38
● Bird Migration, p.68
● Fish Migration, p.74

Scientists have always believed that the mineral magnetite (iron oxide) could only be created in magma chambers, at high pressures and temperatures. No one imagined that some animals might actually synthesize it. But during the early 1960s, Prof. Heinz Lowenstam at the California Institute of Technology (CalTech) made a remarkable find. He discovered an animal that produced magnetite within its body.

While studying chitons, a type of primitive mollusk, he found that the teeth on their ribbon-like rasping tongues were composed of magnetite – also termed lodestone. It seemed that the chitons synthesized this mineral themselves.

Some animals are like living compasses, able to align themselves to magnetic north or find their way home over long distances. They are using the Earth's magnetic field to orient themselves – but how?

But why should chitons produce this unexpected substance? What purpose did it serve? Further studies revealed that in the wild state, and especially during summer, Californian chitons sitting on rocks tended to align themselves to the north. When specimens were placed inside artificial

The chiton, a primitive mollusk, has a tongue (inset) that can detect magnetic north because it contains iron oxide.

The waggle dance performed by bees when they return to the hive tells others in the colony where to find nectar and is dependent on the bees' ability to read the Earth's magnetic field.

of magnetite. These chains, called magnetosomes, clearly played some part in its powers of geomagnetic detection.

The bodies of honeybees also contain magnetite. In the 1970s, Princeton University zoologist Dr. Joseph Kirschvink showed that the magnetite lies in bands of cells in each segment of the bee's abdomen. It is most concentrated just below the ganglion (a compact mass of nerve cells).

Magnetosensitive birds

The most famous magnetosensitive creatures may be birds – and none more so than homing pigeons.

Homing pigeons use the Earth's magnetic field to travel back to the coop.

chambers in which the Earth's geomagnetic field was canceled out, however, the chitons became disoriented, aligning themselves at random rather than toward the north. Presumably, their magnetic teeth helped them orient themselves correctly when exposed to the earth's geomagnetic field.

A living compass

In 1975, while working at Massachusetts's Woods Hole laboratory, New Hampshire University microbiologist Dr. Richard Blakemore discovered a remarkable new species of mud–dwelling bacterium – one whose orientation was controlled by the Earth's geomagnetic forces. Dubbed *Aquaspirillum magnetotacticum,* this creature was attracted downward not by gravity, but by magnetism. When Blakemore applied artificial magnetic fields to vessels of mud containing specimens, the bacterium changed direction according to the direction of the magnetic field. Microscopic examination of *A. magnetotacticum* revealed that its elongated body contained chainlike structures of crystals composed

European robins will fly in the direction they should migrate even without visual signals, but they become disoriented if they can't sense the Earth's magnetic fields.

Even if deprived of familiar landmarks and sunlight, so that they cannot use the Sun to help them find their way, the pigeons can still return – if their magnetic sense is not tampered with. However, if small magnets are attached to their heads, or they are taken to release points in special containers in which the Earth's geomagnetic field is canceled out, the birds become disoriented when they are released. And pigeons fitted with head magnets that reverse the polarity of the magnetic field fly off in the opposite direction from that of their home.

Orienting on the wing

Artificial magnetic fields can also throw migratory birds off course. The American indigo bunting (*Passerina cyanea*) orients toward geomagnetic north during migration but, if exposed to an artificial magnetic field, the birds will faithfully reorient each time this field's horizontal component is changed, so that they are always aligned to it.

As yet, no avian magnetoreceptor has been

Researchers have discovered magnetite in the brains of brown trout, showing that they, too, are magnetoreceptive.

conclusively identified. However, a small but mysterious black-colored structure containing magnetite and nerve fibers is located between the brain's dura mater (outer membrane) and the skull of pigeons and various migratory passerines. Magnetite packets are also found in the necks of these birds.

Fishy feeling

Birds and bees aren't the only animals who are able to use magnetoreception. Undersea creatures are also sensitive to magnetic pull.

The sea slug (*Tritonia diomeda*), for instance, is known to align itself precisely at an angle of 87.6° east to the Earth's north-south magnetic axis.

In 1997, the first known magnetoreceptors – directly linking magnetite to neural connections and activity – were found in vertebrates. A team of zoologists from Auckland University, led by Dr. Michael Walker, had been studying this mysterious sense in trout, and knew that a region of its skull contained magnetite.

Recording neural activity from that region, they discovered that a specific subgroup of nerve fibers within a branch of the trigeminal cranial nerve called the ros V nerve fired in response to changes in the surrounding magnetic field. They also found magnetite in a tissue layer directly beneath the trout's olfactory (smell) organs. When they injected a colored dye into the ros V nerve's newly exposed magnetosensitive fibers, the dye revealed that the fibers terminated and ramified all around the magnetite-containing cells within the trout's olfactory tissue.

Enhanced Vision

Animals can navigate under conditions that would be impossible for humans to mimic without sophisticated equipment. This is because some animals can perceive light in the ultraviolet portion of the electromagnetic spectrum, and other animals can also discern the electric component of polarized light within this same portion. Some can even "see" the Earth's geomagnetic field. Humans have none of these perceptual abilities.

To understand the way that animals perceive light, it is necessary to understand light itself. Ordinary light, such as sunlight, vibrates at right angles to its direction of travel. Each vibration

From the ability of bees to perceive polarized light to that of certain birds to see the Earth's magnetic field, animals are able to use remarkable visual powers when traveling the globe.

consists of an electric and a magnetic component, forming a pair. When sunlight passes through the Earth's atmosphere, it is scattered by air molecules. Most of this scattering occurs in the blue, violet, and ultraviolet portion of the spectrum. For this reason, the sky looks blue to us. Moreover, this scattering has an unusual effect upon the incoming sunlight – it confines the sunlight's vibrations to a single plane, and this sunlight is now known as polarized light.

Light patterns in the sky

Although we cannot see it, polarized light forms distinctive patterns in the sky, which look like black rainbows or concentric rings, depending upon the portion of the sky being viewed and the relative position of the sun. The position of the Sun is important because the pattern of polarization at any one point in the sky depends upon its position relative to the Sun. And as the sun moves through the sky, the pattern of polarized light changes, almost like the hands of a clock sweeping around its face throughout the day. This phenomenon has been harnessed by a number of different animals that normally use the Sun's position as a compass. Since they

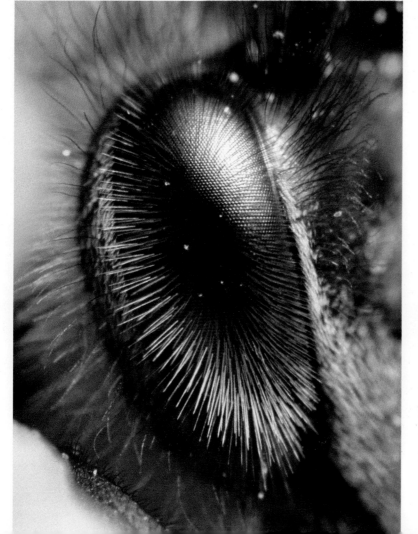

The upper region of the compound eyes of honeybees are sensitive to polarized light, allowing the bee to navigate by the Sun's position in the sky.

can also perceive the electric component of polarized light, they are therefore able to navigate successfully even when the Sun is obscured by clouds – as long as a portion of blue sky containing polarized light patterns is still visible. This remarkable technique seems to work because these creatures compare the pattern of polarized light that they see within one portion of sky with a brain-coded chart of the entire sky pattern.

Baffling the bees

Bees have an amazing ability to discern and employ polarized light. Their talents were discovered by German zoologist Prof. Karl von Frisch in the late 1940s. He revealed that if the polarization plane of polarized light is reversed by reflecting light with a mirror, bees will orient in the opposite direction from the normal one. And if direction-rotating plane filters are applied to the light, the bees will faithfully reorient themselves in line with whichever new polarization plane is imposed. Later studies by Von Frisch obtained comparable results with certain other insects, including fruit flies (*Drosophila* spp.) and flesh flies (*Sarcophaga* spp.).

Photosensors in the squid's eye can collectively perceive polarized light in exactly opposite directions.

The view from the top

Different species use different methods for detecting polarized light. The structures that perform this function in the honeybee are those ommatidia (lenses in the compound eye) that are found at the top of the bee's eyes, forming a region known as the POL (polarization sensitive) area. The flesh fly uses not only these dorsal ommatidia but also the dorsal ocelli (simple photosensitive cell patches on the fly's head). In certain relatives of bees, the larvae can also detect polarized light. Although larval insects lack compound eyes, they do possess ocelli, and in these particular larvae the ocelli situated to the side are sensitive to polarized light.

But insects cannot detect this form of light in all wavelengths. Bees, for instance, are particularly sensitive to those wavelengths of ultraviolet light just beyond violet light. Hence these are the wavelengths within which they can sense polarized light with the greatest clarity.

Experiments conducted by Zurich University biologist Dr Rüdiger Wehner with the Tunisian desert ant (*Cataglyphis bicolor*) showed that out of

ANIMAL PROFILE

The Horseshoe Crab

EYE DETAIL

The first aquatic species shown to be able to perceive polarized light was the horseshoe crab (*Limulus polyphemus*), a sea-dwelling chelicerate arthropod whose compound eyes were found by Dr T. H. Waterman in 1950 to contain an area that could analyze light polarization. Since then, Waterman's continuing studies have revealed that many aquatic insects, crustaceans, fishes, and even mollusks such as squid and octopuses exhibit similar abilities that allow them to reduce glare or dazzling reflections caused by bright sunlight, just as we do by wearing polarizing sunglasses.

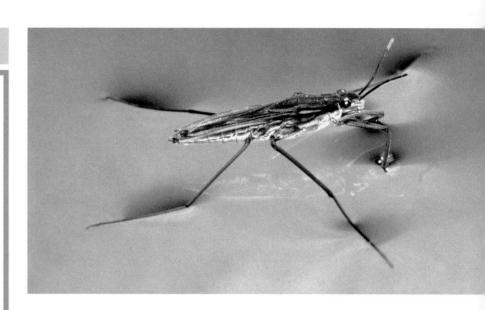

the 1,000 ommatidia in each compound eye, 80 per eye are dedicated to receiving polarized light within the ultraviolet wavelength band, and each receives it from a different point in the sky. That is, one ommatidium receives it from 270°, another from 180°, and so on. Within the compound eye, one region, the retinula, is directly sensitive to polarized light.

A bird's eye view

Some migrating and homing birds can perceive polarized light. In pigeons, a specific retinal region of the eye's upper visual field views the sky for polarized light. This retinal region contains unusual photoreceptors known as double cones, one function of which is to detect polarized light.

Birds also possess an even more remarkable visual talent – they can actually see the Earth's magnetic field. Their magnetic vision is so far outside our own experience that it is not easy to imagine what the Earth's magnetic field might look like to the birds.

Most scientists theorize that the bird's perception of the magnetic field looks like two color-coded spots overlying the bird's normal vision. These dots correspond to the north and south poles, but can be seen by the bird only in certain wavelengths of light, usually the violet end of the visible spectrum. They may vanish entirely in light wavelengths at the red end of the spectrum, depending upon the species.

Pond skaters (*Gerris lacustris*) have specially polarized compound eyes to block out the glare of the Sun reflected off the water they live on.

Like many birds, the indigo bunting (*Passerina cyanea*) can see not only polarized light, but also the Earth's magnetic field.

Whale Strandings

see also:
● Ultrasonic Hearing, p.22
● Bird Migration, p.68
● Animal Hypnotists, p.122

Whales use the Earth's magnetic fields to accomplish feats of astonishingly accurate underwater navigation as they travel the oceans of the world. But, for reasons we don't yet understand, sometimes something goes terribly wrong. The pitiful sight of the world's largest mammals stranded on beaches unable to return to deep water has increased the determination of scientists to try to find the cause. But the mammals' behavior remains a profound maritime mystery.

The world's largest mammals have an astounding ability to navigate the Earth's vast oceans, but sometimes it fails tragically. Just what is it that leads them to disaster?

Reports of mass whale strandings date back many centuries, and have been recorded worldwide. Numerous explanations have been offered – from the prosaic to the poetic, from the decidedly implausible to the eminently feasible – but there is still no universal agreement as to which, if indeed any, is likely to be correct. Some believe that beached whales must suffer from a kind of brain infection, which leads to disorientation, or that they might have a parasitic infestation of the inner ear that prevents them from receiving the unique sonar echoes that tell them where they are. This theory is not unlike the one proposed to explain the bizarre dancing behavior of foxes when in close proximity to their prey.

Drawn to the land

More dramatic is the suggestion that whales beach themselves in order to commit suicide. Another hypothesis holds that some primitive instinct causes whales to seek safety on land – a response dating back to prehistoric whales, which were terrestrial.

The most plausible explanation, however, is that strandings result from some external interference or confusion arising from the whales' electromagnetic navigational skills. Magnetic storms on the Sun, for instance, are known to create havoc with the magnetic components of bird migration. Human sources of magnetic waves, such as radar and possibly even television or radio signals, might also be responsible.

Magnetic variations

A last theory proposes that certain costal changes might have blocked the whales' ancient migration paths. This theory leads to what is perhaps the most likely source of navigational error – coastal locations in which the lines of geomagnetic variation (magnetic valleys) that normally run parallel to the coast are blocked by an island or outcrop of coastline. In these

At this spot on the western coast of Tasmania, a site of frequent whale strandings, whales lie beached with no way of getting back out to deep water. The cause may be a geomagnetic anomaly.

There are always willing helpers who hope to prevent the death of stranded whales. But the animals' size often makes this impossible.

locations, whales using the coast's magnetic valleys to navigate close to the shore would unexpectedly find themselves swimming into dangerously shallow waters, or even coming ashore. Their heavy bodies press lethally on their lungs and, no longer buoyed by the waters of their aquatic domain, they wait to die.

Accident "black spots"

Dr. Margaret Klinowska, a marine mammalogist at Cambridge University in England, has identified a number of "black spots" – specific locations where whales become stranded on a regular basis. One is near Bicheno, on the coast of Tasmania, Australia. Three separate mass strandings of pilot whales (*Globicephala* sp.) have taken place at this site within 12 months from late 1991 to September 1992. Despite rescue attempts, more than 430 whales died.

This is a region in which the coast's magnetic valleys run across it instead of parallel to it. Klinowska also noted that oceanic species, such as pilot whales, are the ones that most often become stranded, rather than coastal species. A simple explanation for this may be that those whales that normally spend their lives traveling the oceans will have little or no local knowledge of coastline geography, making them more likely to fall victim to the shore's geomagnetic traps.

ANIMAL PROFILE

The Harbor Seal

Echolocation is well known in toothed whales (odontocetes) and bats. Claims that seals and sea lions (pinnipeds) also use this mechanism were backed by zoologists Dr. Deane Renouf and Dr. M. Benjamin Davis of the Memorial University of Newfoundland, Canada. Their recordings of common (harbor) seals (*Phoca vitulina*) in the field and in captivity indicated that the species used echolocation when visual stimuli were absent, producing at least two types of signal.

Electricity Generation

see also:
● Electrosensitivity, p.55
● Electromagnetic Enigmas, p.58
● Fish Migration, p.74

Some fish generate enough electricity to kill their prey, whereas others produce electricity for less violent purposes, using it to help them navigate. Different fish generate electricity using organs modified from different muscles, but they all use the same method to produce electricity.

A fish's electric organs are composed of electroplaques – flattened cells stacked in vertical columns like piles of coins. Each electroplaque normally produces little more than 0.1 volt, but, since the individual cells are linked in series per column and the columns themselves are linked in parallel, the overall charge is greatly increased.

Seawater conducts electricity more efficiently than freshwater, so saltwater species of electric fish do not need to generate such high voltages as their freshwater counterparts in order to produce the same current. To generate the higher voltages needed to overcome the inherent electrical

An electric ray can generate up to 200 volts of electricity to stun or kill its prey.

Some underwater creatures pack a punch that is literally shocking. The ability of the electric eel to stun or kill prey with a high-voltage blast is immediately obvious, but other fish use their electric powers in more subtle ways.

resistance of freshwater, electric fish living in this habitat have much taller columns of electroplaques than marine species of electric fish, although they have fewer columns overall.

Electric sea stunners

The most potent marine species of electric fish is the torpedo, also known as the electric ray, the majority of which live in the Mediterranean and the subtropical Atlantic. Its power to generate electricity has been known since ancient Greek

and Roman times and stems from a pair of large electric organs located in its big round pectoral fin, which is just behind each eye. Large torpedoes can generate a fish-killing jolt of up to 200 volts. In Roman times, physicians used this electric charge as a cure for patients with headache or gout by strapping a living torpedo ray to the sufferer's head.

Much weaker voltages are generated by other fish, including bottom-dwelling marine rajid skates, whose electric organs are in their tails. In the west Atlantic, electric stargazers, which are related to perch, hide in the sand, with only their eyes protruding, waiting for their prey to come close enough to be seized. Their electric organs are located in deep pits behind the eyes, and are used for defense as well as for stunning prey.

The mighty electric eel (*Electrophorus electricus*) can produce a 550-volt blast out of its tail.

Freshwater shocks

The freshwater species that produces the most powerful electrical discharge of all is the Amazon electric eel (*Electrophorus electricus*). Measuring up to 10 feet (3 m), it has three electric organs. Of these, two are used for navigation and prey detection. The third, and largest, is a formidable weapon. Split into two long, lateral halves, it discharges out of its tail, releasing up to 550 volts into its freshwater habitat.

The shock stuns its prey, which consists of fishes and frogs, but is also powerful enough to kill humans and even horses if they are present in the water when the eel discharges.

Africa's freshwater electric catfish (*Malapterurus electricus*) can discharge up to 350 volts from an electric organ surrounding its body. Like the electric eel, it uses this high-voltage jolt to stun prey as well as to deter would-be attackers. Interestingly, this species is also very sensitive to the Earth's magnetic field. In captivity, it responds to magnetic currents generated several hours before an impending earthquake.

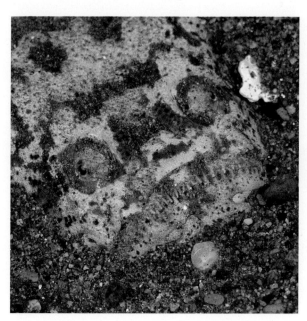

The crafty stargazer fish (*Uranoscopus* sp.) lies hidden in the sands, ready to stun passing prey with the electric organs located between its eyes.

Electric navigation

Two other fish, the mormyrids and the knifefish gymnotids, use their electric organs to navigate. These organs create an electric force field that surrounds the fish as it swims, and is modified by the relative conductivity of objects in the fish's immediate surroundings. The fish detects and interprets these electrical fluctuations through electro-receptors embedded in its body, so that it has a constantly changing electrical image that enables it not only to navigate effectively around obstacles in even the darkest water but also to sense nearby prey, and anything else coming its way.

The mormyrid, or elephant-trunk fish (*Gnathonemus petersi*), generates electricity, which it uses to navigate.

The mormyrid's detection mechanism is so sensitive that it can distinguish between different species of fishes, and also between different sexes of its own species. In 1992, studies were conducted by Dr. Christian Graff from Pierre Mendès-France University in Grenoble, France, and Dr. Bernd Kramer of Germany's Regensburg University, using mormyrids specially trained to respond to certain signals. The studies revealed that these fish could even distinguish between different same-sex individuals of their own species. They detected and recognized the unique characteristics of pulse and frequency emitted by each individual.

The navigation system of mormyrids and knifefish gymnotids is like the echolocation used by bats. In some mormyrids, the electric organs are derived from muscles at the tail's base, but in gymnotids they mostly derive from flank muscle.

Hidden depths revealed

The fishes in the Amazon river's dark, deepwater zones have remained mostly unknown – until now. Recently, Arizona University ichthyologist Dr. John Lundberg has led a major investigation using deepwater nets. By February 1997, his team had caught 125,000 fishes comprising more than 240 species, many of them new to scientists. Two of the most bizarre are a pair of predatory species of electricity-generating fish that use their electricity to navigate the Amazonian abyss. Dubbed *Magosternarchus duccis* and *M. raptor*, they bite off and devour the tails of other electric fishes. Because their victims' tails soon regenerate, these fishes' very peculiar food source remains undiminished.

To "see" in murky waters, the electric knifefish (*Sternarchus albifrons*) creates an electric force field as it swims.

Electrosensitivity

see also:
● Exotic Senses, p.38
● Electricity Generation, p.52
● Electromagnetic Enigmas, p.58

Animals do not generate electricity just to navigate and to stun or kill their prey – different members of the animal kingdom have found various ways to use their electrosensitivity.

Although sharks do not have electricity-generating organs, they do have numerous electrosensitive organs known as the ampullae of Lorenzini. These tiny jelly-filled structures are located just beneath the skin and open through external pores onto the surface of the shark's snout. They can detect electrical fields as minute as 0.005 millivolt, produced by the muscles of prey that are nearby. The ampullae of Lorenzini are so sensitive that they can help the shark find flatfish hidden in the sand.

The great white shark (*Carcharodon carcharias*), which rolls its eyes back out of harm's way when

Electric powers aren't just restricted to eels and torpedo rays. Other members of the animal kingdom, from sharks to snakes and even platypuses, also get a charge out of life.

opening its jaws to bite its victim, is guided during that brief period of blindness by the electrical information provided by these tiny organs. They enable it to home in to even very weak electrical fields in order to ensure the accuracy of its initial bite. In the hammerhead, the ampullae of Lorenzini are profusely scattered across its grotesquely broad head, so they are able to scan the widest possible area for the telltale

The great white shark (*Carcharodon carcharias*) homes in on its victims with the help of electro-sensitive organs.

electrical traces emanating from their favored prey, stingrays, which hide on the sandy sea floor.

Snake, rattle, and roll

Three facets of rattlesnake behavior and physiology – silent rattling, tongue scanning, and tribo-electricity – have long perplexed herpetological researchers. Now it seems they may be linked to the generation of electricity.

The purpose of the rattlesnake's rattle has traditionally been believed to be for scaring off potential aggressors. Why then do even rattlers who can't yet rattle go through the motions? A juvenile specimen whose rattle has not yet developed sufficiently to make its familiar sound still vibrates it enthusiastically. This mystifying phenomenon is known as silent rattling.

Tongue scanning is the name given to another odd behavior performed by snakes. It occurs when a snake waves its tongue above an object, its twin tips flicking up and down without touching it. Snakes directly touch objects with their forked tongues when feeding or tracking prey, but before doing so they practice tongue scanning. This process was thought to be a way of collecting olfactory particles from the air, but might it also serve a second, very different purpose?

A third mysterious phenomenon is tribo-electricity, the process of generating electricity through friction. Like other dry-skinned land animals that slide across the earth's surface, rattlesnakes acquire a positive electrostatic charge through friction. Yet whereas other such creatures have hairs, bristles, or spines that serve as multiple discharge points, rattlesnakes and other serpents do not. They appear able not only to acquire but also to retain an electrostatic charge.

Shocking revelations

In 1997, zoologists Dr. Theodore Vonstille and W. T. Stille, both from Florida's Envi-Sci Center, proposed a fascinating new theory linking these three anomalies in a paper in the journal *Nature*. They performed a series of experiments with detached rattlesnake rattles (obtained from road-kill specimens). Attaching one of these structures to a static voltmeter, they showed that, when stationary, a rattle would not produce a voltage. When vibrated 60 times per second, however, it yielded positive charges of 50 to 100 volts, suggesting that, when a rattlesnake vibrates its rattle, it generates electrostatic charges.

Australia's duck-billed platypus has been shown to find its way underwater using electro-receptors in its bill.

Rattlesnakes may use their rattles, their tongues, and the positive electrostatic charge picked up as they slide across the dry ground to create an electric sixth sense.

Vonstille and Stille proposed that the rattlesnake's electrostatic charge may serve as an aid to navigation. According to their theory, the snakes may use tongue scanning to read the electrical charges of the landscape as they travel. Electrostatic charges would cause the scanning tongue tips to be repelled by other positive charges and attracted to negative charges. Differences in environmental charge levels could be detected by sensory nerve endings or other sensory cells.

Dead giveaway

Sensitivity to electrostatic charges could also be useful in leading the snake to potential prey. Since moist air is a good conductor of the electric charges that are present on the Earth's surface, the airborne plumes of moisture exhaled by animals could theoretically be detected by snakes, thus giving away the animal's location. As the moisture plumes take on static charges from the Earth, the snake's tongue could detect the charge, helping the snake to find its prey.

Unfortunately, snakes are notorious for responding poorly, or not at all, to rewards or negative reinforcements in experimental situations. It is therefore difficult to devise ways to test this theory. Even so, the concept of rattlesnakes with an electrostatic sense that is in some ways like the distant touch sense yielded by the lateral line system of fishes is so intriguing that it should be worthy of spending the time to design experiments to examine it.

All charged up

When a platypus (*Ornithorhynchus anatinus*) dives underwater, it closes its eyes, ears, and nostrils – so how does it detect the fishes, shrimps, and frogs that it preys on? By the early 1980s, the traditional belief – that it simply sensed its prey's movements – was rejected by an Australian National University team of researchers headed by German zoologist Dr. Henning Scheich. He decided to explore the sensational possibility that the platypus, like the shark, may be sensitive to the electrical impulses produced by its swimming prey.

Discernible discharge

No mammal had ever been shown to possess this quality. In 1986, however, the team announced that when a tiny live 1.5-volt battery was placed on the floor of a pool containing a platypus, the animal unerringly swam up to the battery and attacked it with its bill. But when a dead battery was placed in the same pool, the platypus ignored it completely. Since both batteries were stationary, they did not create any water currents, and the platypus could not see, hear, or smell them. The aquatic creature must therefore have been reacting to the live battery's minute electrical discharge. Later studies confirmed this remarkable discovery by revealing the presence of tiny electroreceptors all over the platypus's bill. Interestingly, these are linked to the trigeminal cranial nerve, whereas in all electrosensitive fishes the corresponding receptors are linked to the auditory cranial nerve.

Electromagnetic Enigmas

see also:
- Electricity Generation, p.52
- Bird Migration, p.68
- Insect Migration, p.72

A number of controversial cases involving instances of electrical phenomena in the animal kingdom continue to perplex mainstream zoology even today.

For example, electrical phenomena caused by animals may help to explain some UFO – unidentified flying object – sightings. Over the years, many different solutions have been offered for these sightings, ranging from weather balloons, luminous clouds, and rare optical phenomena to misidentified sightings of celestial bodies such as the planets Venus, Mars, and Jupiter. One of the most intriguing explanations, however, must surely be the possibility that some accounts of glowing aerial spheres are actually sightings of electrified swarms of insects.

Electrifying entomology

In the 1960s, Norton Novitt, an amateur scientist from Denver, Colorado, conducted a series of experiments that lent weight to this theory. Novitt attached winged ants to a ping-pong ball that was then connected by a thin wire to a static generator inside a darkened room. Once the generator was switched on, the ants' bodies became luminous, glowing brightly. In the wild state, ants commonly initiate their nuptial flights shortly after thunderstorms, which cause very strong atmospheric electrical fields. Accordingly, during

The electromagnetic powers of some creatures can give rise to startling effects, from false UFO sightings to the ability to find water.

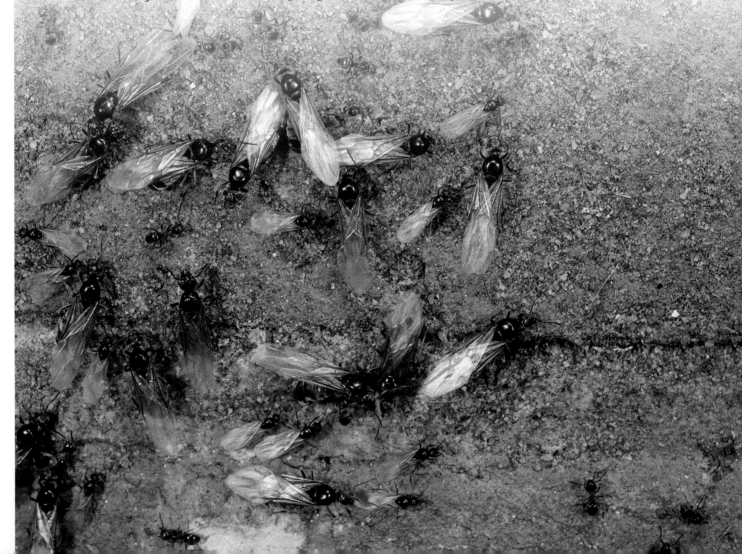

such conditions, swarms of winged ants might indeed glow – quite possibly emitting sufficient light to be readily visible at night, and, in turn, to be mistaken by some observers for alien spacecraft.

Certain species of moth will also glow in electrical fields, including the spruce budworm moth (*Choristoneura fumiferana*) of Canada, whose enormous migratory flocks can measure up to 60 miles (96 km) long and 15 miles (24 km) wide. If such a vast swarm were to take to the sky following a thunderstorm, the total amount of light that it could emit while traveling through the highly charged air would be more than adequate to convince eyewitnesses not familiar with this species' swarming activity that they had seen a "real" UFO.

When they are ready to mate, ants take to the air to find partners, flying in great swarms just after a heavy thunderstorm.

Animal water witches

Dowsing is the unexplained ability of certain people to sense the presence of subterranean water sources or mineral deposits. One popular explanation,

ANIMAL PROFILE

Shocking Insects

The following short report was published in 1881 by a journal called *The English Mechanic*, but remains as mystifying today as it was then:

"Certain insects are known which give something like an electric shock to anyone touching them. The *Redivivus* [*Reduvius*] *genatus* or 'wheelbug' of the West Indies, is one so described by Kirby and Spence. Two other examples have been lately recorded in the Entomological Society, by Mr. Yarrell. A letter from Lady de Grey, of Groby, referred to a shock caused by a beetle, one of the Elateridae [click beetles], and extending from the hand to the elbow. The other case is that of a large hairy lepidopterous caterpillar in South America. Captain Blakeney, on touching, had an electric shock so strong, that he lost the use of his arm for a long time, and his life was even considered in danger."

These accounts are mysterious because there is no known species of insect that can actively give off an electric shock. A sudden sting or skin irritation might, however, give the impression of an electric shock. Since *Reduvius*, the assassin bug, has a sharp, stabbing beak and since certain species of caterpillar have hairs containing highly irritating substances, it is possible that some people might think that they had received a shock from one of these creatures. Click beetles, however, do not sting, so it remains a mystery how anyone could think that they have received an electric shock from a click beetle.

THE MONGOLIAN DEATH WORM

The inhabitants of the southern reaches of Mongolia's Gobi desert fear a mysterious wormlike beast, the *allghoi khorkhoi*, or Mongolian death worm. Unknown to science, this elusive beast is up to 5 feet (1.5 m) long, and can apparently kill either by squirting a lethal corrosive venom or using a method that seems to involve electrocution.

The nomads tell of camel herds that have stepped on sand concealing a death worm, only for each camel to drop dead as soon as one of its hoofs touched the worm. During the 1990s the celebrated Czech explorer Ivan Mackerle led two expeditions to the Gobi in search of this dreaded creature. Although his team did not find a death worm, they gathered a lot of data regarding it from the local people, including an account of a party of American scientists who had visited the region many years before. One of the scientists, while idly prodding some sand with an iron rod one evening, abruptly dropped to the ground, dead – having unwittingly touched a death worm in the sand with the rod. If these stories are true, the only mechanism by which the death worm can kill in this way is indeed electrocution.

To date, all known species of electricity-generating animal are fishes, and hence dwell in water – a good conductor of electricity. By comparison, sand is a much poorer conductor. Perhaps, however, if the death worm actually exists and does indeed kill by electrocution, it does not generate electricity internally but externally – via friction. This phenomenon, called triboelectricity, occurs when the external body surface (in this case probably scaly if, as seems likely, the worm is some form of reptile) rubs against the desert sand as it moves through it.

supported by Russian research into this controversial subject, is that dowsers are very sensitive to small changes in the Earth's magnetic field. Moreover, there is a concentration of magnetite whose function is so far unknown within the cranial bones forming the nasal cavity in humans.

Some researchers claim that other species also practice dowsing. There are many records on file, for instance, of elephants traveling far from their normal feeding territories during periods of drought in search of water, excavating drill holes with their trunks in seemingly barren areas lacking any visible sign of water, yet successfully locating water within those holes.

Moreover, Trevor Beer, a naturalist based in Exmoor, England, has suggested that birds employing their geomagnetic sensitivity during migration may actually use their bills as divining rods, dowsing the earth's natural magnetic field as they fly over it through the sky.

Elephants have been known to find water by digging holes in the ground with their trunks during droughts.

Earthquake Prediction

see also:
- Infrasonic Messages, p.25
- Electrosensitivity, p.55
- Hibernation, p.100

There are countless records on file, some dating back many centuries, that tell of animals behaving abnormally before a major quake strikes. Animals seem to notice early warning signs of an earthquake even before it can be detected by today's sophisticated seismological equipment.

Although western scientists remain somewhat skeptical of this phenomenon, their counterparts in the East readily accept that many different kinds of animal can sense oncoming earthquakes. The monitoring of animal behavior to see if it can be used as an early warning system for earthquakes has long been accepted as a valid area of research in China and Japan. But can animals detect earthquakes, and if so, how?

Many animals behave oddly just before an earthquake. Can they sense something we can't? Different species of animal may be alerted by their powerful secret senses to the early warning signs of an impending quake.

Not surprisingly, the creatures that have attracted the majority of attention as quake detectors are those most closely associated with humans – whether as pets or vermin. Dogs seem particularly sensitive to an earthquake's cryptic clues. In the days leading up to the massive quake that devastated Calabria on the Italian mainland in

Dogs around the world have been recorded howling and barking just before earthquakes have struck.

1783, dogs in Messina, Sicily, barked and howled hysterically, eventually creating so much noise and disturbance that an official order was issued to shoot them all. Many were duly killed, but the remainder continued to howl and bark – until the quake abruptly hit the area.

And this is not the only record of dogs sounding the alarm before an earthquake. On February 20, 1835, in Talcahuano, near Concepción, Chile, the howling dogs did not wait to be shot – instead, they ran out of town. Later that same day, a major earthquake razed Talcahuano. A similar pattern of abnormal canine behavior was documented a few hours before an earthquake that occurred at San Juan, Argentina, in 1942. And throughout the evening preceding the infamously catastrophic San Francisco quake of 1906, dogs howled loudly and unceasingly, to the bewilderment but also consternation of their unsuspecting owners, as many later recalled. More recently, the same scenario occurred before the Assisi quake of 1997, and up to four days before the violent quake at Ismet, Turkey, in 1999. The distraught behavior of dogs and other livestock in the Chinese city of Haicheng in 1999 led the authorities to order its evacuation – saving many lives, because later that same day Haicheng was hit by an earthquake.

Rats on the run

While rats are only rumored to leave sinking ships, there is documented proof that they will sometimes desert a city before it is struck by an earthquake. During the early hours of February 9, 1971, two policemen patrolling a section of California's San Fernando Valley were astonished to encounter huge groups of rats racing down the traffic-free roads leading out of the city. Moreover, when they alerted their colleagues, they learned that similar rat packs had been observed doing the same thing at the opposite end of the city. Just before 6 A.M. that morning, the police – and everyone else in San Fernando – learned why, when the city was struck by a monstrous earthquake.

Aerial and aquatic earthquake detectors

Birds and water-dwelling beasts are also frequently reported quake prophets. While the dogs were fleeing Talcahuano on February 20, 1835, the town's skies were full of panic-stricken gulls, circling wildly and screaming continually. This also occurred with gulls at Iquique, Chile, some hours before a quake struck there in 1868. And less than 12 hours before a quake occurred at Montana's Hebgen Lake on August 17, 1959, all of the

When the Snakes Awake

Snakes are adept at sensing an oncoming earthquake, coming out of hiding in good time to escape. Indeed, this dramatic behavior inspired the title of Berlin Free University scientist Prof. Helmut Tributsch's book on animal quake prediction (*When the Snakes Awake*, 1982).

So acute – and compelling – are a snake's powers of quake prediction that snakes will wake from hibernation and crawl out into a cold, snow-covered world if they detect the hidden early-warning signs of a quake. Six weeks before China's Haicheng quake of February 4, 1975, snakes came out of their burrows; many froze to death on the snow.

Two notable cases occurred within just a month, in the same country. Early on July 26, 1976, a ditch in Ninghe County, roughly 25 miles (40 km) from the city of Tangshan in China's Hebei Province, was found to contain a writhing mass comprising hundreds of snakes. Less than two days later, Tangshan was wrecked by a massive quake. Similarly, in August 1976, many snakes mysteriously emerged from burrows in Sichuan Province's Jiangyou County – just before a major quake hit the neighboring counties of Pingwu and Songpan.

Creatures as diverse as seagulls and rats have been known to desert an area hours before it is hit by an earthquake.

waterbirds normally residing here in dense populations took to the air and disappeared.

Japanese fishermen have often reported disorientation among fishes and aquatic invertebrates, in freshwater and even in the deep sea, that makes them easier to catch. There are numerous cases on file, for instance, of catfish physically jumping out of their ponds before a quake, and of eels migrating overland from one pond or river to others farther away just before a quake strikes. An unexpected abundance of octopuses in shallow water was reported in Japan's Oga peninsula before this area was shaken by a quake in 1939. Several deep-sea species were caught at or near the surface just before quakes hit Tokachi-Oki on May 16, 1968 and Uwajima three months later, including two oarfishes (*Regalecus glesne*), a 17-foot (6 m)-long giant squid, a deep-sea *Nemichthys* snipe eel, and a 5-foot (1.4 m)-long lancetfish (*Alepisaurus borealis*).

One of Japan's leading quake researchers, Osaka University physicist Prof. Motoji Ikeya, has tried to test animals' sensitivity to earthquakes. Since electric fields are generated in the earth before a quake and Ikeya had read reports of catfish leaping out of ponds before a quake, he tested these fishes' electrosensitivity. His experiments revealed that they display violent agitation even when exposed to electrical fields as small as 4–5 volts/meter. And he found that eels were even more sensitive. Yet when he placed his own finger into a tank containing these fields, he could not feel anything.

Early warning signs

An earthquake is preceded by ground vibrations that snakes, insects, and spiders can probably feel since they are close to the ground and very sensitive to these tremors. There are many cases on file of these creatures behaving abnormally, emerging from their nests or hideaways in disorder, just before an earthquake. Some quake-associated movements of underground gas yield infrasonic waves, and these could be detected by pigeons and birds that use low-frequency sound waves as guides on their long-distance journeys.

Although different animals seem to respond to different early warning signs, many of them may feel the accumulation of positive electrical ions in the air. These positive ions build up before quakes due to massive pre-quake compression of subterranean rocks. Animals as diverse as dogs, snakes, birds, and even catfish and other aquatic species might all be able to detect these ions.

Humans, even if they once could detect ions, may no longer be able to. However, some people become depressed and even ill if exposed to positive ions, such as those found in some hot dry winds. It may be that these people have a remnant of ancestral earthquake sensitivity.

Weather Prophets

see also:
- Electrosensitivity, p.55
- Electromagnetic Enigmas, p.58
- Earthquake Prediction, p.61

Animals are better at forecasting the weather than humans are due to their sensitivity to various meteorological cues, including those of an electromagnetic nature. Researchers have long wondered how insect-eating bats that live in dark, deep caves seemingly sealed off from basic knowledge of the weather can nonetheless accurately sense when rain will make flying insects swarm in the outside world. Recently, it was discovered that these bats can sense a specific meteorological stimulus to which the insects respond.

Bat researcher Dr. Ken Paige of the University of Illinois's Institute for Environmental Studies noted that flying insects were most common when air (barometric) pressure was low (except in heavy rain). During these conditions eastern pipistrelle bats inhabiting caves in western Illinois came outside in large numbers. When the air pressure rose, however, insect numbers declined, and fewer bats exited the caves. The bat's barometric sense may be due to the Vitali organ in the middle ear – bats are the only mammals with this organ.

Hideaway bees

Insect "weathermen" rely heavily upon their electromagnetic sensitivity. Bees, for instance, are very responsive to electrical discharges in the air that occur just before a thunderstorm, ultimately causing lightning, which in turn generates electromagnetic waves. These waves stimulate bees to return swiftly to their hives and remain inside until the storm is over. The electromagnetic cause of their behavior was confirmed in an experiment in which artificial electrical fields triggered the same behavior in the insects as thunderstorms.

> The ability to forecast weather is not limited to human meteorologists. Many members of the animal kingdom are also adept weather diviners.

When the American ground squirrel, or prairie dog, hears an approaching thunderstorm, it builds a circular dyke around the entrance to its burrow to keep it from being flooded.

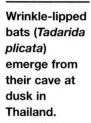

In New Zealand, the nuptial flights of certain moths are so influenced by the positive ion accumulation in the atmosphere that precedes thunderstorms that they can be used as an accurate guide to future weather conditions. At first, scientists had assumed that the environmental cues responsible for their activity were temperature and humidity, but experimental studies found that ionization was in fact the cause.

Birds also use electromagnetic cues. The swift (*Apus apus*), for example, spends most of its life on the wing and therefore needs to be able to predict the weather in order to avoid bad conditions. By sensing atmospheric ionization, the swift can detect an electrical storm before it arrives and elude danger by flying at right angles to its path, returning only once the storm has ended.

Although humans can hear thunder, to certain creatures, such as birds, elephants, ground-dwelling rodents, and various insects, this sound is even more dramatic because they can detect the infrasonic component we cannot hear. Since infrasonic sound tends to travel greater distances through the air than the wavelengths audible to

our ears, animals who can hear it can detect approaching thunderstorms much earlier than we can, and hence take appropriate evasive action. American ground squirrels, or prairie dogs (*Cynomys* spp.), for example, build a circular dyke to keep rain from flooding their underground burrows. Some animals can even hear the infrasonic component of air turbulence caused by rain clouds.

Swifts spend virtually their entire lives on the wing and use electro-magnetic cues to detect and avoid storms.

Legendary leeches and frog forecasters

Some people have tried to use the early-warning system of animals to predict the weather. Frogs were once kept as living barometers, and a 19th-century inventor used leeches to ring a literal warning bell when a storm was on its way. Perhaps inspired by a folk legend that claims that leeches stay at the bottom of ponds in sunny weather but rise to the surface when a storm is about to begin, he constructed a vertical tank of leeches, with a tiny bell that was triggered whenever the leeches rose to the surface.

Frogs were once kept as living barometers, becoming darker when rain was due as the pigment cells (melanophores) in their skin expanded due to the humidity.

CHAPTER THREE

FANTASTIC JOURNEYS

Long before Homo sapiens *became long-distance voyagers and explorers, many species of animal were already highly accomplished navigators and globetrotters – through land, sea, and air. From wildebeests that trek across Africa to whales that voyage from pole to equator to terns that travel from North to South Pole and back again in a single year, animals undertake journeys that are truly superhuman. The vast migrations they perform continue to amaze scientists and put our own mechanically assisted journeys to shame, even in today's sophisticated age of world travel.*

Bird Migration

see also:
● Infrasonic Messages, p.25
● Tidal and Annual Rhythms, p.96
● Brood Parasitism, p.170

How birds travel the globe to their breeding and feeding grounds is an enigma that scientists are now close to unraveling.

Even tiny birds can make giant journeys. Hummingbirds, for example, fly up to 3,700 miles (6,000 km) from their summer haunts in southern and eastern North America to their central Mexican wintering grounds; these distances equal those covered by much bigger birds, such as cranes and geese.

Many different avian species travel vast distances during migration; in doing so, they all use a complex system of navigation that relies on a wide range of external cues and innate knowledge to keep them on course. True migration involves both an outward journey and a return journey.

The long-distance traveler par excellence of the bird world is indisputably the arctic tern (*Sterna paradisaea*). During the northern hemisphere's summer, this small seabird breeds in the Arctic, sometimes nesting within 450 miles (720 km) of the North Pole, thus experiencing the 24-hour daylight present there. As soon as winter begins, however, it commences an incredible marathon flight south, traveling from pole to pole until it reaches the Antarctic Circle, where summer is just beginning. Daylight once again lasts 24 hours.

Depending upon the route that the bird follows, this flight can cover up to 12,400 miles (20,000 km), yet can take under three months. And that is only half of the arctic tern's record–

The Arctic tern has the longest migratory journey of any creature, following the summer Sun from the North Pole to the South Pole and back again in a single year, making a journey that totals in excess of 24,800 miles (40,000 km) round-trip.

beating journey. As soon as winter approaches in the Antarctic, this remarkable bird heads north again, covering another 12,400 miles (20,000 km) or so during the return to its Arctic breeding grounds. By dividing its entire year between the constant daylight of the far north and far south, the arctic tern experiences more daylight in a year than any other organism.

Within the space of a year, therefore, it has flown roughly 24,800 miles (40,000 km) – the greatest distance between breeding seasons traveled by any bird. Since it does this each year of its adult breeding life, which can last over 30 years, a single arctic tern can conceivably fly more than 621,300 miles (one million km) in its lifetime.

The mystery of migration

How birds successfully navigate over such vast distances, locating their breeding or wintering grounds unerringly from afar, was once one of the animal world's greatest enigmas. Generations of researchers, however, have peeled away the layers of mystery that shroud this phenomenon, revealing many (though still not all) of its secrets.

There seem to be two principal components at work in a bird's ability to migrate: Innate knowledge and learned experience. Cuckoos famously take no part in the rearing of their offspring. Yet young cuckoos successfully migrate to their species' winter feeding grounds, even though

The white stork spends winters in Africa, returning to Europe to nest each spring.

they have never been there before. Clearly, then, they possess genetically inherited navigational knowledge concerning the distance to, and compass orientation of, their grounds.

Birds use the Sun and Moon like compasses. They seem to have an inherent basic knowledge regarding the Sun's position and also, in night-flying species, those of the Moon and certain stars (notably the Pole Star cluster in northern

ANIMAL PROFILE

Albert the Albatross

Birds can take a wrong turn when migrating, but few have ever strayed farther than a certain black-browed albatross (*Diomedea melanophris*). Native to the South Atlantic, this species needs powerful air currents to sustain its soaring flight and so cannot cross the doldrums, a belt of very light winds at the equator. In June 1967, British bird-watchers were amazed to see a black-brow among a colony of gannets in Scotland. This lone male, dubbed Albert, returned there each spring for the next two years, but the gannets always rebuffed him. He then moved to a gannet colony on the Shetland island of Unst, and reappeared there every spring for over 20 years. In 1996, however, Albert failed to reappear and is now believed to be dead.

Snow geese fly in a V formation as they travel on their lengthy journey between their nesting colonies in the Arctic tundra and their winter feeding grounds on the Gulf of Mexico.

signposts during future migrations. They may also note infrasonic acoustics generated by wind passing over mountains and tall buildings or coming from natural features such as waterfalls, and possibly even the echoes of their own calls. All manner of visual, topographic features will be used as landmarks during daytime flying, together with more sophisticated, learned astronomical indicators in the hours of darkness. Some birds may even somehow use the Earth's own spinning force – the Coriolis effect – in navigation.

Massive flocks

The movements of some species are exceptional not because of the vast distances they cover but because of the colossal size of the flocks. The most extraordinary example is unquestionably the red-billed quelea (*Quelea quelea*). For good reason, the quelea is often called the feathered locust. This small, seed-eating species is a relative of the finches and is the world's most abundant wild bird, with a total population currently estimated at around 10 billion, and a total adult breeding population of one-and-a-half billion.

A single flock of queleas can contain millions of birds. Although they normally eat the seeds of wild grasses, queleas also find the cultivated cereal crops of farmers to their taste. When a flock of this size descends upon farmland, they can strip it bare in just a few days. Queleas will travel up to 1,000 miles (1,600 km) in search of food in order to fuel their prolific reproduction. These birds produce up to four broods a year, each hatching in under two weeks. Adult queleas that have already raised one brood often move to another region to raise the next one, displaying a form of breeding migration.

Since the quelea is extremely destructive to agriculture, affecting the economies of over 20 African countries, many measures have been tried to reduce its numbers. Although approximately one billion birds are killed each year by methods including poisoning and nest destruction, this species breeds so efficiently that no long-term reduction in its total number has yet been seen.

Another (formerly) superabundant species, the North American passenger pigeon (*Ectopistes migratorius*), was hunted into extinction by 1914 despite a total population estimated at 5–10 billion

hemisphere birds). Since birds can see polarized light, they can navigate even when the Sun is hidden by clouds.

Before they make their first migratory flight, young birds explore their home territory to familiarize themselves with landmarks and other local features for use as recognition aids on their return journey (a method of navigation that is termed piloting). The Earth's geomagnetic force may also be used. All of these navigational modes are governed by the birds' own internal biological clock, detecting and responding to daily and seasonal environmental rhythms.

Migratory maps

Adult birds rely not only upon their innate navigational knowledge and biological clock, but also upon additional data acquired during previous migrations, so that they can modify their routes and correct for displacement of navigational clues if necessary. This additional data takes many forms, including clues of an olfactory, auditory, visual, and possibly even gravitational nature. For example, researchers have provided evidence that homing pigeons may respond to olfactory signals, creating a veritable "smell map" that guides them back to their coops. Other birds may well use the scent of meadows or the sea in a similar way.

Pigeons and a number of other species probably take notice of animal-related sounds too, in localities they fly over and use them as aural

This warbler is feeding its larger cuckoo nestling (an imposter who has tricked its adoptive parent into nurturing it). The cuckoo will later embark on a genetically programmed migration.

Intriguingly, the eastern bar-tailed godwit (*Limosa lapponica baueri*), a wading bird, exhibits a similar but more subtle behavior that appears to assist its long-distance migration. As revealed in 1998 by Groningen University researcher Dr. Theunis Piersma and Dr. Robert Gill from the U.S. Geological Survey, before setting out on its 6,800 mile (11,000 km) migration from Alaska to New Zealand, this bird builds up huge amounts of fat to sustain it on its flight. In order to provide itself with enough room to house all of this extra fuel, yet also keep its weight down for flying, the godwit absorbs up to 25 percent of the tissue comprising its liver, kidneys, and alimentary canal. Only when the bird completes its migration are these organs reformed in their entirety. This is the first time that partial organ absorption and subsequent reconstitution has been documented in a species of migratory bird. Other species may also do this to fuel them on long journeys where there are few opportunities to feed en route.

birds in 1800. It would appear that this species could reproduce effectively only when present in huge flocks. Once these had been reduced below a certain critical level, extinction became inevitable.

Strange sustenance

A grotesque phenomenon known as autophagy or autocannibalism, in which an animal eats portions of its own body, can be used as an aid to migration.

This huge flock of red-billed queleas descends on water in Namibia. When they land on farmers' fields, they live up to their nickname (the feathered locust), eating all the crops in their path.

Insect Migration

see also:
● Bird Migration, p.68
● Irruptions and Invasions, p.82
● Tidal and Annual Rhythms, p.96

Although they are often far smaller than birds and may also appear much more delicate, insects are capable of undertaking some highly impressive feats of migration and swarming. Many species of butterfly journey great distances between their breeding and wintering grounds. To navigate they use an innate celestial knowledge, and they are probably also stimulated by olfactory and visual cues, just as birds are.

The most famous butterfly migrant is the American monarch or milkweed butterfly (*Danaus plexippus*). During the early summer across much of North America, this large, slow-moving orange-hued butterfly lays its eggs on the underside of the leaves of milkweed plants. After hatching, the monarch caterpillars feed on the leaves for about a month before pupating. A week or so later the mature butterflies emerge. For the rest of the summer, the butterflies are content to sip nectar from

Small in size and often fragile-looking, insects undertake some of the toughest migrations on record, sometimes, as in the case of locusts, causing great damage along the way.

garden and countryside flowers. At the onset of fall, however, enormous flocks of monarchs take to the air and fly south, to Florida, southern California, Mexico, the West Indies, and Central America. Monarchs that live in South America fly even farther south in the fall.

At their winter destinations, monarch butterflies settle in vast numbers on the branches of evergreen trees, where they remain in a torpid state throughout the winter. In the spring, those that have survived the winter begin their return journey north to their summer grounds. On the way, they breed, sometimes passing through as many as three generations before reaching their destinations.

Despite their relatively fragile form, monarchs can attain flying speeds of up to 9 miles (15 km) per hour, and cover immense distances. The longest recorded journey for a monarch is 2,132 miles (3,432 km), which is the straight-line (and hence minimum) distance covered by a female specimen originally

Monarch butterflies settle on trees in Mexico, where they look like living flames. Several million have been counted on a single acre.

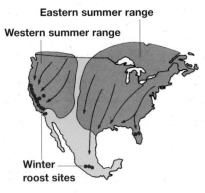

Eastern summer range

Western summer range

Winter roost sites

Wintering in southern California and Mexico, monarchs migrate north in spring, heading south again the next winter.

tagged and then released on September 6, 1986 in Canada's Presqu'ile Provincial Park, near Brighton, Ontario, and recaptured on January 15, 1987 on a mountain close to Angangueo, Mexico.

Other butterflies and moths also make incredible journeys. The painted lady (*Cynthia cardui*), the hawk moth (*Erynnyis ello*), the large (cabbage) white (*Pieris brassicae*), and clouded yellow (*Colias croceus*) are all famous for either their long journeys or huge swarms.

A plague of locusts

From the earliest times, crops grown in semiarid regions of Africa, Asia Minor, and western Asia have been devastated by locust swarms. The desert locust (*Schistocerca gregaria*) is especially destructive, but like other locusts it lives a sort of Jekyll and Hyde existence. For much of the time, it is a harmless grasshopper, living a solitary life, doing no harm to agriculture, and laying eggs that hatch into fresh generations of normal grasshoppers, wingless at first but gradually developing wings as they mature.

If environmental conditions confine these grasshoppers into concentrated breeding sites, however, a disturbing transformation occurs. The juvenile grasshoppers begin forming groups. Then, groups close to one another combine to form ever-larger congregations, and eventually an immense "army" is produced. These gregarious yellow grasshoppers develop longer-than-normal wings, enabling them to fly farther and faster. Once

airborne, they move through the skies in vast clouds, guided by the Sun and wind, seeking food and able to fly across a continent to find it.

In 1889, one such swarm reported over the Red Sea was estimated to contain 250 billion locusts. The all-time record is claimed for a terrestrial swarm spied in South Africa during 1784, which covered over 1,900 square miles (5,100 square km). Because each locust can eat its own weight in food each day, locusts can cause human famine and death on a grand scale. Ultimately, however, even the biggest swarm will disintegrate, sometimes due to weather fluctuations. And when eggs from these locusts hatch, the juveniles will be normal grasshoppers – the rampaging Mr. Hyde turned into the passive Dr. Jekyll again.

This locust swarm in Africa, feeding on a grass called sedge, is made up of millions of individuals (inset).

Fish Migration

see also:
- Sensitive Smell, p.28
- Refined Taste, p.31
- Electrosensitivity, p.55

From salmon who can leap waterfalls in a single bound to tuna as streamlined as a speeding bullet, many fish are masters of migration.

Both freshwater and seawater fish migrate. Their migratory journeys to their spawning grounds can be split into four broad categories, based upon the nature of the journey: from freshwater to seawater, from seawater to freshwater, from one region of seawater to another, and from one region of freshwater to another.

Most species of eel always live in the sea, but anguillid species, including the European eel (*Anguilla anguilla*), mature in freshwater and then migrate to the sea to spawn. This type of migration is termed catadromous.

European eels begin life in the Sargasso Sea of the North Atlantic, hatching from their eggs as a ½-inch (10 mm)-long larval form called the leptocephalus. Scientists once believed that these larvae were a wholly separate species from the adult eel. As the larvae grow larger, they drift farther out from the Sargasso, carried passively across the Atlantic by the Gulf Stream until, three years later, they reach the European coast. Entering estuaries,

they metamorphose into the familiar elver or "glass eel" stage, after which they begin their upstream migration in vast hordes, seeking rivers in which to live, so bringing to a close their migration's outward-bound phase. In the process, they have covered a distance of up to 3,100 miles (5,000 km).

They remain in the river for a number of years until they have transformed into fully mature adult eels. Curiously, adult European eels journeying downstream to reach the sea again are almost never seen. In their North American counterpart, however, adult eels are regularly reported moving downstream. When they reach the eastern coast of North America, they begin the final phase of their migration – heading for the Sargasso Sea where they spawn, thereby completing their life cycle.

Those specimens that do complete their life cycle use many environmental cues to navigate during their migration. Not only are eels highly sensitive to olfactory stimuli, they also respond readily to small fluctuations in water movements, seismic activity, and even to the minute electrical

■ Breeding ground   ■ Migration path

The European eel is spawned in the Sargasso Sea, then spends three years drifting across the Atlantic to the shores of Europe.

fields generated by water currents. The eel larvae are also helped by ocean currents; North American eels move up the east coast, whereas European eels move across the Atlantic on the Gulf Stream.

Intriguingly, some researchers have speculated that the North American and European eels may not be separate species at all. They also theorize that few if any European eels complete their migration cycle, and that the North American version may actually give rise to both forms in the Sargasso Sea. Critics of this theory have pointed out that the two species have differing number of vertebrae. However, experiments have shown that the eel's vertebral count can be modified by environmental influences; eels reared in higher water temperatures have fewer vertebrae.

Spawning salmon

Fish that migrate from the open ocean upstream into freshwater rivers for spawning are said to be anadromous. The most famous of these anadromous fish is the salmon. These fish are noted for the

This male Atlantic salmon leaps up a waterfall on its way to its spawning grounds upriver. Only the fittest salmon survive the journey.

lengthy, arduous journeys they make back to their birthplaces in freshwater streams and rivers from the ocean where they spend their adult lives.

The Atlantic salmon (*Salmo salar*) begins its life in a river, in the wild mountain streams of Norway or Scotland, hatching from an egg there in springtime. The salmon usually spends up to four years in the river before beginning the outward phase of its marathon migration as a smolt (a young salmon ready to migrate to the sea), traveling downriver to the ocean. During this period, the smolt's physiology adapts to enable it to live in seawater.

Once in the ocean, it spends up to four years traveling and maturing before setting off on its return journey as an adult salmon, retracing its path upstream to the very river in which it hatched as many as eight years before. The salmon's extraordinary ability to locate the river where it was born is due to its highly developed olfactory sense, which enables it to distinguish between different rivers by scent.

Survival of the fittest

Because salmon swim against the water current when journeying upstream, and often need to leap over waterfalls and other natural (as well as all manner of human-made) obstacles, it is a long and exhausting journey and only the fittest specimens survive to reach their rivers and spawn. This process weeds out the weakest fish, ensuring that none but the best survive to pass on their genes to the next generation.

Moreover, in the Atlantic salmon, after spawning has taken place some adult females actually make their way back to the sea again, where, albeit exhausted, they eventually recuperate and live on. In Pacific salmon (*Oncorhynchus* spp.), however, the adults die after spawning.

During their migration, salmon travel widely, some as far north as Greenland, others to the sea around Norway, sometimes covering over 3,500 miles (5,600 km).

Traveling tuna

Although they never leave their ocean habitat during migration (and are thus referred to as oceanodromous fishes), tuna can sometimes undertake even lengthier migrations than even those masters of migration, the salmon and eels. After spawning in the seas off Florida and the Bahamas during late spring and early summer, and in the Mediterranean during mid-summer, the bluefin tuna (*Thunnus thynnus*) sometimes undertakes immense migrations north. These

journeys are closely associated with the movements of its prey, which include other, smaller fishes such as herring and mackerel.

In order to study the tuna's migratory habits and to ascertain the routes taken and distances traveled, scientists have tagged individual tuna using special devices called darts, which are attached to their bodies. These darts contain detailed information concerning the fish and its original whereabouts and are to be sent back to the scientists by anyone who catches these tagged fishes.

One specimen, dart-tagged in 1958 off Mexico's Baja California, was caught five years later 300 miles (483 km) south of Tokyo, Japan. This means that the minimum (i.e. straight-line) distance that it had swum during those intervening years was 5,800 miles (9,335 km) – but it had almost certainly covered a much greater distance than that, as it is highly unlikely that a tuna (or any other fish) would swim between two such widely separated locations in a straight line.

From lake to river and back again

Freshwater fish that remain in freshwater to migrate include such species as carp, barbels, minnows and catfishes, as well as North America's formidable garpike.

These freshwater migrations tend to mean that the fish move from deep, slow-moving lakes or rivers to faster-flowing but shallower tributaries for spawning purposes in order to avoid encountering predators. They readily recognize their own specific spawning grounds, and actively seek them out each year when the time comes to spawn again, perhaps using olfactory clues to find their way. After spawning the fish will journey back to their original bodies of water to complete their life cycles.

The bluefin tuna swims north from its breeding grounds in search of prey, sometimes traveling up to 6200 miles (10,000 km) on its journey.

Mammal Migration

see also:
- Whale Strandings, p.50
- Electromagnetic Enigmas, p.58
- Irruptions and Invasions, p.82

Although there are far fewer long-distance travelers among the mammals and reptiles than among the birds, insects, and fishes, they include some creatures that make spectacular migratory journeys whether by land or by sea.

From little lemmings to mighty whales, a wide range of different mammals undertakes migrations each year, often in search of food.

The most incredible voyages are those accomplished by certain species of aquatic marine mammal, particularly members of the whale order. Indeed, the gray whale (*Eschrichtius robustus*) undertakes the longest confirmed migration of any mammal, aquatic or otherwise.

The gray whale's summer feeding grounds are in the waters of the Bering Sea between Alaska and Siberia, whereas its winter breeding grounds are off Baja California in northern Mexico. These two marine areas are separated by a distance of up to 6,200 miles (10,000 km), but the gray whale swims this in a speedy 90 days, twice a year, during its annual migration cycle.

A whale of a trip

Recently, cetological research has indicated that humpback whales (*Megaptera novaeangliae*) may well cover comparable, if not even greater, distances during their migrations, performing such maritime marathons as traveling from the Caribbean to Greenland and Iceland, from Hawaii to Alaska, and from the Antarctic Ocean to Colombia in South America.

In 1998, a zoological team from the Sea Mammal Research Unit at Scotland's St. Andrews University and the Australian Antarctic Division announced that their satellite-tracking studies of elephant seals (*Mirounga leonina*) from Macquarie Island had revealed that within four to six weeks of taking their very first swim in the sea, the young will journey out as far as 620–1,240 miles (1,000-2,000 km) in search of squid and other food – a feat made even more remarkable by the fact that, as young pups, they have no previous experience of where to find the food to fuel them on their journey.

Whether from the northern or southern hemisphere, humpback whales follow the same annual migration pattern, moving from the krill-rich waters of the poles to the warm waters of the equator to give birth.

- ■ Summer feeding grounds

- ■ Winter feeding grounds

The Alaskan fur seal lives in colonies at their breeding grounds in the north. The females travel south each winter to feed in Southern California.

Female Alaskan fur seals (*Callorhinus ursinus*) are also long-distance travelers, journeying some 3,100 miles (5,000 km) southward each year during September and October to southern California's warmer coasts for the winter (the males remain in northern waters by the Aleutian Islands). During the spring, however, they return to their colder breeding grounds in the Bering Sea's Pribilof and Commander Islands, and Japan's Sakhalin Island.

Mass migrations on land

Several species of hoofed mammal, including springboks, gnus, and the American bison, formerly undertook mass migrations comprising millions of individuals. But since these species were hunted to near-extinction before the 1900s, they no longer exist in sufficient numbers to accomplish this. Smaller-scale migrations do, however, take place.

One much smaller species of herbivorous mammal that still undergoes periodic swarming on a spectacular scale is the lemming. Displaying a formidable reproductive rate – more than 100 offspring can be born to a single pair within six months – a population of Norwegian lemmings (*Lemmus lemmus*) can expand very dramatically. In doing so, the lemmings deplete their food supply within a given area of the Scandinavian tundra and scrub that comprises their normal habitat. Once

The blue gnus, or wildebeests (*Connochaetes taurinus*), surmount many obstacles on their mass migrations. Here, they are about to cross a river.

the population size reaches 40-100 individuals per acre (100-250 individuals per hectare),which tends to occur every three to five years, emigration ensues, whereby a sizable horde of these volelike rodents travels southward in search of food, expanding their population's range by 120 miles (200 km) or more as they go.

Accidental death?

During this mass migration, many lemmings die. Others, suffering from the effects of acute overcrowding (such as aggression toward one another and general disorganization within the horde), become frenzied and exhausted – to the extent that some drown in rivers or even plummet over cliff tops into the sea. These lemmings are not running over cliffs due to any suicidal impulse (although such claims frequently appeared in early nature books). Rather, the lemmings are unable to change course in time. Some researchers have claimed, in addition, that because food is so scarce,

An illustration from an old book shows migrating lemmings leaping into a river. It was once believed that lemmings deliberately committed suicide, but this is a myth.

lemmings may be forced to eat certain species of toxic plant, and that these are partially responsible for inciting their frenzied behavior. The lemmings' population fluctuations are usually mirrored by comparable fluctuations in the populations of their predators, particularly owls and arctic foxes.

Migrating mammals on the wing

Bats, the only mammals equipped with the power of true flight, are, like their counterparts in the bird kingdom, able to journey considerable distances in their travels. Some exhibit true migration – flying from their summer breeding grounds to their wintering grounds. These bats then turn around six months later and return home to breed again.

Australia's gray-headed fruit bats (*Pteropus poliocephalus*) travel more than 1,000 miles (1,600 km) between October and December during their southward migration from Queensland to Victoria. They make stops along the way to snack upon paw-paw fruits.

Similarly, the American red bat (*Lasiurus borealis*) migrates from Canada and much of the northern United States down to the southernmost regions of the United States and even to islands as far from the mainland as Bermuda 560 miles (900 km) away, often in single-sex flocks. Moreover, adult females will each carry up to three infants (collectively weighing more than their mothers) during their mass migration.

Gray-headed fruit bats roost in trees in summer in New South Wales.

Other Migrations

see also:
● Sensitive Smell, p.28
● Refined Taste, p.31
● Tidal and Annual Rhythms, p.96

Many reptiles and amphibians migrate over relatively short distances. During the breeding season, frogs, for instance, often migrate merely from one pond to another one fairly close by, rarely traveling more than a couple of miles. They use the Sun, Moon, and stars as overhead signposts to guide them on their way. Some aquatic reptiles, however, are much more adventurous.

Reptiles and amphibians migrate far and wide. Some, such as the sea turtles, make incredibly long journeys across entire oceans, whereas others, like frogs and crabs, make short but sometimes spectacular trips to mate.

Most notable among these are the sea turtles. These turtles feed in the deep sea but nest on the tropical beaches on which they were born, often thousands of miles away. Loggerheads (*Caretta caretta*) hatch from their eggs in Japan but spend the next two years swimming 6,200 miles (10,000 km) across the Pacific Ocean to their feeding grounds off

The green sea turtle lives off the coast of Brazil but migrates to Ascension Island to mate and lay eggs. The adults then return to Brazil, leaving the young to incubate, hatch, and find their own way home alone.

Mexico's Baja California. Then, after spending five years there, feeding and maturing, they set forth on their return journey to Japan. Other extra-long-distance voyagers are the green turtles (*Chelonia mydas*), one population of which commutes between its nesting grounds on Ascension Island and its feeding grounds off the Brazilian coast – a distance of 1,400 miles (2,250 km). Similarly, the leathery turtle (*Dermochelys coriacea*) lives in temperate waters around the world, even though it builds its nests and hatches its eggs on tropical beaches of the Atlantic, Pacific, and Indian Oceans

■ Feeding grounds

up to 3,100 miles (5,000 km) away. It is believed that sea turtles are guided during their migratory navigation by taste and smell cues in the surrounding seawater.

The most abundant reptiles on Earth are sea snakes, and the yellow-bellied sea snake (*Pelamis platurus*) may well be the most abundant species of them all. It is widely distributed through the Pacific and Indian oceans, and is well known for drifting passively (often several thousand at a time) on the surface. It cannot enter the Atlantic due to upwellings of cold water. However, as first proposed by Dr. Monty Priede in 1990, if global warming elevates sea temperatures, these thermal barriers may cease to exist, permitting this snake to invade the Atlantic, which could in turn bring it as far north as the shores of Great Britain and New England.

March of the Christmas crabs

Each year at the rainy season's onset, the land crab (*Geocarcinus natalis*) of Christmas Island undertakes an amazing mass migration. Millions of these small blue-backed, red-legged crabs emerge from their forest-floor burrows and march across this tiny Indian Ocean island situated 870 miles (1,400 km) northwest of Australia toward the sea, invading houses, cars, and any other obstacles that stand in their way. Once they have reached the shore, they feed en masse, before returning to their forest homes in the island's interior to mate. After mating, the female crabs make the trek back to the sea, entering it to lay their eggs, before making their way back to their forest burrows where they remain until the next rainy season.

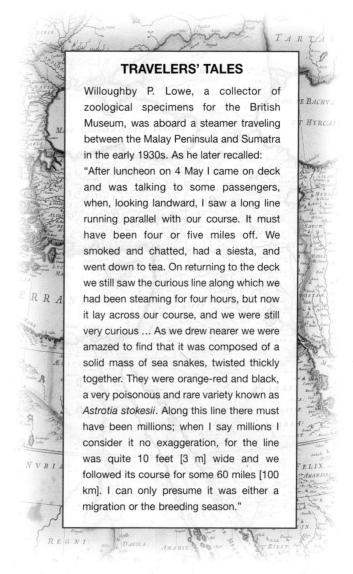

TRAVELERS' TALES

Willoughby P. Lowe, a collector of zoological specimens for the British Museum, was aboard a steamer traveling between the Malay Peninsula and Sumatra in the early 1930s. As he later recalled: "After luncheon on 4 May I came on deck and was talking to some passengers, when, looking landward, I saw a long line running parallel with our course. It must have been four or five miles off. We smoked and chatted, had a siesta, and went down to tea. On returning to the deck we still saw the curious line along which we had been steaming for four hours, but now it lay across our course, and we were still very curious ... As we drew nearer we were amazed to find that it was composed of a solid mass of sea snakes, twisted thickly together. They were orange-red and black, a very poisonous and rare variety known as *Astrotia stokesii*. Along this line there must have been millions; when I say millions I consider it no exaggeration, for the line was quite 10 feet [3 m] wide and we followed its course for some 60 miles [100 km]. I can only presume it was either a migration or the breeding season."

Irruptions and Invasions

see also:
- Magnetoreception, p. 44
- Bird Migration, p. 68
- Mammal Migration, p. 77

Mass movements of birds can take surprising species to far-flung lands. In invasions, these strangers remain, whereas in irruptions, they stay for only one season.

Animals can suddenly move in vast numbers far beyond the areas in which they usually live (their range). These movements are often termed irruptions or invasions. Although frequently confused with one another, these two terms have quite different meanings. Irruption is an unusual form of migration in which the proportion of individuals moving, distance traveled, and destinations all vary from year to year. Typical migration, in contrast, is regular – it occurs during the same season each year, and features a fairly constant number of individuals moving between fixed breeding and wintering areas. Invasion is different from irruption. It is the expansion of a species' distribution by successfully colonizing new areas outside its normal distribution range. Invasions are permanent movements of animals into new areas, whereas irruptions are temporary.

Taking wing to find food

By its very nature, irruption is common among birds, especially certain northern species. It is often associated with irregular food supplies, such as seeds, fruit, and prey that are abundant at some times and not at others. Crossbills, for instance, periodically irrupt in response to a scarcity of conifer seeds within their normal distribution range in the conifer forests of the northern hemisphere. These birds will travel great distances beyond this range during years in which food is scarce. No less than 67 separate irruptions of the common crossbill (*Loxia curvirostra*) into southwestern Europe were recorded between 1800 and 1965.

Several northern birds of prey, notably such species as the snowy owl (*Nyctea scandiaca*), short-eared owl (*Asio flammeus*), North American great horned owl (*Bubo virginianus*), rough-legged buzzard (*Buteo lagopus*), and goshawk (*Accipiter gentilis*), undergo comparable irruptions during

The crossbill feeds by prying the seeds out of pine cones with the specialized beak from which it gets its name.

The snowy owl is among the many birds of prey that periodically irrupt when food in their normal range is scarce, and competition for what prey there is becomes too fierce.

those years in which their prey's numbers are at their lowest ebb within their species' normal cycle of abundance-rarity. Moreover, because during previous years when prey was abundant the owls' birth rate increased, so their population now has to live on less prey. The birds are thus forced to leave their traditional grounds in search of food.

Over the years, Britain has witnessed a temporary influx of some exotic avian species due to irruption. One of the most interesting is Pallas's sandgrouse (*Syrrhaptes paradoxus*). These curious seed-eating birds are related to pigeons and doves. Under normal conditions, the species breeds in the steppes of southern Russia and eastward from the Caspian Sea. In 1863, however, a spectacular irruption occurred that brought sizable flocks of Pallas's sandgrouse as far west as Britain. The first recorded arrival comprised a flock of 14 birds spied on May 21 in Northumberland; within just a few days, flocks had been recorded in most of the counties along the eastern coast, with others spreading westward. Some individuals even reached Ireland, and one was shot in the Outer Hebridean island of Benbecula on October 13 — 250 miles (400 km) from where they were first seen. Several

nests, moreover, were discovered as far afield as Denmark and the Netherlands.

In early 1888, there was another major irruption, with immense flocks traveling through western Europe, reaching Britain by May. Collectors ultimately wiped them all out — despite an act of parliament that was passed to protect them. Several nests and fledglings were found in Britain, and some birds even overwintered successfully — twice, in a few cases, thus surviving into 1890. A few lesser irruptions of Pallas's sandgrouse were later recorded, the last notable one being in 1908, with none in recent years.

Westward ho!

During an invasion, birds expand their distribution range. Some of these cases are very dramatic, but few have been more so during modern times than the comprehensive invasion of western Europe by the collared dove (*Streptopelia decaocto*) as summarized by John Gooders in his classic book *Birds That Came Back* (1983): "Until 1928 it was resident in the Balkans with a range that extended eastwards to India. Then from the area around Belgrade it started spreading in a north-westerly

Limit of range in:	
	1930
	1938
	1945
	1955
	1965
	1970
	1975
	Today

Originally a native of eastern and southern Asia, the collared dove has now successfully colonized all of central and western Europe, southeastern Scandinavia, and the British Isles.

direction ... within twenty-five years it was noted at 468 places in Europe where it was previously unknown, including some Scandinavian sites 1,200 miles from Belgrade. It reached Hungary in 1932 and Czechoslovakia in 1936. By 1938 it was recorded in Austria and ten years later was well established. In 1943 it was present in Germany and reached Munich by 1948. In 1949 it was breeding in Switzerland and reached the Vosges area of France the following year. Others, meanwhile, had reached Denmark in 1948 and southern Sweden in 1949 – a spectacular leap-frogging of huge uncolonized areas to the south. It was present in Holland in 1950 and the first birds arrived in Britain at Manton in Lincolnshire in 1952, the same year that it reached Norway ... The first breeding [in Britain] took place in a garden in north Norfolk in 1955, when two pairs were present. In the following season three pairs bred in the same general area, and another was present at Gomshall in Surrey. By 1957 it was breeding in Lincolnshire, Kent and in Morayshire ... Additionally, individuals were noted in a variety of areas including Kent, Essex and the Isles of Scilly."

By 1965 this extraordinary species could be found throughout most of England, much of Wales and Scotland, coastal Ireland, and even the Outer Hebrides and Shetlands. It has been estimated by ornithologists that Britain harbored 3,000 pairs in 1964, with more than ten times this number less than a decade later. Today, the collared dove is one of Britain's most common species – its exceptional success at invasion is due to its hardy nature, profound reproductive capacity, and ability to live in association with humans.

ANIMAL PROFILE

The Cattle Egret

The story of how the cattle egret (*Bubulcus ibis*) spread across the world is a lesson in global domination. This heron-related species was indigenous to Africa and India. Like the collared dove, it is able to live alongside humans and livestock. The cattle egret had invaded South America by the late 1800s, Australia by the early 1900s, and both Europe and North America by the early 1950s.

Psi-Trailing

see also:
- Magnetoreception, p.44
- Mammal Migration, p.77
- Psychic Animals, p.192

Perhaps the most extraordinary, and mysterious, animal journeys of all are those featuring lost pets that have inexplicably found their way back home (or to their owner) despite having to travel considerable distances through unfamiliar terrain. In some cases the owner had moved since losing them – so these pets actually tracked their owners to houses that they had never even seen before. This thoroughly baffling homing ability is known as psi-trailing.

Rovers that returned

Some determined dogs, in successfully finding their way home, have undertaken journeys every bit as remarkable as anything experienced by the animals in Sheila Burnford's well-loved novel *The Incredible Journey* (1960).

Pets are capable of traveling thousands of miles when lost, even from one country to another. Scientists remain confounded by their built-in homing devices, such as psychic trailing.

Some claim that these seemingly miraculous returns are simply cases of mistaken identity, whereby wishful owners mistake look-alike strays for their lost dogs. But in two well-documented cases, distinctive scars have provided positive identifications. One concerns a collie called Bobbie, who was lost in Indiana in 1923 and yet found his way home to Oregon. The other involves a German shepherd dog named Nick who found her way home from the deserts of Arizona across rivers and mountains to Washington State.

Bobbie, a collie owned by Mr. Brazier of Silverton, Oregon, was lost in Wolcott, Indiana, in August 1923. Six months later, Bobbie came home and was identified by a scar. He had journeyed 3,000 miles (4,800 km) across rivers and mountains, even passing through a farm where he had lived as a puppy.

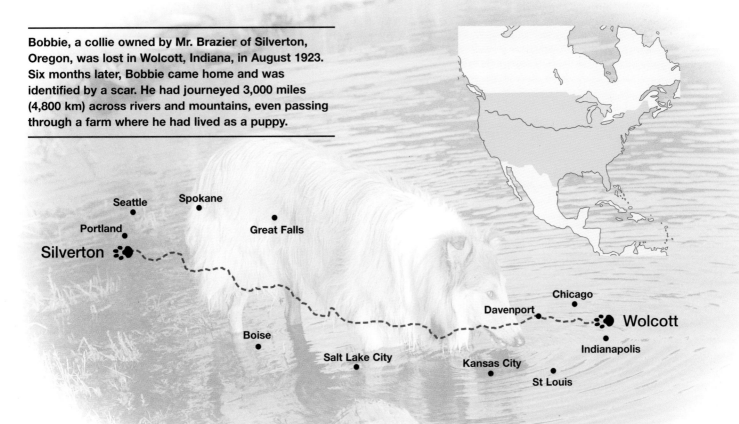

Seattle · Spokane · Great Falls · Portland · Silverton · Boise · Salt Lake City · Kansas City · St Louis · Davenport · Chicago · Indianapolis · Wolcott

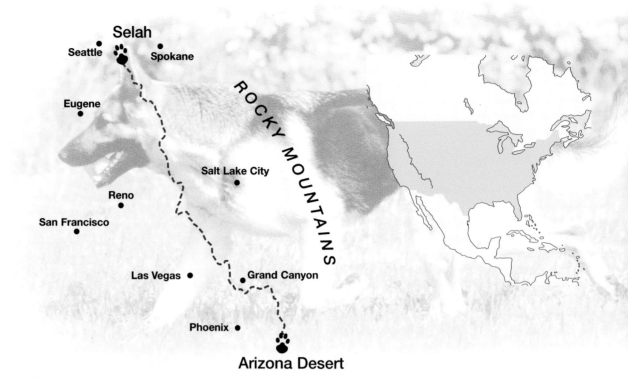

In 1979, Nick, a German shepherd dog, was lost in Arizona. Four months later, she returned to Washington, 2,000 miles (3,200 km) away. Nick would have traveled through the Grand Canyon and across rivers and mountains to get there.

Other notable psi-trailers of the canine kind include an Australian fox terrier called Whisky, who journeyed 1,860 miles (3,000 km) from Darwin to Melbourne in 1973; and Fido, who, after spending two years traveling 990 miles (1,600 km), tracked down his owner, Lise Deremier, in 1989, even though she had moved from Mons in Belgium to Gijon in northern Spain.

In 1995, a border collie called Blake was abducted when thieves stole his master's car. Blake was abandoned in Downhan Market, Norfolk. It took him just five days to travel over 50 miles (80 km), reaching Letheringsett, only a mile from his home at Holt. There he was noticed by villagers, who contacted his owner, Tony Balderstone. In this case, because the dog had been gone for such a short time, there is little chance that mistaken identity could have played a part.

The cats that came back

Feline practitioners of psi-trailing are also well documented. In 1986, Linda Thompson and her black-and-white cat, Sam, moved from Beaver Dam, Wisconsin, to Tucson, Arizona. A year later, however, Thompson moved back to Beaver Dam, but to a different house. She decided not to take Sam, leaving him at the Tucson Humane Society to be adopted by a new family. In 1991, four years after returning to Beaver Dam, she happened to visit the person who now lived in her

In 1997, Jap left her new home in North Carolina and traveled 650 miles (1,050 km) back to her old home in Indiana.

original home there and, to her great surprise, she discovered that Sam was living in the garage. Somehow, during the previous four years he had found his way back to his former home, journeying about 1,500 miles (2,400 km) from Tucson to Wisconsin.

In 1981, a cat called Minosch trekked a similar distance after being lost by his owners during a vacation in Turkey. Minosch turned up safe and sound (albeit in a somewhat bedraggled condition) just 61 days later at their home on the island of Sylt in northern Germany.

A heartwarming case of psi-trailing took place in 1992 and involved a tabby called Scrooge, owned by 6-year-old Aurelie Assemat of Grugny in France. Two years earlier, Aurelie had suffered grave injuries after falling from a fourth-floor window, which confined her to a wheelchair and left her almost blind and unable to speak. In the hope of providing her with some solace and focus, her parents gave Aurelie a little cat, Scrooge, whose warm embrace became her greatest joy. Tragically,

however, in August 1991, during a family vacation in the French countryside 620 miles (1,000 km) from Grugny, Scrooge became lost. After a fruitless search the family had to return home without their pet. During the months that followed, Aurelie grew ever sadder, spending all her time staring fixedly at Scrooge's empty basket – until, on 9 July, 1992, 312 days after he had disappeared, Scrooge scratched at the door of the Assemat family's home. As soon as he was let in, he ran to Aurelie, contentedly rubbing himself against her legs. Aurelie was so overjoyed that she called out to Scrooge by name – the first words that she had spoken since her terrible accident two years earlier.

This cat, Pluto, was found in an empty cottage that was for sale. Liking him, some potential buyers took him to their home, but the cat trailed over 20 miles (32 km) to get back to the cottage, so the family bought the property and moved in with him.

On the track of psi-trailing

The term "psi-trailing" was coined by Dr. J. B. Rhine, a parapsychologist at Duke University, who has researched this baffling phenomenon for many years. Initially, he assumed that the most dramatic cases might simply have involved mistaken identity – the animal that had unexpectedly turned up at the pet owner's home was not the pet that had been lost but merely another animal that looked similar. However, in such cases as those of Bobbie and Nick, where the returned animal could be positively identified by a scar or other mark, this explanation is clearly untenable.

Rhine then considered the possibility that olfactory stimuli were acting as guides – but discounted this, too, when faced with instances of animals finding their way home over truly immense distances. Furthermore, it seems likely that something more than orthodox navigational mechanisms, such as using topography, celestial markers, or geomagnetism, is involved because there are cases where a pet has found its owner even when the owner has moved away since the pet was lost.

Eventually Rhine concluded that in some still-undefined way, the pet must be able to focus directly upon its goal, whether that is its home or its owner, as upon a beacon, ignoring any intervening distractions.

Dr. Rupert Sheldrake has postulated that pets are linked to their owners and home environments by an invisible network of energy known as a morphic field, which seems to act like an elastic band, pulling pet and owner back together if stretched too far.

ANIMAL PROFILE

Homing Horses

Tango, a 21-year-old half-thoroughbred, and 24-year-old Badger, a Welsh Cob, had lived for most of their lives in the same paddock in Skirmett, Buckinghamshire, in England. Just after they had been moved to another farm about 10 miles (15 km) away, the gate blew open in a storm and the horses wandered off. Later that day, their owner learned that they were back in Skirmett. Traveling overnight on country roads, over completely unfamiliar terrain, the horses had found their old home.

CHAPTER FOUR

TIME CYCLES

*The world's natural rhythms are all of
profound significance to animals – so much
so that some creatures have evolved special
internal biological rhythms that mirror them,
and which therefore control many fundamental
aspects of their behavior. Whether
it's changing tides, the phases of the Moon
or the cycles of both days and years,
there are animals that react to them.
The study of time with regard to biological
organisms and processes is known as
chronobiology. In increasing order of
period length, the four cycles are:
tidal (12.4 hours), daily (24 hours),
lunar (29.5 days), and annual (365 days).*

Circadian Rhythms

see also:
● Exotic Senses, p.38
● Tidal and Annual Rhythms, p.96
● Extreme Endurance, p.110

Some animals' body clocks allow them to stick to a rigid daily routine, even when they cannot tell whether it's day or night.

The most obvious biological rhythms are those that have evolved to deal with – and which therefore correspond to – the natural external daily cycle: the succession of day and night within a 24-hour period. These are referred to as circadian rhythms.

True circadian rhythms are endogenous (controlled internally). That is, even when external conditions are made constant artificially (rather than remaining cyclical), circadian rhythms persist for some time, whereas non-circadian ones vanish.

In each 24-hour cycle, locusts are active during daylight hours but inactive throughout the dark hours. Superficially, this resembles a true circadian rhythm. If, however, they are subjected to constant light or dark, this cycle of activity is swiftly lost. In the same daily cycle, the American cockroach (*Periplaneta americana*) is active only during the first few hours of darkness. However, even if it is kept under constant light or darkness, its cycle continues, demonstrating that it is endogenous.

On first sight, circadian rhythms seem to be the same as various physiological patterns that mirror the external daily cycle, but genuine circadian rhythms can be distinguished from these in four fundamental ways: they are endogenous, can be synchronized by external factors, are not affected by body temperature, and can be conditionally disrupted if the animal's external conditions are disrupted artificially.

Recognizing the rhythm

After a few days of being shielded from the major components of the daily environmental cycle (for example, light/dark and temperature change), an animal's circadian rhythms will begin to be less rigid. Some become slightly shorter than 24 hours, others slightly longer – hence the term "circadian," which means "approximately a day." Thus when the North American flying squirrel (*Glaucomys volans*) is kept in constant darkness, its circadian locomotion rhythm free-runs, eventually displaying a 23.5-hour

The gliding habits of the flying squirrel are disrupted by external factors such as light or dark.

The American cockroach carries on regardless of daylight or darkness.

cycle, which is its inherent periodicity. As soon as the animal returns to a normal 24-hour regime, the light/dark and temperature cycles synchronize its circadian rhythms so that they exhibit a periodicity of precisely 24 hours again. This ability of external factors to synchronize such rhythms is called entrainment. The external factors are called Zeitgebers (from the German words "time" and "giver").

Camels' body temperatures fluctuate more when they cannot find water to drink.

When African camels (*Camelus dromedarius*) do not get enough water, their body temperature's amplitude (the difference between its highest and lowest values) increases from 3.6°F (2°C) to as much as 10.8°F (6°C). But its circadian periodicity stays the same; although body temperature influences many physiological processes, it does not affect circadian rhythms.

A mosquito's circadian activity in low light will become less pronounced if the light is artificially intensified. So circadian rhythms can be disrupted by certain artificial external conditions.

What controls circadian rhythms?

If a sparrow's pineal organ is surgically removed, it immediately loses its circadian rhythms. As soon as the organ is transplanted back, it regains them. If the replacement pineal organ comes from a bird with different rhythms, the recipient immediately exhibits the donor's rhythms instead of its own.

Moreover, if a sparrow's eyes are shielded from all light, its circadian rhythms are unaffected, but if an opaque substance is placed over its skull above the pineal organ, it loses its cycle. In birds, the hormone melatonin establishes the periodicity of circadian rhythms and is secreted by the pineal organ. It receives photo-stimulation from photoreceptors in the brain, not the eyes.

Very similar results to those from the pineal-transplanting experiments in birds have been obtained with silkworm pupae when their brains have been transplanted. Without a brain, pupae lose their cyclical adult-emergence behavior, but regain it once the brain is transplanted back, and gain that of a different species if given that species' brain. It seems that in this case, too, behavior is controlled by the release of hormones. But in some cases, nerve cells in the brain's optic lobes seems to be the primary influence.

In mammals, part of the mid-brain known as the hypothalamus contains two small collections of cells called the suprachiasmatic nuclei, which act as biological clocks and, in conjunction with the pineal organ, hold the key to establishing circadian rhythms. These nuclei are entrained by external light entering through the eyes, but they exert their effect not via hormonal activity (as in birds and some insects) but rather by direct neural action.

THE PHOENIX

The ritual suicide and resurrection of the mythical Egyptian phoenix happens in a regular 500-year cycle. The bird builds a splendid nest which is ignited by the Sun's rays, creating a blazing inferno. The phoenix then dances at the very heart of the flames until it is consumed by the fire. A new phoenix, as magnificent as its predecessor, rises from the ashes and molds together the remains of the nest within a capsule of aromatic leaves and myrrh to form an egg. The phoenix places its egg on the altar of the Sun God as a sacred offering – and then it departs for another 500 years before beginning its cycle of fiery death and rebirth all over again.

TIME CYCLES

Chronobiology is the study of time as it affects biological organisms and processes. Four environmental time cycles are of profound significance to animals – so much so that the animals have evolved special internal biological rhythms that mirror these cycles and control many fundamental aspects of their behavior.

Complex relationships exist between this crucial quartet of time cycles and the corresponding rhythms displayed by animals. In increasing order of period length, these four cycles are those of the tides (12.4 hours), the Earth's rotation (24 hours), the Moon (29.5 days), and the Earth's orbit round the Sun (365 days).

TIDAL CYCLE 12.4 HOURS

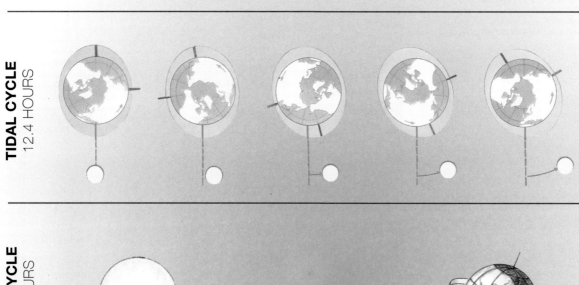

The Moon pulls on the Earth, forcing the part of the planet facing it into an oval shape. This causes the water facing the Moon and that on the other side of the planet to bulge outward, creating high tides twice a day.

DAILY CYCLE 24 HOURS

The Earth rotates on its axis, creating night and day. However, these cycles are not regular but are longer or shorter according to which hemisphere is closer to the Sun – getting longer in summer and shorter in winter.

LUNAR CYCLE 29.5 HOURS

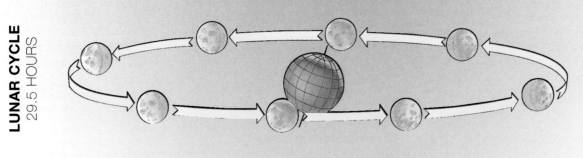

The Moon's phases reflect where it is in its orbit around the Earth. From new moon it becomes crescent, then first quarter, then gibbous. Full moon occurs halfway through, then gibbous, then last quarter and crescent.

YEARLY CYCLE 365 DAYS

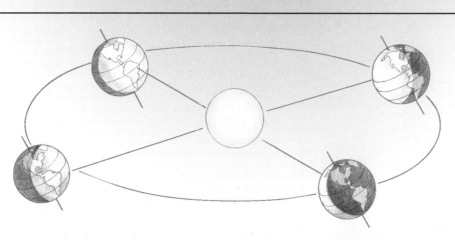

The Earth's orbit around the Sun gives rise to migration, hibernation, and even changes in plumage at different times of the year. As our planet tilts on its axis, seasons change and days lengthen and shorten.

Lunar Cycles

see also:
- Ultrasonic Hearing, p.22
- Tidal and Annual Rhythms, p.96
- Unexpected Vocalists, p.154

Even though it is 238,700 miles (384,400 km) away, and its light (or, to be precise, the sunlight reflected off its surface) is 300,000 times fainter than the Sun's direct light, the Moon has a profound and often baffling influence upon the behavior of many animals. In some cases, the

---

Australian coral spawn with a change in the Moon.

From swarming mayflies to seas filled with headless worms, the phenomena linked to the phases of the Moon are astounding.

Moon wields its influence through the tides, which are created by its gravitational pull upon our planet; in others, it is via its light. And in cases that have been investigated, evidence for certain animals having lunar rhythms that are endogenous (controlled internally) has been obtained.

Underwater snow and fishes that dance

A spectacular lunar-triggered outburst of mass marine reproduction occurs every year along Queensland's Great Barrier Reef, which is made of coral – at the same hour, on the same night, and at the same time, almost precisely a week after the full moon in late November/early December. At this time virtually all the millions of coral polyps comprising this massive natural structure discharge

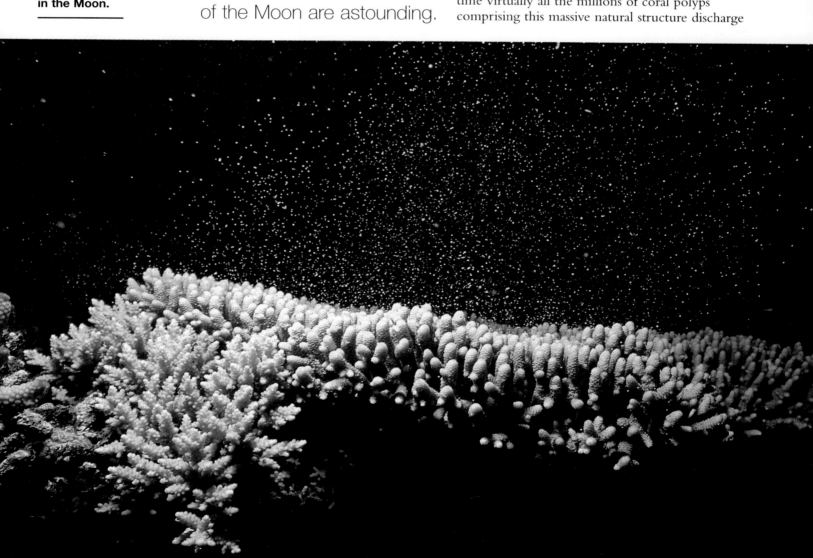

**Grunion
spawn on a
California
beach before
returning to
the sea.**

their bundles of sperm or eggs simultaneously – creating a veritable underwater snowstorm, except that the "snow" drifts upward rather than downward as eggs and sperm meet and fertilize.

Equally famous are the Moon-engendered mating gyrations of the grunion (*Leuresthes tenuis*), a slender silver-scaled fish native to the coast of California. Spawning occurs up to eight times per season, but it always begins three to four nights after a new or full moon, during a high spring tide, when the spawning females strand themselves high up on the shore's sandy beach. Here they gyrate madly while mating with males that have surfed onto the beach alongside them, and which are now entwining their bodies around them, fertilizing the eggs as they are laid. The females bury their eggs in the sand, then, accompanied by the males, return to the sea on the outgoing waves. The eggs remain buried until uncovered by the next high tide, stimulating them to hatch, whereupon the waves carry the young grunion seaward with them.

A frenzied waltz of headless worms

The Pacific palolo worm (*Eunice viridis*) and its West Indian relative (*E. fucata*) exhibit one of the most incredible examples of reproductive behavior on record, which is intimately linked to the lunar cycle. These two annelid species are polychaete worms, and normally remain secure within tubes

excavated by them in coral or under rocks, with their heads at the open end of their tubes – until the breeding season, that is.

When this period approaches, the rear half of each worm transforms dramatically, developing fast-growing reproductive organs. The worm itself reverses its position within its tube, so that it is now pointing head-down, with its highly modified posterior half-projecting out of the tube. Once the reproductive organs are fully developed, the posterior body half breaks off from the rest of the worm (which remains inside its tube but realigns itself so that its head is at the tube's open end again), and swims up toward the sea's surface – almost as if it were a separate animal in its own right. Indeed, it has even developed a pair of primitive eyes to assist it in locating the surface.

As it swims, the worm's posterior body half undergoes a further transformation, its internal structures and segmentation breaking down, so that when it reaches the surface it is nothing more than a writhing bag of either sperm or eggs (the sexes are separate in these species). At the surface, the bag bursts, releasing its contents – and, bearing in mind that millions of palolo worms have all undergone this radical metamorphosis at precisely the same time, the sea is soon awash with a mass of sperm and eggs, yielding a vast bout of communal, random fertilization. What makes these worms' reproductive behavior even more extraordinary is the exact nature of this event's timing. It occurs twice a year on the neap tides of the last quarter moon in October and November for the Pacific species, and the third quarter moon in June and July for the West Indian species of palolo worm.

Experiments were performed with a closely related European species, which swarms almost entirely at the time of the new moon. When kept in unchanging light-dark cycles, it was found that this worm's rhythm free-runs, suggesting it is endogenous.

Land animals under the lunar influence

Although most examples of lunar-influenced behavior feature marine species, several remarkable and sometimes very mystifying terrestrial examples have also been recorded.

In the mayfly (*Povillā adusta*), a distinct lunar-based pattern of adult emergence and swarming has been documented. Dr. R. Hartland-Rowe's studies of 22 Ugandan swarms observed between March 1953 and April 1955 at Kaazi, Jinja, and Lake Albert revealed that these swarms appeared within five days of the full moon, with most of them occurring on the second night after full moon. On three separate occasions, swarms were recorded simultaneously at locations roughly 120 miles (75 km) apart. Adult mayflies live only for a few hours, so the purpose of this swarming synchronicity is presumably to bring the two sexes together in order to maximize mating prospects before they die. Studies have shown that this lunar swarming rhythm occurs with specimens maintained in continuous darkness, indicating that it is truly endogenous.

Even the amount of activity exhibited by animals appears to be lunar-correlated in some species. As reported by Dr J. C. Jahoda following studies of specimens in outside enclosures, within any given month the American grasshopper mouse (*Onychomys* sp.) displays maximum activity close to the new moon and minimum activity near the full moon. Moreover, even when maintained under laboratory conditions of constant illumination, temperature, and atmospheric pressure, rats, hamsters, and several other rodents still exhibit a lunar-linked pattern of activity – high during those hours when the moon is below the horizon, and low when it is above.

The size of the pit dug by an ant lion larva is governed by the phase of the Moon.

The adult ant lion looks like a fragile, slow-moving dragonfly; its name is derived from its larva – a rapacious carnivore with huge jaws that digs a conical pit in sand and lurks at the base, waiting to seize any unwary crawling insect that falls into it. Studies conducted by South African entomologists Dr. G. J. Youthed and Dr. V. C. Moran at Rhodes University have revealed that the volume of the pit excavated by an ant lion larva varies according to the phase of the Moon, and is biggest during a full moon. Yet why this lunar-influenced variation in pit volume occurs remains unclear.

ANIMAL PROFILE

Moon-shy Bats

Bats are associated with the Moon, their shadows flitting across it as they fly at night. But the Jamaican fruit-eating bat (*Artibeus jamaicensis*) is lunaphobic. Dr. Douglas Morris of Cornell University found that when the Moon is full the bat stops night feeding and goes to its roosts, only reemerging once the Moon has set. Why? It does this even when the Moon is obscured by clouds, making it unlikely that it is just avoiding light that would make it visible to predators.

Tidal and Annual Rhythms

see also:
● Bird Migration, p.68
● Time Cycles, p.89
● Hibernation, p.100

The pounding of waves upon the shore and the passing of the seasons can affect animals' endogenous (internally controlled) biological rhythms. These tidal and annual rhythms are the shortest and longest of the four time cycles, respectively.

Not surprisingly, many animals exhibit biological rhythms attuned to the ebb and flow of the tides – which have a period of 12.4 hours – in order to enhance their survival prospects in a habitat involving dramatic, cyclical change, one in which they are successively submerged in water, then exposed six hours later to the sun and any predators lurking on the beach.

The common shore crab (*Carcinus maenas*) hides safely beneath stones or within crevices when the tide is out but knows just when to emerge from its hiding place as the waters start to cover the shore once more. It is one of many animals living on the seashore in the intertidal

Crabs that hide as the tide goes out, emerging only once it has started to come in again, are among the creatures whose behavior is governed by a built-in rhythm rather than a fear of predators.

(between tides) zone that exhibits this kind of rhythmic emergence and concealment behavior.

Some tidal rhythms are not endogenous, but are merely triggered by external cues, notably changes in salinity, pressure, and temperature as the seawater flows over the animal or ebbs away from them, and mechanical disruption caused by water flow. However, there are also many verified endogenous tidal rhythms on record, for which external cues serve merely to keep them synchronized with the tides, rather than actually inducing them.

Even when North American fiddler crabs (genus *Uca*) are maintained in total darkness with no tides for 25 consecutive days, they still exhibit their usual tidal rhythm of emergence and

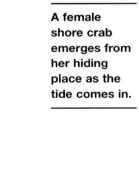

A female shore crab emerges from her hiding place as the tide comes in.

An annual cycle governs the width of the European starling's testicles, which expand or contract with the seasons.

concealment, confirming that this rhythm is truly endogenous. In these crabs' natural seashore habitat the tides occur roughly 50 minutes later each day, and this lag was mirrored by the experimental crabs' tidal rhythm studied in the early 1970s by Dr. J. Palmer. Unlike shore crabs, fiddler crabs emerge during low tide to seek mates and perform territorial displays, and remain hidden beneath the water surface at high tide.

Annual rhythms

With a period of 365 days, annual rhythms cause all manner of behavioral phenomena that occur only once each year, including the migration of creatures in every corner of the globe, hibernation during winter, and even annual changes in plumage and coat color.

Because of the long time period involved, it is not always practical to conduct experiments about whether annual rhythms exhibited by animals are merely induced by external factors or are genuinely endogenous, because this would involve maintaining the specimens under artificial conditions of constant light or darkness or temperature for several years in order to observe whether the rhythm persists.

Nevertheless, the presence of endogenous rhythms has been verified in a number of very different species. The annual molt cycle of both the garden warbler (*Sylvia borin*) and the blackcap (*S. atricapilla*) has been shown to be endogenous in laboratory experiments. Both birds were maintained in constant conditions of 12 hours of light followed by 12 hours of darkness for over two years – thus a regime lacking any seasonal light variation. Their annual moult cycle persisted.

Changes in the width of European starlings' (*Sturnus vulgaris*) testicles have been shown to be governed by an annual endogenous rhythm in laboratory experiments. Similarly, even when kept in constant darkness for several years, the carpet beetle (*Anthrenus verbasci*) retains its annual rhythm of adult emergence from the pupal state. And sika deer (*Cervus nippon*) continue to shed and regrow their antlers annually regardless of the light regime imposed upon them.

ANIMAL PROFILE

Periodic Cicadas

Three species of cicada (genus *Magicicada*) with remarkable rhythms live in the United States. In the south, nymphs spend 13 years underground before emerging within a few days of each other and transforming into adults. In the north, the nymph stage lasts 17 years. What causes the synchronized emergence? Above-ground environmental cues, such as temperature or light, are unlikely to trigger it because they have much shorter cycles. These insects' emergence rhythms may be endogenous, but their length makes it difficult to confirm this. However, recent studies suggest that the cicadas may use cues from nearby tree roots (such as sap quality, which varies cyclically) to time their emergence.

CHAPTER FIVE

SLEEP AND SURVIVAL

Many animals have evolved incredible mechanisms for avoiding adverse environmental conditions, such as extremes of cold or heat and shortages of food and water. They survive by entering comatose states of suspended animation sometimes only marginally removed from death, and are able to remain like this for time periods ranging from a few hours to several months if necessary. Other creatures, by contrast, have developed the ability not merely to endure but actually to thrive in conditions far too extreme for most other life forms to survive, even on a short-term basis.

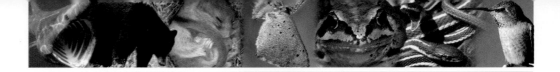

Hibernation

see also:
- Earthquake Prediction, p.61
- Insect Migration, p.72
- Tidal and Annual Rhythms, p.96

Hibernating animals are often said to sleep through the winter, but the process of hibernation actually involves a complex series of physiological changes.

Dormice (right) may spend as much as half the year in hibernation, but they do wake up occasionally. Hedgehogs (below), however, are renowned for taking hibernation to the extreme. Once their big sleep starts, they do not wake until spring.

To stay awake and remain active during the winter, animals have to increase their metabolic rate in order to stay warm. To do so, they need to eat more. But the energy-rich foods that would enable them to survive are in short supply in the barren months of winter. In all probability, they would eat less rather than more in these months, and possibly die as result. The way many small (but not tiny) mammals, such as rodents, bats, and, in temperate zones, medium-sized insectivores, as well as a few Australian marsupials, cope with this deadly paradox is to bypass it completely, through the protective mechanism of hibernation.

The big sleep

Hibernation does not happen overnight. Preparation takes several weeks, during which time the animals feed more than normal, building up layers of fat that will serve as vital food stores to sustain them during the hibernation period. Some species, such as dormice (actually named for their hibernating prowess — "*dormir*" is French for "to sleep"), hibernate for up to six months, and northern Alaska's Barrow ground squirrel (*Spermophilus parryii*) may spend as much as nine months in hibernation. Such long periods of sleep require substantial fatty layers. Bats, for example, can increase their total body weight by as much as a quarter during this fattening-up process.

Hedgehogs, which are probably the most extreme hibernators known, undergo a whole series of physiological transformations prior to hibernating. Their blood's potassium content increases, and their reproductive organs decrease markedly in size, as they will not be needed during hibernation. So, too, do certain endocrine glands, including the thyroid, the anterior portion of the pituitary, and part of the adrenals, whose functioning also diminishes.

Once their fat layers have been amassed, the animals become more sluggish as the time for hibernation approaches. Hibernation itself is usually

Fat Speeds Arousal

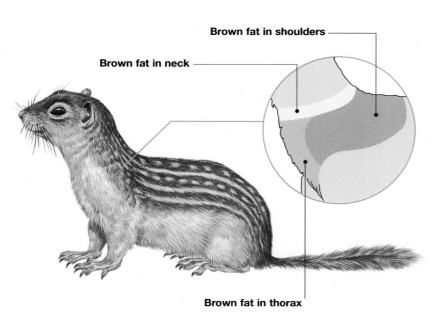

Brown fat in shoulders

Brown fat in neck

Brown fat in thorax

Ground squirrels, which replenish their fat supplies regularly during hibernation, can awaken from their deep sleep in less than three hours. In this time, large amounts of fat are burned as fuel to raise the body temperature. This is accompanied by intense shivering and muscle contraction, which also generate heat. Much of the heat is derived from oxidation of brown fat, a kind of fat that contains many energy-producing cells. As much as 57 percent of the brown fat in ground squirrels is around their shoulders, with 14 percent in their neck, and most of the remainder in their thorax. This substance acts like an electric blanket, releasing heat to the heart and major blood vessels to warm them and speed the circulation of oxygen to the brain and other anterior organs, and then to the posterior body regions. During arousal, the anterior skeletal muscles receive over 16 times more blood than their counterparts in a fully awake animal, powering their shivering to produce heat for raising the body's temperature.

triggered by a drop in the environmental temperature below a certain critical level for the species concerned. When this happens, the animal, usually by now ensconced within hibernating quarters, seemingly falls into a deep sleep. In reality, however, this state is much more profound than any normal sleep.

The animal's breathing rate decreases dramatically (some bats take only a single breath every two hours). So, too, does its heart rate (from over 1,000 beats per minute in a bat in flight to 25 per minute during hibernation). Its circulatory rate also slows, so that its skin and extremities soon become cold to the touch. A hibernator's body temperature can fall by as much as 36°F (20°C), until it is scarcely above the prevailing environmental temperature, and the animal often looks as if it is dead.

In reality, its body's internal regions, especially those nearest to the heart, are still warm, and its vital physiological processes – although functioning in a much lower gear than normal – are still adequate to ensure survival. Temperature regulation is controlled by the hypothalamus in the brain, which prevents the animal's body temperature from falling too low during hibernation, even if external temperatures fall to abnormally cold levels.

A bat's metabolism slows down almost to a stop during hibernation as its breathing rate decreases and there is a dramatic fall in its body temperature.

Unable to feed because of the absence of pollen in winter, some butterflies go into a state of hibernation, awakening in spring when flowers start to be more plentiful.

Having said that, the American red bat (*Lasiurus borealis*) can survive even if its body tissues freeze when the outside temperature falls as low as 23°F (-5°C).

Some species, such as dormice, ground squirrels, and bats, actually wake up at regular intervals throughout their months of hibernation to urinate and defecate and sometimes even to replenish their fat layers by feeding on whatever suitable nutrients they can find.

More extreme hibernators such as hedgehogs, conversely, remain asleep throughout the winter. During this prolonged period of inactivity, to protect their internal system from attack by the bacteria inhabiting their gut, large numbers of white blood cells accumulate around their blood vessels and in the stomach lining as barriers to bacterial invasion.

Wake-up call

Surprisingly, waking up from hibernation can be more dangerous for the hibernator than surviving the long cold months asleep. The danger occurs because arousal requires a significant rise in metabolic activity. In the case of species such as hedgehogs, arousal occurs only at the end of hibernation. Since hedgehogs remain asleep throughout hibernation and do not replenish their fat stores at all during the hibernation period, this is precisely the time when their fat levels are at their lowest.

Fuel is used rapidly to heat the body during the awakening period. As a result, if a hibernating animal is woken by some unexpected external stimulus but does not replenish its fat supplies before sinking back into hibernation again, it is in danger of prematurely exhausting its supplies and dying. For this reason, hibernating hedgehogs should never be disturbed or woken up.

ANIMAL PROFILE

The World's Only Hibernating Bird

Birds are not supposed to hibernate. But on December 29, 1946, Dr. Edmund C. Jaeger, a biologist from California's Riverside City College, made an astonishing discovery. Walking along a canyon in California's Chuckwalla Mountains, he saw what seemed to be the body of a dead bird wedged in a rocky hollow in the canyon's wall. After lifting the bird's body out of its crevice, however, Jaeger was amazed to find that it was still alive – comatose and cold to the touch, yet clearly alive. It was a poorwill (*Phalaenoptilus nuttallii*), a nocturnal species related to the nightjar, and it seemed to be hibernating. Certainly, its heartbeat was scarcely discernible, and its body temperature was 73°F (23°C) lower than normal.

Anxious to learn more, Jaeger returned on several occasions during the next few days, and the bird was always there. Finally, however, after being handled by Jaeger several times, it woke up sufficiently to fly away. Eleven months later, Jaeger revisited the canyon, and the bird was back in its crevice, dormant once more. He ringed it and studied it thereafter for several years. He revealed that it did indeed hibernate, for an average of 88 days each year.

Subsequent studies by fellow researchers with other poorwill specimens confirmed this species' extraordinary status as the world's only known species of hibernating bird, despite the fact that it does not possess brown fat, as hibernating mammals do.

Moreover, a poorwill needs only about two-thirds as much energy to sustain it during hibernation as it would need to maintain its normal body temperature. Also, it requires just ¼ ounce (7 g) of fat to keep it alive during 70–100 days of hibernation. This amount would sustain it for only one week if it were attempting to maintain its normal body temperature of 104°F (40°C). Hibernation is, therefore, an energy-efficient means of survival for this species when the temperature outside falls.

Summer Hibernation

see also:
● Hibernation, p.100
● Extreme Endurance, p.110
● Carnivorous Vegetarians, p.118

A few animals beat the heat of summer by entering a state of suspended animation called estivation.

Whereas some creatures hibernate to avoid the cold, adverse conditions of winter, certain others undergo a similar process when faced with unusually elevated temperatures during the summer or severe periods of drought. This "summer hibernation" is known as estivation and, although less common than true, winter hibernation, it has been recorded in several different types of animal. In some cases, in response to drought, it can last for years.

Cocooned from life

Undoubtedly the most famous estivators are lungfishes, notably the West African lungfish (*Protopterus annectens*) and the Congolese lungfish (*P. dolloi*). These species normally inhabit swamps and streams, but during hot weather their watery abodes can dry out completely and remain dry for several months. Thus, as soon as a drought begins, the lungfish digs down into the soft mud at the bottom of the watercourse, creating a tubular breathing burrow with a wide chamber at the base.

Here it remains once the level of water in its swamp or stream falls below the upper end of the burrow (which is sealed by a porous lid allowing the inward passage of air), sheltered and protected from the heat outside.

Even without water, the lungfish will not dry out because it rapidly secretes vast quantities of thick mucus around itself, which hardens to form a protective cocoon inside the chamber. Able to breathe the air filtering down into its chamber, the lungfish can stay entombed in this state for many months if necessary. Indeed, live specimens have been removed from mud-encapsulated cocoons that had been dug up then stored out of water by scientists for more than four years. The lungfish

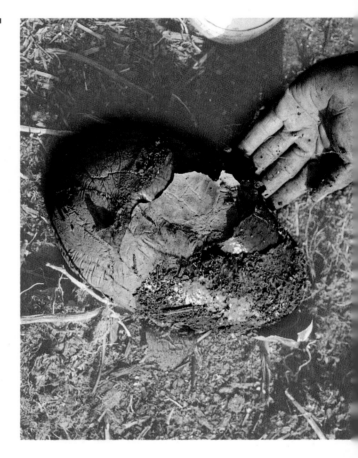

were still alive – somewhat emaciated, certainly, but not fatally so.

As soon as the drought period is over, and the newly arrived rainy season has restored water to its swamp, the African lungfish will reemerge from its cocoon and begin to feed as normal. However, water returning to the dried-out muddy swamp is not the only way to wake up a lungfish.

Even the sound of rain falling on the mud can be enough to stimulate the fish's reemergence. Villagers in parts of the Sudan, for whom lungfish are a popular delicacy, trick the fish into coming out of their underground chambers. Just before the rainy season begins, the villagers walk over dried-out swamps where lungfish are likely to be snugly ensconced in their cocoons beneath the mud, and make loud tapping noises with their fingers on gourds. These sounds are sufficiently similar to the noise made by rain beating down on the mud to induce the lungfish into stirring from their estivating stupor. As they stir, they produce distinctive grunting sounds. When the villagers hear them, they swiftly dig through the mud and seize the unsuspecting lungfish.

The eel-like South American lungfish (*Lepidosiren paradoxa*) also estivates within a tube-linked chamber in swamp-bottom mud, but unlike its African relatives it does not produce a cocoon. However, not all lungfishes can estivate – the Australian lungfish (*Neoceratodus forsteri*) dies if its river home dries up.

True survivors

During estivation, the lungfish's metabolic activity falls markedly, as in true hibernation, helping it survive longer. The lungfish also relies on certain physiological specializations in order to survive what can be a very prolonged period of physical confinement within its cocoon. Unable to obtain food, it derives its energy instead via a process of auto-cannibalism – known as autophagy – whereby it actively digests portions of its own body tissues – in particular its muscles. Indeed, one specimen that was examined just before it sealed itself away, and then again after six months of encapsulation, was found to have shrunk in length from 16 inches (40.6 cm) to 14 inches (36.5 cm), and to have diminished to 9 ounces (289 g) from its original weight of 12 ounces (374 g). Yet within two months of having emerged from its cocoon, this specimen had regained its original dimensions.

Even more remarkable is the lungfish's ability to withstand the potentially lethal effect of its own highly toxic waste products. Since a cocooned lungfish cannot discharge its urea, its kidneys recirculate this substance's water content but retain the toxic component. Hence they have

African lungfish (inset) estivate in dry conditions. When dug up, the mucus cocoon that surrounds them is visible.

ANIMAL PROFILE

Tenrecs

Certain mammals are known to estivate. Perhaps the best-known examples are tenrecs – Madagascan insectivores related to hedgehogs. During abnormally hot summer weather, they enter a state of inactivity resembling hibernation. Moreover, when outside temperatures plummet, they undergo true hibernation, becoming stiff and cold to the touch. This behavior has been noted on a number of occasions with captive zoo specimens of tenrecs maintained in countries with cooler average temperatures than that of their tropical Madagascan homeland.

evolved an incredible tolerance to it, and can store concentrations of up to 20,000 parts per million of urea with no harmful effects. In stark contrast, a mere 10 parts per million of urea is generally fatal for the vast majority of other vertebrates. Once a lungfish has emerged from its cocoon into water, its kidneys release the stored urea and it returns to normal life.

Other summer hibernators

Land crabs avoid upper extremes of temperature by remaining in a state of dormancy within their burrows until conditions become more favorable. Similarly, earthworms estivate during especially hot summers – hollowing out chambers in deep soil and coiling up inside. And certain land snails, particularly desert dwellers, seal themselves inside their shells to avoid desiccation in dry conditions, secreting a special membrane across their shells' opening that reduces evaporation; they can remain encased for years if need be until rain returns.

Torpor

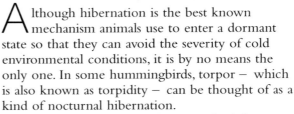

see also:
● Earthquake Prediction, p.61
● Insect Migration, p.72
● Hibernation, p.100

Although hibernation is the best known mechanism animals use to enter a dormant state so that they can avoid the severity of cold environmental conditions, it is by no means the only one. In some hummingbirds, torpor — which is also known as torpidity — can be thought of as a kind of nocturnal hibernation.

For such tiny creatures, hummingbirds have an exceedingly high metabolic rate and, because they feed mostly while they are in flight, they expend considerable amounts of energy on feeding. Yet, because of their very small size, they are unable to store significant quantities of nutrients in their bodies. This does not cause any problem during the daytime because, as long as the environmental temperature is normal, there is more than sufficient food in the form of flower nectar and tiny insects for the hummingbirds. But what happens at night?

A sleep lasting from a night to several months helps some animals to survive either cold or a lack of food.

Living without midnight snacks

To begin with, hummingbirds cannot see in the dark to find food. And even if they could, the flowers whose nectar serves as their primary food source close up at night, and day-flying insects conceal themselves. Yet because the environmental temperature falls at night, in order to sustain their high metabolic rate and body temperature the hummingbirds would actually need to eat more food at this time than during the day. Clearly, this conflict would prove lethal, so each night

Torpidity helps hummingbirds to survive cool nights when they are unable to feed.

hummingbirds enter a torpid, dormant state similar to that of winter hibernation, during which their body temperature falls drastically, by as much as 54°F (30°C) in some species. The next morning, however, once the environmental temperature has risen to its usual daytime level again, so, too, does the hummingbirds' body temperature, and they emerge from their torpor to resume their typical feeding activity. This effective physiological strategy is known as heterothermy.

The environmental temperature at which torpor is induced often varies inversely with altitude. In other words, the higher the altitude of the habitat, the colder it must be to induce torpor. The Andean hillstar (*Oreotrochilus estella*), which inhabits mountainous regions at 12,500–13,800 feet (3,800–4,200 m), enters a torpid state only when the environmental temperature falls as low as 44°F (7°C), but the purple-throated carib (*Eulampis jugularis*), living at heights less than 5,000 feet (1,500 m) above sea level in the Lesser Antilles, becomes torpid when the environmental temperature is lower than 68°F (20°C).

A true hibernating bird?

Certain other avian species, such as African mousebirds, swifts (especially nestlings), and swallows, can become torpid for up to a few days at a time if necessary, generally during adverse weather conditions when food is scarce or even

unobtainable. However, this state is not as extreme as the true hibernation displayed by the poorwill (*Phalaenoptilus nuttallii*), a nocturnal species closely related to the nightjar. The poorwill is the only bird known to hibernate, doing so for about 88 days per year.

Moreover, shrews, which include among their number the tiniest mammalian species alive today, can become torpid for a time during adverse conditions. Just like hummingbirds, they possess an extremely high metabolic rate and body

Shrews use torpid sleep to help them to survive harsh winters.

Black bears, such as this male, wake up often during winter to search for food.

ANIMAL PROFILE

The Basking Shark

Torpor or hibernation in fish is rare, but the most remarkable case features the basking shark (*Cetorhinus maximus*). It swallows great quantities of plankton, straining it from the water via specialized filters called gill-rakers. A common sight drifting just beneath the sea surface during the plankton-rich summer months, these sharks are rarely seen during the winter, when plankton is scarce. This is because they descend to deeper waters where, scientists assumed, they spend the season in a torpid state. However, when scientists examined two basking sharks during winter they lacked gill-rakers and thus couldn't feed. This unexpected finding suggests that basking sharks hibernate, shedding their gill-rakers and regrowing them in spring.

temperature, and live permanently on the edge of starvation. Unlike hummingbirds, however, shrews can see and hunt food at night, as well as during the day, and are even active during the winter.

Winter sleeping

Bears are often said to hibernate, but this is not strictly true. For although they do sleep through much of the winter inside their dens, the physiological process involved is far less extreme than that of true hibernation, and is best referred to as winter sleeping or winter denning. During fall, bears consume greater quantities of food, especially fruit, than normal and build up layers of fat, just like true hibernators. Similarly, once they retire to their dens at the onset of winter and go to sleep, their breathing and heartbeat rates drop significantly, and their oxygen consumption falls to a little under 50 percent of normal. However, their body temperature falls by merely a few degrees, rather than plummeting to only a little above the environmental temperature, which is what happens in genuine hibernators. Moreover, bears wake up frequently during the winter and leave their dens to find food, often for several days at a time. Adult

female bears have even been known to give birth to cubs in the cold season. This would not happen if they were truly hibernating.

Using mud as insulation

Amphibians, reptiles, and insects are cold-blooded (poikilothermic) animals, and they are so called because they are unable to regulate their own body temperature, which fluctuates in direct relation to the environmental temperature. This means that at night, and especially during the winter, the body temperature of these creatures falls dramatically. As a result, during such periods they become increasingly sluggish, and seek hideaways in which to avoid predators and to conserve precious body heat. For if the environmental temperature falls too low, and their body temperature plummets accordingly, they are in grave danger of dying from hypothermia. Frogs seek to avoid this fate by burying themselves in mud at the bottom of ponds during the winter. Here they stay warm and, by becoming torpid, require less oxygen. This means that they can survive by breathing through their skin, which requires less energy, rather than through their lungs.

Thousands of red-sided garter snakes share the same dens to help to conserve body heat during the long winter months.

Snakes, meanwhile, choose to conceal themselves during the winter months in underground dens (hibernacula). The depth of these dens is directly linked to the level to which the environmental temperature usually falls at this time of year – as is the length of the snakes' period of torpor. Snakes will often congregate in great numbers at this time to help to conserve as much of their body heat as they can. They will even share their hibernacula with other poikilotherms, such as lizards, tortoises, and toads.

Mating follows the big sleep

Every year thousands of red-sided garter snakes (*Thamnophis sirtalis parietalis*) return to the Interlake area of Narcisse, Manitoba near Lake Winnipeg in Canada. Dens there – which can include anything from an underground limestone cave to tree roots, sewers, and rock piles – are often home to as many as 10,000 snakes at any given time. The creatures enter the dens in early September and reemerge in May, when they perform a frenzied three-week mating ritual before dispersing to nearby marshes for the summer months.

Despite these efforts, approximately 80 percent of the red-sided garter snake's young will not survive their first winter.

Pause for growth

Juvenile insects often undergo a period of suspended development and growth which may be accompanied by a decrease in their metabolic rate. This is known as diapause. It also occurs in adult insects that survive the winter (often referred to as overwintering), such as various species of butterfly and beetle. In these cases the diapause can be thought of as a hibernation mechanism.

During overwintering diapause, fertilized eggs that were produced during the fall by the females are retained internally, and their development is halted, while still at an early stage, until the spring. Then, once the adult insects have emerged from this torpid state, their eggs ripen and are laid.

Extreme Endurance

see also:
- Hibernation, p.100
- Summer Hibernation, p.104
- Parasitism, p.165

Within the animal kingdom are creatures who can survive freezing, boiling, desiccation, acid baths, and even high doses of radiation, thanks to special adaptations.

Some animals are able to survive environmental conditions far more extreme than any that humans can normally endure (even when assisted by sophisticated protective apparatus).

Cool creatures

An internal antifreeze stops some animals from freezing in sub-zero temperatures. Some Antarctic fishes and certain species inhabiting Scandinavian fjords, as well as the Alaskan blackfish (*Dallia pectoralis*), are said to be freezing-susceptible because their bodies do not form ice crystals even in sub-zero temperatures. The blood of Antarctic ice fishes of the genus *Trematomus* has a glycoprotein that functions very efficiently in preventing the formation of ice crystals; indeed, it is 200-500 times more effective than salt. The glycoprotein lowers the temperature at which ice crystals enlarge, while having no effect upon the temperature at which they melt.

Glycerol acts as an effective antifreeze compound in the blood of some insects, rising in concentration in larvae of the parasitic wasp *Bracon cephi* before the onset of winter, and falling again in spring. In 1997, biologists from Pennsylvania's Slippery Rock University revealed that the spring peeper (*Pseudacris crucifer*), a tiny species of North American frog, produces glucose during frosty weather to concentrate its body fluids and so reduce ice crystal formation, enabling it to survive for up to three days with almost half of its total body fluid frozen. It returns to a fully active state in only a day after thawing out.

Certain insects, moreover, can even survive the formation of ice crystals within their bodies. One

Deep-frozen Fish

The Alaska blackfish (*Dallia pectoralis*), which lives in ponds and streams in Alaska, was once thought to be able to survive being frozen solid in ice. Although this claim has been refuted, scientists now know that as long as ice crystals do not come into contact with any part of its body (which would result in fatal necrosis setting in), the blackfish can indeed survive for as long as 30 minutes at temperatures as low as -4°F (-20°C). This is because its body fluids can undergo supercooling – cooling to below their normal freezing point – without freezing, as they do not contain any mechanical nuclei or "seeds" that would induce the formation of ice crystals.

example is the larva of the midge *Chironomus*, which can be repeatedly frozen to a temperature as low as -13°F (-25°C) and thawed again without suffering any ill effects. Experiments have shown that at 5°F (-15°C), up to 90 percent of its body fluid is frozen. Such creatures are said to be freezing-tolerant.

Some like it hot

One of the world's most famous heat-tolerant animals is the Devil's Hole pupfish (*Cyprinodon diabolis*), once found only in a single hot-water spring pool in Ash Meadows, Nevada, called Devil's Hole, whose temperature remains stable at 93.2°F (33.9°C). This fish's upper lethal temperature is as high as 107°F (43°C). Related species inhabit similar springs in Death Valley, California, and in Arabia.

In 1923, several specimens of a small but very peculiar crustacean, lacking eyes and with only very primitive limbs, were discovered living in the hot spring of Hel Hamma close to Tunis, Tunisia, near the ruins of an ancient Roman bath. These were shown to belong to a radically new species,

subsequently named *Thermosbaena mirabilis*, because it can withstand water temperatures of 97.5-117.5°F (36.5-47.5°C). Yet even this is nothing in comparison with the thermophilic tolerance of certain very special deep-sea creatures.

During the mid-1970s, an amazing discovery was made on the ocean floor off the Galapagos Islands. Located here were vents in the seafloor through which water heated by the earth's molten magma was spurting. And surrounding these vents

The pupfish lives in hot springs in California.

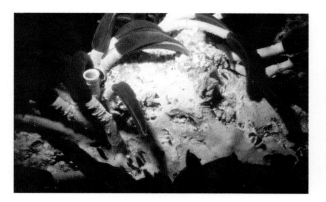

These tube worms live in a Pacific hydrothermal vent, where the water is scalding hot.

ANIMAL PROFILE

Surviving Radiation

In radiology, a rem is defined as the dosage of radiation that will cause a specific, measured amount of injury to human tissue. During an entire lifetime, humans are normally exposed to doses of no more than 16 rems, while a lethal dose would be 800 rem or more.

However, cockroaches are able to withstand rem doses spectacularly in excess of this. According to Iowa State University entomologist Dr. Donald Lewis, the lethal rem dose for the American cockroach (*Periplaneta americana*) is 67,500 rems, whereas for the German cockroach (*Blatella germanica*) it is 90,000-105,000 rems, enabling this latter species to survive the radiation that would be released during a thermonuclear explosion.

Another remarkable example of radiation survival is the ability of ants to wander around inside active microwave ovens without suffering any ill effects. In this case, however, the secret is not any built-in immunity, but the inherent design of the oven – the emitted radiation waves are spaced a certain distance apart to cook the food. Fortunately for any ants that happen to find their way inside, they are smaller than the distance separating the radiation waves and can therefore avoid them. In any event, these insect interlopers tend to stay close to the oven's walls, which remain cooler than elsewhere inside.

was a rich abundance of exotic life-forms never before seen by humans, including giant clams, spaghetti-like acorn worms, siphonophores resembling dandelion clocks, and, most spectacular of all, enormous vestimentiferan worms (*Riftia pachyptila*), encased within vertical white tubes, with huge red petal-like tentacles sprouting out of the upper end of these tubes like strange alien flowers. All of these species were adapted to survive not only the immense barometric pressures found in the ocean's depths, but also the unexpectedly high water temperature near the vents.

Certain vents took the form of dark chimney-like edifices, known as black smokers or chimneys of hell, which belched forth smoky metal-rich water heated to temperatures of up to 662°F (350°C). However, similar, paler versions, known as white smokers because the water they pumped out was creamy, were associated with a wide variety of thermophilic species, most notably a remarkable polychaete called the Pompeii worm (*Alvinella pompejana*). Living inside tubes attached directly to the walls of the white smokers, its posterior body portion can tolerate direct contact with heat measured at 176°F (80°C). It is as if the worm were sitting on a hot plate.

Indestructible water bears

The ultimate expression of endurance in the face of extreme external conditions is the ability of certain animals to enter an incredible near-death state of suspended animation known as cryptobiosis. The most famous of these animals are a group of tiny creatures called tardigrades. Also known as water bears due to their vaguely bear-like appearance (notwithstanding their eight legs), and distantly related to crustaceans and spiders, these enigmatic little invertebrates normally inhabit the water film surrounding the leaves of mosses and lichens. Should this habitat lose its dampness, however, as in unusually dry seasons or drought, a tardigrade will pull in its legs, lose up to 85 percent of its body's total water content, shrivel up, and enter into a cryptobiotic state.

During this time, it neither feeds nor moves, and its metabolic rate plummets dramatically so that it is only barely alive. The tardigrade will remain like that until its habitat gains water again – even if this takes several years. Only then will the tardigrade rehydrate by absorbing water and transform back into its normal active state.

Without cryptobiosis, a tardigrade would live only for around 18 months, but since it can become cryptobiotic several times, its total lifespan can be extended by as much as 60 years, and

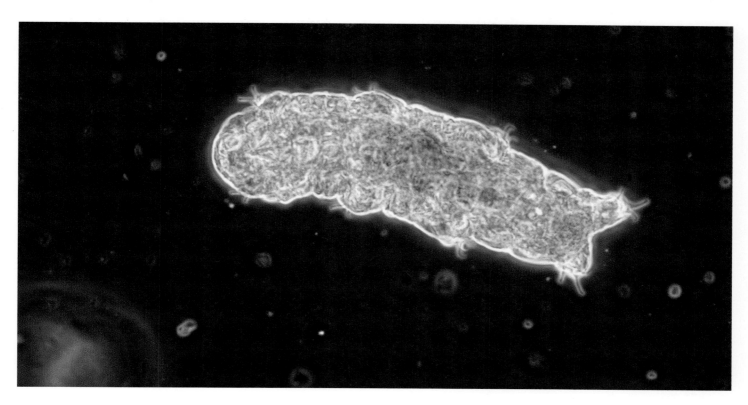

occasionally even longer. Remarkably, some tardigrades discovered in a cryptobiotic state on a piece of moss that had been kept dry in a museum for 120 years came back to life when the moss was moistened.

Most incredible of all, however, is the virtually indestructible nature of tardigrades while they remain in cryptobiosis. In laboratory experiments, cryptobiotic specimens have been chilled in liquid helium to -457°F (-272°C), which is only marginally above absolute zero. They have also been heated to temperatures exceeding 300°F (149°C), exposed to radiation doses far in excess of the lethal dose for humans, immersed in vats of liquid nitrogen, concentrated carbolic acid, hydrogen sulphide, brine, and pure alcohol, and even bombarded by deadly streams of electrons inside an electron microscope. Yet when removed from all of these incredibly hostile environments – which would have proven fatal for any other form of animal life – and moistened with water, these astounding creatures recovered.

They simply emerge from their cryptobiotic state, rehydrate themselves, and amble away on their four pairs of stubby claw-tipped legs, completely unharmed. Even today, the physiological

mysteries behind the tardigrades' unparalleled powers of endurance during cryptobiosis remain unsolved.

Some nematodes, or round worms, undergo a similar, though less profound, form of cryptobiosis. As demonstrated by Newcastle University researcher Prof. Conrad Ellenby during a series of classic experiments, they become wholly desiccated when confronted with unfavorable external conditions, yet they revive fully when moistened.

The water bear, or tardigrade, is a microscopic creature that can enter a form of suspended animation.

To survive hostile conditions, the nematode can dry out and enter a state of crypto-biosis.

Entombed Animals

see also:
● Exotic Senses, p.38
● Torpor, p.106
● Extreme Endurance, p.110

Some of the most remarkable discoveries in the annals of natural history have been found when hollow rocks were split open to reveal a toad or occasionally some other small animal entombed – alive – inside. How did they become entombed, and how do they survive in this state, without any apparent source of nutrition?

Toads in holes

A well-documented incident featuring a toad found in a hole inside a completely sealed rock took place in 1835, when John Bruton noticed a slab of rock fall off a wagon traveling near a railway cutting close to Coventry. As the slab hit the ground, it broke across the middle, exposing a hole at its center. Out of that newly revealed hole fell a live toad. Unfortunately, however, before a very startled Bruton was able to do anything, the toad hit the ground with such force that it damaged its head. Bruton kept the injured amphibian on display in his office workplace for the next ten days until it died of its head injuries.

Common frogs like this one have sometimes been found in rocks far below the ground.

Many cases of toads trapped in stones have been recorded in recent centuries, but how did they get there? Nature can be stranger than fiction, as shown by amphibians found in seemingly impossible situations.

More recently, in 1982, a team of railway workers extending a track near Te Kuiti, New Zealand, were trimming through a layer of sedimentary rock known as mudstone when one of them found a small cavity in the rock. The tiny chamber was 14 feet (4 m) beneath the surface of the ground. As the amazed workmen looked closer, they discovered a living frog ensconced inside the rock that moments before had been buried beneath tons of earth. A second live frog was subsequently discovered in another cavity within this same layer of rock.

This is the only preserved example of a toad in stone, but, because it was donated by a suspected hoaxer, it may be a fake.

TRAVELERS' TALES

In 1886, zoologist Dr. Albert Günther documented one of the most unusual zoological specimens in his personal collection. It was an old shell from a pearl-producing bivalve mollusk called *Margarita margaritifera*. When it was studied very closely, a tiny, perfectly preserved specimen of a small fish known as a fierasfer (*Carapus acus*) could be seen embedded in the iridescent shell wall. It had been sealed inside by a thin layer of nacre – the substance from which pearls are produced. Fierasfers often live inside pearl shells, but normally remain within the two halves of the mantle. However, this nacre-enveloped specimen had ventured between the mantle and the shell. Presumably, therefore, in so doing it had irritated the mollusk, which had immediately secreted nacre to ease the irritation and inadvertently entombed the unfortunate fish.

One of the eyewitnesses to these enigmatic finds was L. Andrews, the railway's works supervisor, who affirmed that it was impossible for the frogs to have fallen into the holes – they were definitely inside them when the rock was split open during trimming.

Famous faker undermines authenticity

Perhaps the most infamous example is also the only preserved example, now on display at the Booth Museum in Brighton, England. It consists of a hollow flint nodule, inside which is the mummified corpse of a toad. Apparently, it was discovered when the nodule was cracked open by workmen in a quarry at Lewes, East Sussex, England, in 1899. But is it authentic? Maybe not. This intriguing specimen was donated to the museum by none other than Charles Dawson, the prime suspect behind the Piltdown Man hoax. (In 1912, the fossilized bones of what was thought to be a prehistoric human were found in East Sussex. Hailed as the evolutionary "Missing Link," it was proven to be a hoax by modern dating methods in 1953.)

Still, there are many other, much more reliable records of incarcerated toads on file, as well as numerous depictions of such discoveries. Bob Skinner's book, *Toad in the Hole* (1986), is an invaluable compilation of source material on this mystifying subject.

But if such cases are indeed genuine, how can they be explained? One theory some scientists have put forward is that the toad enters the rock when still very young and small, through a pore (common in rocks such as limestone) or via a channel that leads inside. Once inside the stone cell, it becomes trapped if it grows any larger before attempting to get out again. Its own smell may be enough to lure tiny insects inside the stone, and the toad could feed on these. Air could easily penetrate through the rock's pores or channel. And rain seeping in would also sustain the toad during its enforced encapsulation.

If it entered a state of torpor, as happens when toads become dormant during adverse environmental conditions, its metabolic rate would plummet, enabling it to survive for a much longer period than if it remained in its normal, fully active state.

Canned frog – the real thing?

A remarkable modern-day incident that makes the whole subject of entombed animals timely again and offers support for the scientific explanation of this phenomenon features a discarded Cherry Coca-Cola ring-pull can, found by schoolboy Paul Astbury of Rhyl High School, Wales, in 1995. While clearing away some rubbish near a pond in the school's quadrangle, Paul picked up the discarded can. He was very surprised to find a frog squatting inside – a creature that was much larger than the ring-pull hole. So how had it managed to get inside the can? After examining both the can and the frog, David Wilson, head of science at the high school, stated that the frog must have entered while still a tadpole, and had subsequently grown too large to escape. He believed that it survived by feeding on insects entering the can. This case offers a highly pertinent, parallel scenario to the more familiar version featuring rock-entombed toads.

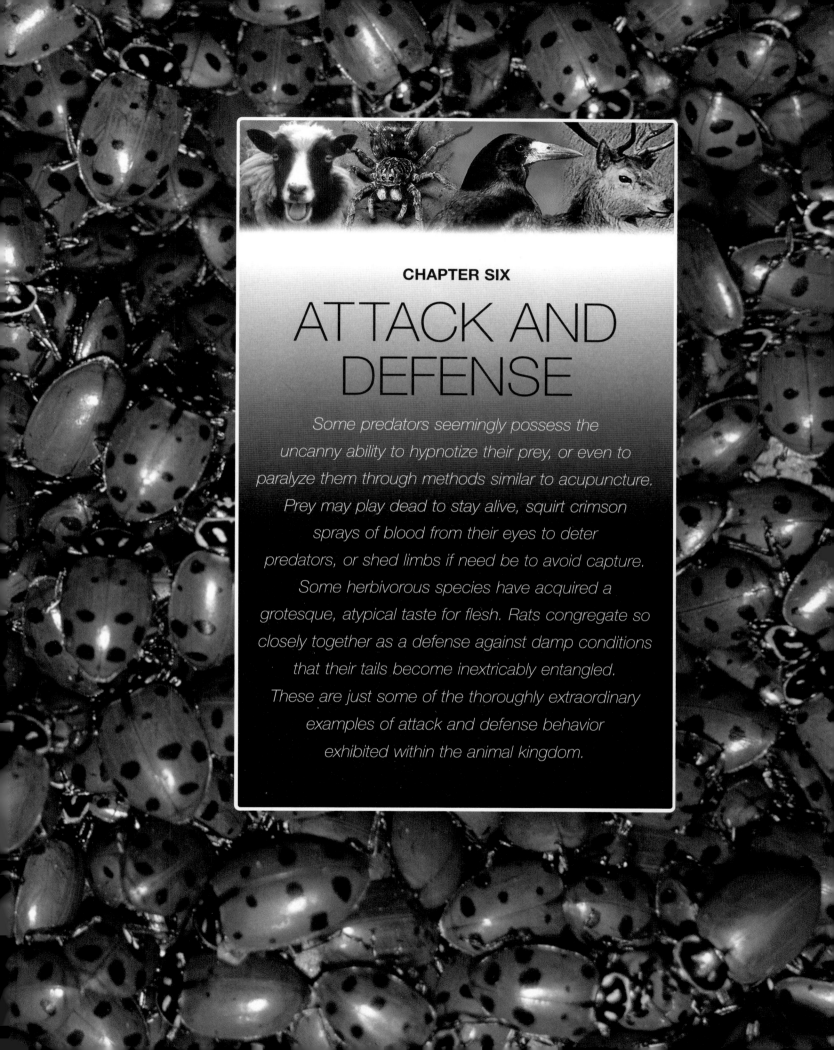

CHAPTER SIX

ATTACK AND DEFENSE

Some predators seemingly possess the uncanny ability to hypnotize their prey, or even to paralyze them through methods similar to acupuncture. Prey may play dead to stay alive, squirt crimson sprays of blood from their eyes to deter predators, or shed limbs if need be to avoid capture. Some herbivorous species have acquired a grotesque, atypical taste for flesh. Rats congregate so closely together as a defense against damp conditions that their tails become inextricably entangled. These are just some of the thoroughly extraordinary examples of attack and defense behavior exhibited within the animal kingdom.

Carnivorous Vegetarians

see also:
- Mammal Migration, p.77
- Living Together, p.159
- Dangerous Friends, p.163

Environmental conditions can transform normally placid, plant-eating herbivores into lethal, merciless devourers of flesh and blood.

On one of Scotland's western outposts, the island of Rhum in the Inner Hebrides, there are more than 300 red deer (*Cervus elaphus*). Although they are the same species as those found on the Scottish mainland, the red deer of Rhum exhibit a macabre dietary deviation that sets them far apart from others of their species.

These ostensibly mild-mannered herbivores have acquired a murderous interest in the chicks belonging to the large population of Manx shearwaters (*Puffinus puffinus*) that nest on the ground around this island. Quite simply, the deer frequently bite off the heads of these unfortunate young birds in order to chew their bones. A detailed study, conducted by Glasgow University zoologist Dr. Robert Furness, confirmed the behavior and his findings were reported in 1988.

When an animal's diet becomes deficient in certain minerals, it uses any means it can to fulfill its needs – animals that are normally herbivorous can even be driven to consume flesh or bones in a quest for essential nutrients.

The reason for this bizarre activity appears to be that Rhum, which is only a small island, is deficient in certain minerals – in particular calcium and phosphorus – that the deer require to sustain their dietary balance and metabolism. Elsewhere, deer circumvent this problem by chewing their own shed antlers, or even the bones of dead deer. On Rhum, however, which is amply supplied with defenseless shearwater chicks that make easy prey, the red deer have become carnivorous. They kill the birds to supply themselves with bony material to chew on and are therefore able to obtain the minerals they require.

Killer sheep

Nor are decapitating deer the only unexpected perils faced by seabirds nesting on Scottish islands. Following his grisly revelation on Rhum, Furness listened to local farmers' tales of feral sheep living

When their diets lack essential minerals, red deer on the Scottish island of Rhum become carnivores. The normally herbivorous beasts bite the heads off Manx shearwater chicks so that they can chew on their bones, which are rich in calcium and phosphorus. The chicks are easy prey because they nest on the ground.

on the tiny island of Foula, the most westerly member of the Shetland Islands. Investigating such stories, he discovered that these seemingly passive creatures have also resorted to attacking birds, and for the same reason as their cervine counterparts on Rhum – to obtain the minerals, notably phosphorus, that they require. However, they do this in a different fashion. The Foula sheep attack the chicks of nesting arctic terns (*Sterna paradisaea*), and even some skua fledglings, but, instead of biting the birds' heads off, they sever their wings and legs to chew on, leaving the chicks alive but fatally mutilated.

In the most recently revealed episode of Britain's gruesome saga of carnivorous herbivores, Durham University zoologists Dr. James Robinson and Dr. Keith Hamer announced during 1999 that the same scenario was occurring on the island of Coquet in Northumberland. Here, however, the carnivorous culprits were even more innocuous than deer and sheep – this time they were rabbits. As on Foula, arctic tern chicks were discovered with severed legs, and sometimes wings, too, and the only creatures that inhabit the island and would be capable of inflicting such injuries are rabbits. The zoologists assume that, as with the deer and sheep, they are resorting to these extreme measures in order to supplement their intake of minerals.

Drawing blood from a feather

No less bizarre than the discoveries revealed here with typically herbivorous mammals are those first uncovered in 1964 relating to birds. While studying nesting boobies (seabirds closely related to gannets) on Wolf (Wenman) Island in the Galapagos archipelago, ornithologists Dr. Robert J. Bowman and Dr. Stephen L. Billeb were amazed to observe small finches surreptitiously pecking at new feathers on the tails of moulting boobies and then drinking the blood that seeped from the wounds created by their pointed bills.

Known, aptly, as the sharp-billed ground finch (*Geospiza difficilis*), this species is normally a seed eater, but on Wolf Island it has acquired a taste for blood. This was corroborated dramatically by naturalists Friedemann and Heide Köster while filming the birdlife here in 1983. A year earlier, they had successfully filmed these finches' blood-thirsty activities, but during their return visit, they happened to prick themselves on some cactus spines while working. As soon as the sharp-beaked finches discovered this, they flew up to them, alighted on their arms and legs, and began pecking their flesh as they eagerly attempted to drink the blood oozing from the wounds caused by both the

Certain sheep have been known to chew the legs and wings off arctic tern chicks.

cacti and their own beaks. It must have looked like a scene from Alfred Hitchcock's film *The Birds*.

And as if that were not horrific enough, in October 2000, reports emerged from Argentina that flocks of gulls were habitually attacking migrating whales swimming off the Patagonian coast. The gulls were seen dive-bombing the whales and tearing chunks of flesh from their backs whenever the mighty sea mammals surfaced for air. Dr. Roger Payne, an American whale expert, stated that this opportunistic feeding behavior could be so distressing for the whales, up to 2,500 of which migrate here to breed each year, that in future years they may avoid this region completely and journey elsewhere to breed.

The sharp bill of a ground finch pecks at a booby to draw, then drink, its blood.

Spider Attack

see also:
● Carnivorous Vegetarians, p.118
● Symbiosis, p.160
● Dangerous Friends, p.163

An unusual white-tailed spider that bites when disturbed was the prime suspect for a nasty flesh-eating condition that baffled doctors in Australia. Only when a spider detective got to work was the real cause of the illness revealed.

Not jumping to conclusions is among the first rule for all naturalists, and nowhere was this shown to be more important than in Australia. The island continent had an ongoing problem that threatened the health of its inhabitants and seemed to be related to one of the many species of indigenous venomous spider.

For years there were widespread reports of a mysterious spider whose bite when attacked or disturbed caused devastating results – ulcerating, cyanotic (discolored bluish-gray) lesions that progressed in some cases to such profound rotting of skin and flesh (necrosis) that the underlying bone was exposed. In certain cases, the spider's victim needed to undergo plastic surgery to repair the extensive, disfiguring tissue damage that was caused by the bite.

The common Australian white-tailed spider was thought to be the cause of a flesh-eating disease.

This horrific condition is known medically as necrotizing arachnidism, in recognition of its spider connection, but recent research suggested that Australia's arachnids may well have been taking the blame for the misdeeds of a much more insidious miscreant. But who was the real flesh-rotter?

Until as recently as the early 1990s, the white-tailed spider (*Lampona cylindrata*) was at the head of the list of suspects who might be responsible for causing necrotizing arachnidism. Both the condition and the species are widespread – this very common spider with a gray or black hairy body and white tip is found in most parts of Australia, often roaming inside houses. It is likely to come into frequent contact with humans, and is also well known for biting.

Nevertheless, the accounts of victims who went to the hospital or visited natural history museums to discuss their bites with experts did not match this species' behavior. In instances of spider bites where the white-tailed spider was known to have been the species responsible (when, for example, the victim had shown the presence of mind to capture the offending arachnid and bring it along for identification), any effects resulting from such bites invariably proved to be short-lived and hardly visible. It thus became clear (and was duly confirmed via biochemical analyses) that the white-tailed spider's venom was very weak, and therefore could not be the cause of the devastating tissue damage that is characteristic of necrotizing arachnidism.

Seeking the solution

So what was the identity of the phantom flesh-rotter? Could it be a species of spider still undiscovered by science? One of the world's leading experts on spiders and spider venom, Dr. Struan Sutherland, notes in his book *Venomous Creatures of Australia* (revised 1994) that new species of Australian wolf spider are regularly being discovered. Indeed, the venomous fiddleback spider (*Loxosceles rufescens*) remained undescribed by science until as recently as 1974, when it was discovered in a western suburb of Adelaide, South Australia's capital city. Sutherland brought

The Australian wolf spider may look frightening, but the soil it lives in may be more dangerous than its bite.

the mystery surrounding the species that induced necrotizing arachnidism to the attention of a congress of the International Toxicology Society held in Brisbane on July 14, 1982. Then, eight years later, he made an unexpected discovery that offered a highly significant yet surprising hitherto-unsuspected insight into the condition's secret agent.

A secret in the soil

In 1990, Sutherland published a report revealing that after examining a necrotizing wound, he had successfully isolated a species of bacterium called *Mycobacterium ulcerans*, often found in soil. What makes this achievement so important in relation to the long-running saga of the phantom flesh-rotter is that if *M. ulcerans* infects a wound, the outcome is a large, expanding area of necrosis – whose appearance matches exactly that seen in cases of necrotizing arachnidism.

It was as if a veil had been lifted suddenly. There was no unknown species of deadly spider awaiting exposure, because spider venom was not in fact responsible for the flesh-rotting disease. Instead, spiders were simply the vectors – that is, the eight-limbed modes of transportation – for this dreadful condition that had baffled doctors for so many years. The true culprit was the bacterium *M. ulcerans*. Any species of spider that lives in soil is likely to harbor it on its large chelicerae (biting jawparts). Consequently, if a soil-inhabiting spider bites someone, the virulent bacterium will be transferred directly from the spider's chelicerae into the victim's bloodstream and surrounding tissues.

Wolf spiders (*Lycosa* spp.) live in soil and the ground, and it is known that they have indeed been responsible for bites that subsequently developed into necrotizing arachnidism. Conversely, the white-tailed spider is most commonly encountered by humans inside their homes, which may well explain why bites from this species rarely (if ever) become necrotic. After years of undeserved notoriety and suspicion, Australia's infamous white-tailed spider and its biting attack or defense behavior can be officially exonerated of the heinous flesh-rotting crime once attributed to it.

Animal Hypnotists

see also:
● Hibernation, p.100
● Unexpected Vocalists, p.154
● Parasitism, p.165

What qualified hypnotists can do to their fellow humans, some predatory animals seem able to do to other animals. There are many intriguing descriptions of the way animals may hypnotize, or "fascinate," their prey.

When on the hunt for food, some carnivores can use tactics that literally stop their victims in their tracks until the moment is right to move in for the kill.

Certain carnivorous mammals, notably mustelids (such as stoats, weasels, and martens) and foxes, indulge in a bizarre activity known as the dance of death. In England in March 2000, David Speight from Bakewell, Derbyshire, reported seeing a stoat (*Mustela erminea*) following a squirrel. Instead of pursuing it normally, the stoat engaged in an extraordinary display, performing sideway leaps and chasing its tail, after which it disappeared into a hedge. The

mammalogist Nigel Dunstone suggests that this behavior may mesmerize the potential victim. During the dance the stoat edges closer to its prey until it suddenly seizes its unwary victim – although in the case recounted by Speight, the squirrel proved immune to the stoat's dance.

The red fox charms its intended prey by spinning around and around, holding its own tail in its mouth.

A rabbit freezes, all movement suspended, as it watches a stoat making its predatory advance on the entrance to the warren. In other instances a stoat may dance frenetically, rendering a rabbit motionless with both fear and fascination.

Not so, however, on February 3, 1919, also in England, when Albert Rowland of West Green, Hampshire, observed a weasel (*Mustela nivalis*) capering and circling in the snow while a rook sat nearby. Throughout its giddy performance, the weasel moved closer to the rook, until it abruptly sprang at the bird. It missed, but, undaunted, it repeated the procedure several times more. Remarkably, the rook never attempted to fly off, and eventually the weasel grasped it by the throat.

Foxes have frequently been spied engaging in a similar activity with rabbits and rodents — a phenomenon often referred to as fox charming. As with mustelids, the fox performs a frenetic dance, spinning around its intended prey, which sits passively until, without warning, the fox pounces.

Scientific opinion remains divided as to whether the dance of death is a voluntary performance. It is now known that the sinuses of stoats and related mustelids are often infested with a parasitic nematode worm (*Skrjabingylus nasicola)*, which causes skull deformities that press on the brain, inducing severe irritation in the host. Some researchers suggest that this may in turn cause the stoat to dance so frenetically, noting that these animals will do so even in the

The eyes of the Egyptian banded cobra may have the power to hold its intended victim in a state of suspended animation until it can inject its lethal venom.

The intent gaze of a golden eagle may be able to fascinate a smaller animal. Its stare is unblinking and mesmerizes the victim.

absence of potential victims. Others claim the dance is a ploy to attract and hold the victim's attention, enabling the stoat to approach it stealthily, and even to attract a potential victim some distance away – explaining why it dances when no victims are close by.

A compelling report by Dr. Maurice Burton and Dr. Robert Burton in their book *Inside the Animal World* (1977) supports the theory that this dance is a deliberate act, and that predators use the dance as a decoy. A crow was seen watching a frolicking Himalayan marten. What it didn't see, however, was the marten's mate approaching it from the rear. When close enough, this second marten seized the unsuspecting crow. The dancing marten then joined its mate to share the kill.

The eyes have it

Sometimes, the predator does not perform a dance, but merely fixes its eyes upon those of its intended victim. In Britain, in 1852, an incident was reported in Somerset by the Rev. Henry Bond.

"As I was walking on the hill-side above West Creech Farm, in Penbeck (the down was scattered with very low furze bushes), my attention was arrested by a cry of distress; it proceeded from a rabbit which was cantering around in a ring, with a halting gait. I watched it for some minutes, but as the circle became smaller and the rabbit more agitated I perceived a stoat turning its head with the rabbit's motion, and fixing its gaze upon it. I struck a blow at the stoat and missed it; its

attention was thus withdrawn, and the rabbit ran away with great vigor in a straight direction."

There are numerous reports of snakes performing this direct, eye-to-eye fascination. The Rev. Bond, who also witnessed such an instance, this time in Dorset, England, later wrote:

"Up the hill above Tyneham, toward the sea, I was struck by the shrill cry and fluttering agitation of a common hedge-sparrow, in a whitethorn bush. Regardless of my presence, its remarkable motions were continued, getting, at every hop from bough to bough, lower and lower down in the bush. Drawing nearer, I saw a common snake coiled up, but having its head erect, watching the sparrow; the moment the snake saw me it glided away, and the sparrow flew off with its usual mode of flight."

A venomous attack?

Some skeptics say snake fascination is nothing more mysterious than eyewitnesses failing to realize that snakes have fixed gazes because they cannot blink, but this ignores the victim's behavior. Others claim that where the victim has been rendered immobile, the snake has injected it with venom. Instances where the victim has fled when the snake's gaze was broken make this theory unlikely.

If you accept the eyewitnesses' accounts, it seems more plausible that the victim is so traumatized by the sight of the predator that its escape instincts are inhibited, but not its curiosity. This causes it to move closer to the source of its fear. Undoubtedly, much has yet to be uncovered in this highly speculative area of animal behavior.

Although much less publicized than such reports of snakes and mammals, predatory birds also mesmerize their prey, according to J. H. Gurney:

"I once saw a golden eagle which appeared entirely to fascinate a rabbit that was put into the large cage in which the eagle was kept. As soon as the rabbit was introduced, the eagle fixed his eye upon it, and the rabbit intently returned the gaze, and began going round the eagle in circles, approaching nearer each time, the eagle meanwhile turning on his axis (as it were) on the block of wood upon which he was seated, and keeping his eye fixed upon that of the rabbit. When the rabbit had approached very near to the bottom of the eagle's perch, it stood up on its hind legs, and looked the eagle in the face; the eagle then made his pounce, which appeared at once to break the charm, and the rabbit ran for its life, but it was too late for it to escape the clutch of the eagle..."

There are also reports of owls fascinating mice and voles, but these, like the eagle account, have yet to be formally accepted or explained.

Playing Dead & Akinesis

see also:
● Hibernation, p.100
● Torpor, p.106
● Animal Hypnotists, p.122

Creatures great and small have long baffled scientists with the way they can feign death or enter a trance-like state when threatened. Although the reasons for doing it might be understandable – animals after all have an instinct for survival – the exact mechanisms involved remain mysterious.

Probably the best-known example of this type of animal escapology is playing possum, which got its name from the dramatic behavior of the Virginian opossum (*Didelphis marsupialis*). Its ability to feign death in the face of possible attack by a predator is now used to sum up the entire phenomenon which also appears in a wide variety of other creatures. Scientists call it thanatosis – after Thanatos, the Greek god of death.

Perplexing the enemy

The ability of opossums to play dead has been well documented. The opossum first tries to defend itself against an aggressor by using its teeth and making savage growling sounds, but if that fails the animal abruptly collapses, becoming totally limp, lying on its side with its head turned down, eyes closed, mouth gaping, and tongue lolling out. Suddenly it ejects a vile-smelling green fluid from its anal glands, the noxious odor of which suggests putrefaction. Incredibly, the opossum does not even flinch if its perplexed antagonist attempts to bite or claw at it. Eventually, faced with what appears to be an unpalatable corpse, the aggressor departs, and only then – on some occasions up to six hours after it first entered its thanatotic state – does the

When an opossum plays dead, it gives a truly amazing performance.

All manner of animals can play tricks as a way of convincing their enemies that they are not worth pursuing. By faking death or going into a trance they put predators off their track and, if they are lucky, live to fight another day.

A dead bug on its back is a common sight, but in fact the sexton beetle rolls over to fake death.

opossum cautiously reanimate itself. This remarkable performance has been formally observed and documented many times by scientists, but there are a number of aspects that remain controversial. For instance, playing possum appears to be a behavioral tactic of only a small percentage of opossums, rather than a sizable majority. In 1967, American naturalist Leonard L. Rue commented: "Of the thousands of opossums that I have handled, only 10 or 12 collapsed as expected. The others tried to escape by running away or by turning around and biting."

Why this behavior's occurrence is limited to just a few animals adds to the mystery. It is not even clear whether it is voluntary or involuntary. Whereas some scientists claim that the opossum deliberately plays possum, others believe the activity is actually akin to fainting, and hence occurs automatically, induced by overwhelming shock caused by the presence of the enemy.

As far back as the 1960s, electroencephalogram studies compared brain activity of opossums in a normal active state, asleep, and playing dead. They

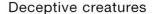
A grass snake in full defense mode writhes and bleeds, but it is only feigning death.

of thanatosis, too, including the grass snake (*Natrix natrix*) and, even more interestingly, the American hog-nosed snake (*Heterodon*), a non-venomous species. When W. E. Bartlett found one on his lawn he described what he witnessed, and later published the account in the journal *Nature* in 1920:

"I approached the serpent in company with a friend to make some investigation of it, and only to interfere with it enough to keep it from crawling away. The creature went through the usual feint of being a dangerous snake that is peculiar to this species, and quickly began to coil and recoil and to hide its head under its body. After it had done this a short time it turned on its back, but continued to writhe as though injured severely.

"Gradually it assumed a position simulating that of a dead snake lying on its back, with its mouth completely inverted and bleeding. This was done in such a way that the head appeared to be completely mashed or severed. The exudate of blood from the entire surface of the mouth was perfect. It was the most complete and well-carried-out feint of a tragic death that I have ever witnessed, and all without the least torture or stroke of any kind from me. I only detained the snake by placing my foot in front of it and turning it back once at the beginning. We left the creature in this apparently killed condition, only to see that it disappeared in a very short time."

Just as human thespians can, the hog-nosed snake also has a tendency to overact. If it is rolled back onto its stomach during its thanatotic display, this shamming serpent will swiftly flip over so that it is lying belly-up again – oblivious to the fact that when a snake is genuinely dead it does not do this.

revealed that when playing dead, the opossum's brainwave patterns correspond with those occurring in a normal active state. That is, to the eye the animal may appear inanimate, but in reality it is fully alert, only waiting for the opportunity to revive and run away. It is therefore all the more remarkable and mystifying that the opossum, while feigning death, can somehow inhibit its normal behavioral and neurological reactions to the bites it receives from a predator.

Deceptive creatures

Many other creatures are known to play dead, including various rodents, frogs and toads, many different insects (from stick insects, giant water bugs, and grasshoppers to longhorn beetles and mantids), and some South American canids (*Dusicyon* spp.).

Certain snakes are skilled performers in the deceptive art

The partridge, a wild game bird, was one of the first animals to be put into a trance.

Going into a trance

Even more bizarre than thanatosis is akinesis, a process by which creatures can be put into a trance. It has yet to be satisfactorily explained. One

Placed on their backs, with their heads tucked under their wings, these pigeons have been put into a trance.

of the earliest records of this phenomenon dates back to 1646 and was performed by the eminent Jesuit scholar Father Athanasius Kircher with a partridge. He bound its legs together and placed the bird on its back, then put a piece of chalk in front of its beak and drew a straight line leading away from it. The partridge promptly froze, remaining motionless.

Subsequent experiments have revealed that the bird does not even need to be tied. As long as it is swiftly and unexpectedly laid on its back, it will become immobile, and will remain in this state for some minutes until "awakening." So, too, will frogs and toads, and a crayfish can be rendered akinetic simply by standing it vertically, balanced on head and chelae (claws) like a tripod.

A most fascinating example of akinesis occurs with cobras. If one is held behind the head, and the top or nape of its head is pressed with a finger, the cobra becomes completely motionless, and when laid down resembles a stiff rod. The fact that cobras can be rendered cataleptic has been cited by some people as an explanation for the biblical account in *Exodus* (4:2-5) in which Moses transformed a living cobra into a rod. Examination of this passage, however, reveals that Moses picked up the cobra by its tail, not its head, before transforming it – an action which would not have induced an akinetic effect.

Paralyzing prey with acupuncture?

In 1986, naturalists Raza Tehsin and J. S. Nathawat presented an intriguing idea about predators causing a paralyzed state in prey. Knowing that livestock thieves in India's Kumbhal Gadh region

The "Fainting" Goats of Tennessee

This extraordinary strain of goat arose in Tennessee during the 1880s, bred selectively from animals that were prone to collapsing when stressed. Farmers saw the genetic manipulation as a way to protect their flocks from coyotes and dogs. The fainting goats became decoys, so that the hardier ones could escape unharmed. The goats do not actually faint. Instead, their muscles lock, causing them to keel over, but they remain conscious. This condition, called myotonia, is due to a recessive gene allele. Such a breed could never survive in the wild, but today it is a popular pet and meat yielder. Continued selection has created goats so sensitive that the mere sound of a loud car engine can be enough to cause them to swoon en masse.

can immobilize a sheep or goat by pulling it to the ground and placing a small weight on its ear, the naturalists did the same, achieving success with an antelope, a young deer, and two rodents. They then speculated that since tigers (and other big cats) normally place one of their canine teeth near the back of their prey's ear when pulling it down, they may be using a form of acupuncture with their fangs on a specific area to induce paralysis.

Reflex Bleeding

see also:
- Insect Migration, p.72
- Spider Attack, p.120
- Playing Dead and Akinesis, p.125

Creatures display various defenses when threatened by a predator. Perhaps the most dramatic of these involve autohemorrhaging or reflex bleeding, in which blood and poisonous fluids are secreted – and sometimes even squirted – to ward off would-be attackers.

Optical blood squirters

Among the most famous, and spectacular, performers of autohemorrhaging are three species of North American desert-dwelling lizard, *Phrynosoma cornutum*, *P. coronatum*, and *P. solare*, which are commonly known (albeit inaccurately) as horned toads. When confronted by a predator, a horned toad attempts a number of defenses.

Initially the lizard will try straightforward intimidation. By inflating its body, the lizard can give the impression that it is much bigger than it really is and, therefore, a greater challenge for would-be predators. If this has no effect, the lizard will then jump forward, hissing loudly at its enemy.

If the predator is still not intimidated, however, and persists in its attack, the lizard has one final, and quite grotesque, defense mechanism. It uses a series of thin-walled, blood-filled spaces called sinuses found within its eye sockets. When the lizard rapidly increases the blood pressure within these sinuses, it causes the sinus walls to break suddenly. The blood is then forced out in jet-like squirts of crimson droplets. Sometimes, the force with which the lizard squirts this eye-ejected blood is so powerful that it can send sprays shooting up to distances of 4 feet (1.2 m). This bizarre squirting can be repeated several times if necessary, which is usually sufficient to frighten off any predator. Also, the squirted blood may contain a distasteful chemical, which would act as an additional deterrent to potential predators.

> Jets of blood, vile-tasting froth, and foul-smelling fluid are some of the more gruesome extremes creatures will go to for the sake of self-preservation – and they usually work.

Horned toad lizards (*Phrynosoma* spp.) are among the few creatures that actually squirt blood as a deterrent.

When grasshoppers of the genus _Dictyophorus_ secrete blood plasma as a defense mechanism, a foul-tasting froth is produced as the blood mixes with air. This is enough to deter even the hungriest of predators.

Ladybugs have a reflex-bleeding mechanism too, but they secrete liquid from their limb joints.

Although scientists know how the lizards achieve this startling behavior, there are still quite a few mysteries associated with _Phrynosoma's_ ability to autohemorrhage, particularly because there does not seem to be any established pattern as to when the lizard resorts to this tactic.

Several researchers, including the eminent American herpetologist Dr. R. L. Ditmars, have handled hundreds of specimens before provoking one to squirt blood, whereas others have experienced this phenomenon after handling only a small number of lizards. Some lizards squirting blood were also found to be molting, but others were not. Nor does there appear to be any sex-related tendency to perform this activity. And for a desert animal normally anxious to preserve as much of its body's fluid content as possible, to lose fluid in this manner is very odd indeed.

Reflex-bleeding insects

A number of insects also release blood in order to deter predators. Some of the most dramatic examples occur among grasshoppers of the genus _Dictyophorus._ When threatened, hydrostatic pressure within the grasshopper's body increases, forcing blood plasma out of weak pores in the body's cuticle. As it emerges, the blood mixes with air and converts into a disgusting froth that covers the insect's body surface. The froth contains a repellent so noxious that any creature brave enough to attempt to eat this vile-looking insect soon drops it and beats a hasty retreat. Once alone again, the grasshopper reabsorbs much of its blood by decreasing its body's internal hydrostatic pressure.

ANIMAL PROFILE

The Firefly

When defending themselves, female fireflies of the genus *Photuris* release droplets of blood from their thorax that contain distasteful substances known as lucibufagins (LBG).

Intriguingly, in 1998, Cornell University biologist Dr. Thomas Eisner revealed that these fireflies do not produce the chemicals themselves but obtain them from the bodies of their prey, males of a related genus, *Photinus*. These are lured to their doom when the female *Photuris* fireflies cunningly mimic the bioluminescent signals of the *Photinus* females.

Beetle juice

Other animals that autohemorrhage come from various insect families within the beetle order Coleoptera. One such creature is the bloody-nosed beetle (*Timarcha* spp.), which forces bright-red blood out around its mouth when threatened. Another is *Lytta vesicatoria* from the oil beetle family, commonly known as the blister beetle. These creatures secrete a liquid called cantharidin which, when in contact with human skin, causes it to blister. The liquid has valuable medical properties, and is often used as a treatment for skin complaints such as warts. Paradoxically, blister beetles' ability to produce cantharidin renders them unable to camouflage themselves, leaving them vulnerable to attack.

Relatives of the blister beetle known as oil beetles secrete a greasy substance that deters predators because of its unpleasant taste.

Death-feigning snakes

There are certain snakes in the world that autohemorrhage and none of them is more effective than the West Indian wood snakes (*Tropidophis* spp.). Related to the great boa constrictors of Central and South America, these snakes perform a series of dramatic acts designed to ward off enemies and hungry predators.

First, they coil themselves up into a tight ball and secrete a truly foul-smelling fluid, which has an odor not dissimilar to that of rotting flesh. At the same time, they turn their eyes bright red by releasing blood into them, although they do not squirt it out in the way that the horned toad lizards do.

Instead, the wood snakes have devised an equally macabre finale to their performance. They increase the blood pressure within small capillaries just inside their mouth. The increasing pressure causes the capillaries to grow ever larger until they burst, sending bright scarlet rivulets of blood trickling down from the snake's mouth.

The alarming effect of this, coupled with the awful stench of the secreted fluid, suggests not only that the creature is dead and in the process of decomposing, but also that it is damaged in some way, or even diseased. As might well be expected, this highly unpleasant sight is normally enough to turn away even the most desperate of predators.

The blister beetle defends itself by irritating skin.

Shedding Limbs

see also:
● Extreme Endurance, p.110
● Reflex Bleeding, p.128
● Rat Kings, p.134

Some animals have an extraordinary and dramatic ability to lose a part of their body in order to avoid being captured.

The shedding of tails, and sometimes other limbs too, is not uncommon in the natural world. Autotomy, as scientists call it, is a clever means of getting away from predators, which are literally left holding a part of the intended victim's body. Not only is the victim able to survive the incident, it is able to replace the lost body part. Species from no less than 11 of the 16 classified families of lizard shed their tails in this way. The secret of the process lies in the structure of a typical lizard's tail. Each of its caudal vertebrae from the sixth onward contains a weak horizontal "break" or fracture plane, which is made of cartilage instead of bone and will snap easily if held. Also, within each vertebra's fracture plane the blood vessels and nerves are constricted, so that if the tail does snap off, blood loss will be minimal. Because the shed tail still contains a functioning neuromuscular system, it will thrash violently for a short time, distracting the predator and enabling the lizard to escape.

Trouble in the tail

There are, however, disadvantages to tail-shedding. Although the lizard can regenerate its tail, the new version is less flexible than the original. In an older lizard the new tail will be shorter and may have imperfections. And, most significantly, a lizard can partially shed its tail only once – the new version cannot be shed because it does not contain separate vertebrae. Its internal skeleton is nothing more than a cartilaginous rod, so it can snap off only at its base, not at any point along its length. Therefore, any future encounter with a predator would involve losing the entire tail.

Sometimes, the regeneration process does not occur properly, causing bizarre results such as forked tails, or two or even three complete tails. This puts the lizard at great disadvantage because it is likely to attract more attention from predators than normal, and the new tail will make it less mobile.

Perhaps the most intriguing disadvantage of tail-shedding is the loss of social standing that it can

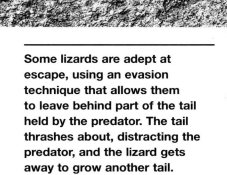

Some lizards are adept at escape, using an evasion technique that allows them to leave behind part of the tail held by the predator. The tail thrashes about, distracting the predator, and the lizard gets away to grow another tail.

A five-limbed starfish resting on a rock is the target of a predator, the painted prawn (*Hymenocera picta*).

The starfish breaks away, leaving the marauder with just a limb. If the painted prawn doesn't eat it, that limb may turn into a brand new starfish.

Having gotten away, the starfish can regenerate the part that was lost to its attacker.

cause to the tail-shedder. In a study of the sociable desert lizard (*Uta stansburiana*), Dr. Stanley Fox and Dr. Margaret Rostker from Oklahoma State University discovered that those lizards that had lost their tails became the subordinates of those with intact tails. They lost breeding and feeding opportunities, as well as territories, and regained their original position within the social hierarchy only once their tails had regenerated.

Salamanders can also shed their tails, but, unlike lizards, the horizontal fracture planes in the tails of these amphibians occur in between the vertebrae, rather than through the vertebrae.

Poor imitations of the original

In some invertebrates, autotomy can involve the loss of one or more legs. Crabs, for instance, are famous for sacrificing a claw if attacked by a predator, which they will then regrow. Indeed, they are willing to lose several of their limbs if necessary to avoid capture, though this willingness decreases markedly with each successive limb loss, for obvious reasons – a crab that loses too many limbs will be unable to move, and therefore will become an easy target for a predator.

As with lizards' regenerated tails, newly made crab limbs are only poor imitations of their originals. They are usually smaller or narrower in form, and significantly lighter. In the case of regrown claws, they are less successful as weapons. But crabs evidently deem this to be an acceptable trade-off since, on occasion, a crab will not wait to be seized and will take the initiative itself. It attacks and grabs the predator with its claws, then deliberately pulls away so these limbs break off. As it scuttles away to regenerate, the predator is left in the painful grip of the crab's shed claws.

A talent for re-creation

Starfishes, which have hard spiny skeletons and five (or more) arms or limbs in a star-like arrangement, are also adept at autotomy when caught by predators. Their subsequent regeneration, however, can be particularly dramatic. As long as the shed limb is not devoured by the predator and still contains a section of the central body disc of the starfish that shed it, this limb has the ability to regenerate into a complete starfish.

Rodent tails

It is a common assumption that among the vertebrates, tail-shedding is limited to reptiles and the lower taxonomic classes. However, certain species of rodent also have this talent. According to the authoritative mammalian encyclopedia *Walker's*

When a predator seizes the eye-catching brush-like tail end of the Australian carnivorous marsupial phascogale, all it gets is a mouthful of hair. The squirrel-like creature escapes to grow more hair.

Mammals of the World (1999), edited by Dr. Ronald M. Nowak, these include deer mice, rock rats, spiny mice, spiny rats, and dassie rats (not to be confused with true dassies, the hyrax subungulates). As with lizards, rodent tail-shedding involves the breaking off of all or part of the tail, allowing the rodent to escape. A partial replacement of the lost tail subsequently develops.

An interesting variation on tail-shedding was revealed in 1997 by Australian zoologist Dr. Todd Soderquist at Monash University, Victoria, while studying a superficially squirrel-like but carnivorous marsupial called the brush-tailed phascogale (*Phascogale tapoatafa*). This arboreal species earns its name from the extensive and unusual black brush of hair on its tail. Soderquist discovered that when cornered by a predator, the phascogale erects this

eye-catching brush of hair, inciting the predator to grab at it. But when it does so, all that it gets is a mouthful of hair, the loss of which is far less important to the phascogale than the opportunity for escape. In any case, the sacrificed hairs are soon regrown and the phascogale's tail is restored to its former glory.

In 1984, a curious report in the media involved a case of aberrant reptilian autotomy. While he was repairing the foundation of his house in Bachero di Cingoli, near Florence, Italy, Mario Angelucci allegedly discovered a two-tailed lizard. Ignoring pleas from biologists at the local university to send his find to them for examination, Mario kept it, believing that it was a sign of impending good fortune. Not long after, he dreamed that a Roman soldier gave him detailed instructions for locating a precise site in his garden where hidden treasure lay buried. Mario lost no time in digging — and unearthed a hoard of 2,000-year-old Roman coins worth $45,000.

Rat Kings

see also:
- Hibernation, p.100
- Entombed Animals, p.114
- Shedding Limbs, p.131

One of nature's most grotesque oddities, the rat king, has no real explanation. Once fraud has been discounted – and tricksters have sometimes made rat kings to fool the unwary – scientists struggle to understand this rare phenomenon.

Rat kings are preserved aggregations of black rats (*Rattus rattus*) linked to one another by their tails. The name comes from *roi de rats*, a possible corruption of the French *rouet de rats* or "rat wheel," and reports of their discovery go back through the centuries.

Nature sometimes throws up truly weird and grotesque occurrences such as rats, or even squirrels, joined together in death by their entwined tails.

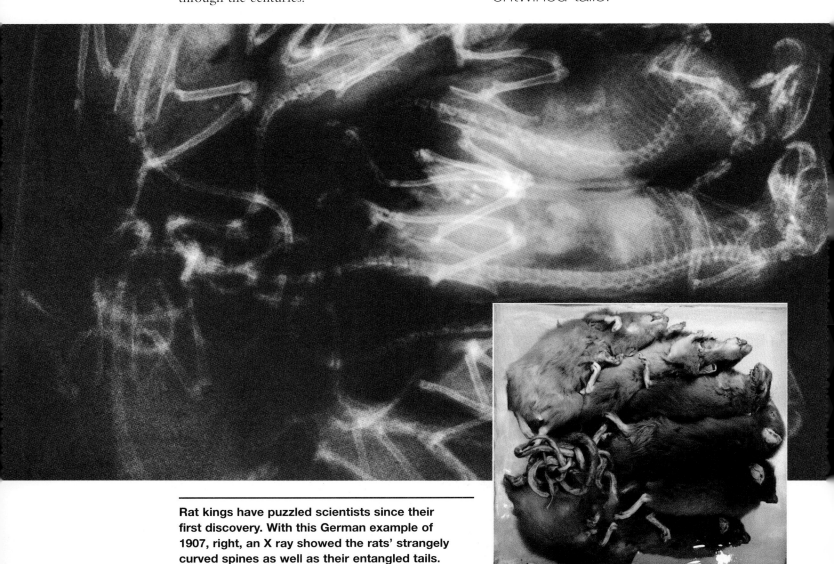

Rat kings have puzzled scientists since their first discovery. With this German example of 1907, right, an X ray showed the rats' strangely curved spines as well as their entangled tails.

More than 50 kings are listed by Martin Hart in his book *Rats* (1982), 38 of which he considers to be genuine. Intriguingly, all but one of these rat kings feature black rats (*Rattus rattus*) and none involves the much commoner brown rat (*R. norvegicus*). Indeed, the only exception to the black rat rule is a king consisting of ten young field rats (*R. brevicaudatus*) discovered on March 23, 1918 in Bogor, Java.

A number of explanations for the formation of rat kings have been offered. The most popular is that rats huddle together in defense against damp surroundings, and their tails, pressed against one another, become sticky and ever more entangled as the rats strive to pull free. Another notion is that a rat king is actually a single litter whose members' tails became entangled in their mother's uterus. However, this explanation seems highly unlikely, as rats yoked together in this way would be unable to obtain food and so could not survive very long.

A knot of tails

The most spectacular example on record was found inside a miller's chimney at Buchheim, Germany, in May 1828. Hairless and desiccated, the king comprised no fewer than 32 rats, probably not adults, and inescapably bound to one another by their Gordian-knotted tails. This exceptional rat king – indeed, rat emperor! – is today a much-valued specimen in the Altenberg Mauritianum.

Equally extraordinary was the discovery by some farmhands in December 1822 at Döllstadt, in eastern Germany, of two rat kings within a hollow beam in a barn roof. One of these kings consisted of 28 rats, the other involved 14. When the rats in both kings were separated, the tail of each rat clearly bore the impression of the tails of the other rats, showing how tightly they had been entwined.

Another famous example was discovered in July 1748 by miller Johann Heinrich Jäger at Grossballhausen (also spelled Gross Ballheiser) in Germany, when an 18-rat king fell from under his mill's cogwheels. Another, found in 1907 at Ruderhausen, near Germany's Harz Mountains, is in the collections of Göttingen's Zoological Institute. Like the one found in February 1963 by farmer P. van Nijnatten in his barn at Rucphen, in North Brabant, Holland, the king was X-rayed, revealing some tail fractures and signs of a callus formation – all indicating that the knot of tails had occurred quite some time before death.

A single mouse king has also been fully confirmed, comprising several juvenile field mice (*Apodemus sylvaticus*). It was found at Holstein, Germany, in April 1929.

A similar phenomenon occurs in cats, as shown in this drawing. Called a crown, the newborn cats – found at Strasbourg in 1683 – had their umbilical cords knotted together.

Mystery of the squirrels

Several squirrel kings have been recorded, though the concept of bushy-tailed squirrels becoming entwined together in this way seems even more unlikely than rat kings.

In a seven-squirrel king found in a South Carolina zoo on December 31, 1951, two of its members were dead and a third was dying. Two other wild squirrel kings have also been found there over the years, and all in cold, snowy weather, implying that the squirrels had huddled together for warmth. A king of six young squirrels was spotted by schoolgirl Crystal Cresseveur in a hedge outside her home in Easton, Pennsylvania, on September 24, 1989. A five-squirrel king, with two albino members, fell out of a tree near Reisterstown Elementary School in Baltimore, Maryland, on September 18, 1991, but these were successfully separated because their tails were linked to one another only indirectly, with sticky tree sap, tangled hair, and nest debris.

In Europe, at least two kings of red squirrels (*Sciurus vulgaris*) have been recorded – one in August 1921, the other on October 20, 1951 (this one was later preserved). In July 1997, what looked at first like a huge hairy spider was spotted under a tree in Brantford, in Ontario, Canada, but closer scrutiny revealed a squirrel king – five young squirrels with tails braided together up to their bases.

Equally remarkable are bird kings. In these, the members are allegedly joined to one another not by entwined tails but by entangled legs. However, there are very few on record. The most famous is a king comprising three young blue tits (*Parus caeruleus*), found barely alive in a nesting box alongside some separate siblings, and documented by the German journal *Natur und Volk* in 1953. When the birds were separated from one another it was found that they had been united by a clump of entangling nest-lining material stuck to their legs.

Bird Parliaments

see also:
- Bird Migration, p.68
- Talking Birds, p.151
- Anting, p.222

One of the most mystifying forms of attack is the so-called bird parliament, in which a single bird—the accused—is surrounded by a group of others, who seem to sit in judgment before sentencing the bird to be pecked to death.

Although most commonly recorded in pre-20th-century natural history tomes, bird parliaments or courts are still often observed and reported even today, most frequently among species belonging to the crow family.

In one example, on the morning of July 14, 1978, David Morris of Abergele in Clwyd, Wales, watched as 80-100 rooks (*Corvus frugilegus*) flew down to a field and formed a circle around a single rook standing in the center. There then followed a raucous cacophony of cawing from the rook court for a while ("as if discussing the case," Morris later remarked), but abruptly this ceased, and there was absolute silence. Then the rooks moved in, attacking the accused en masse. In just a

Crows are considered by many ornithologists to be the most intelligent members of the bird kingdom, but do they really sit in judgment on their fellows?

ANIMAL PROFILE

The Stork

In 1954, naturalist L. W. Hayward revealed in a letter to London's *Mirror* newspaper that storks in Germany quite often form parliaments. He described one case in which the accused was encircled and vociferously "sentenced" by a jury of about 50 fellow storks, then done to death in a matter of seconds.

In a ditch at the base of a hedgerow, a circle of birds comprising chaffinches, blue tits, blackbirds, a robin, and even a much larger magpie had gathered. Confined in the center of the accusers was a solitary male chaffinch. Had the court proceeded to its usual grisly end, the chaffinch may well have been torn apart, but Quinn's arrival made the startled birds fly off in all directions and the chaffinch escaped unharmed.

There have been too many reliable reports of bird parliaments to dismiss the phenomenon as fictitious, but their true nature and function remain undetermined. Crows are widely believed

few minutes the victim had been reduced to a handful of feathers, after which the rooks flew off.

In 1975, Rose Bridgett of Arnold in Nottinghamshire, England, witnessed a crow court in a local field. As in Morris's case, the accused was surrounded by a circle of other crows. In this particular instance they did not physically attack it, but the sheer terror of the occasion seemed to overcome the hapless victim. When the crows flew away, Bridgett found the accused lying dead on the ground, without any visible signs of injury.

Sometimes, the accused belongs to a different species from those in judgment of it – as in a case reported by a *Daily Telegraph* reader to this London newspaper's nature columnist, Dr. Robert Burton, in 1993. On that occasion, a badly bleeding magpie was surrounded by a ring of 30-40 rooks, who attacked it whenever it tried to escape.

What may be a unique multi-species parliament was observed near Frome, Somerset, by Bristol-based ecologist Phil Quinn during autumn 1991.

by ornithologists to be the world's most intelligent birds, and some researchers consider it possible that crow courts are indeed judgmental throngs capable of sentencing a wayward member of the flock.

Others deem it more likely that the victim is a diseased, parasitized, or infirm individual that is culled to preserve the health of the flock – indeed, other nonavian social or gregarious species perform similar rites. Certain cases may even involve the compassionate killing, as opposed to "execution," of a terminally ill specimen.

Yet the fact that some examples involve an apparently healthy victim, and that others feature an atypical multispecies congregation rather than a normal single-species flock, makes this explanation incomplete. Some researchers claim parliaments are a means of reducing competition for food, but this is normally dealt with by straightforward bouts of fighting between individuals. This mass-attack phenomenon is still a perplexing behavioral mystery awaiting a satisfactory answer.

Crows are social birds that live together in large groups.

CHAPTER SEVEN

ANIMAL COMMUNICATION

Humans are not the only
species capable of complex communication.
Indeed, thanks to a number of remarkable
breakthroughs in inter-species communication,
some researchers have been able to converse
with nonhuman individuals, including apes
and parrots, on a scale that would once
have been thought impossible.
Moreover, several animals traditionally
deemed either unable or extremely
unlikely to vocalize have recently been
exposed as bona fide – and sometimes
decidedly vehement – vocalists.

Primate Sign Language

see also:
● Self-Awareness, p.180
● Tool-Using, p.186
● Animal Humor, p.198

The anatomy of their throats precludes speaking to humans, but some apes have been trained to use sign language.

Widely deemed to be the most intelligent nonhuman species on earth, the great apes have always attracted interest from animal behaviorists eager to find some way of communicating directly with our closest relatives in the animal kingdom.

Using sign language

A major problem for researchers trying to train apes to communicate is that their throat structure is ill designed for attempting human speech. Various alternative methods have been investigated. One of these is sign language. A number of researchers in the United States have taught apes to communicate using a version of ASL – American Sign Language or Ameslan. ASL is normally used by deaf people to communicate.

The earliest but most famous ape to learn ASL was a female chimpanzee called Washoe. She made history by becoming the first nonhuman to communicate directly with humans using a human–made language. Her training was undertaken by Professor Allen Gardner and his research associate wife, Beatrice, both psychologists at Nevada University. They began in June, 1966 and, by the time the first phase of this long-term project ended in October, 1970, Washoe had learned more than 130 signs. She began hesitantly, taking seven months to master her first four signs. During the next seven months, however, she added nine more signs to her vocabulary, and an additional 21 during the seven months following those. Moreover, as her vocabulary expanded, so, too, did her ability to combine words to create short "phrases."

During her training, Washoe's ability to communicate with the Gardners and her other teachers, who included deaf people skilled in ASL

Koko "asks" animal behaviorist Penny Patterson for an orange by extending her left arm away from her body (top). She then makes the sign for the word "orange" by rotating her clenched right fist, which is pressed to her lips (bottom).

from an early age, meant that researchers gained many insights into her thought processes. Washoe seemed to have the ability to lie, make jokes, and be consciously aware of herself. She even proved adept at thinking up insults. Once, Washoe had a heated quarrel with a macaque monkey and, when she encountered the macaque later, she signed "dirty monkey" – deftly combining two words hitherto used only separately – to emphasize her dislike of the macaque. Moreover, Washoe proved capable of passing her ability on. Not long after her baby Sequoyah died, she was presented with an orphan chimpanzee called Loulis as a substitute. After taking a few days to accept him, Washoe began teaching him to sign. In time, Loulis acquired a sizable ASL vocabulary learned entirely from his adoptive mother.

Another notable student of ASL was a gorilla called Koko, treated almost like a foster daughter by animal behaviorist Penny Patterson. Her training began at San Francisco Zoo in 1972, but Patterson and Koko later moved to Stanford University. Koko's vocabulary initially increased at much the same rate as Washoe's had done, but after three years it was evident that Koko was even more talented: Koko had acquired 127 signs while Washoe learned only 85 signs in that time.

As with Washoe, communication through ASL with Koko exposed many telling facets of her personality. She revealed much deliberate humor, the ability to lie at times, and often childlike contrariness or boredom if the teaching process became monotonous. Also of great interest was the discovery that Koko understood not only ASL but also spoken English. Moreover, even though she could reply only using ASL, questions posed to her that combined signs and voice elicited better results from her than sign-only or voice-only questions.

Do apes understand?

Many animal behaviorists believe such studies are of immense value in finding out whether animals can truly communicate using language in the sense that humans do. There are other scientists, however, who remain skeptical, including Dr. Herbert Terrace, who was initially impressed by such results, and had experienced success himself in teaching a chimp called Nim to sign using ASL. After meticulously examining videotapes of sessions with Nim and other signing apes, however, Terrace changed his mind. He claimed that the tapes revealed that these apes were not so much signing in an independent, truly communicative manner as merely mimicking their trainers as an effective way to obtain rewards.

He felt that they were signing without a true understanding of what they were saying (just as parrots do when reciting words taught to them). They were, he argued, aware that if they made signs, they would be given food (just as parrots learn that reciting words is a good way to get their owners to feed them). He also thought it likely that trainers might sometimes be overinterpreting the signs of their apes, and be unconsciously prompting their responses.

To find out the truth, double-blind experiments were conducted with these same apes. They signed correctly in response to questions expressed visually, vocally, and using a combination of the two in set-ups designed to exclude the risk of

ANIMAL PROFILE

A True Talking Ape

Cody, a young orangutan from Scarborough's Flamingo Zoo Park in England, is remarkable among communicating apes because he was taught to vocalize. Cody was trained by Keith Laidler and is the subject of his extraordinary book, *The Talking Ape* (1980). Although Cody's throat structure did not allow the enunciation of human speech, he was nonetheless taught to speak, voicing several different one-syllable sounds, each with its own meaning. To achieve this, Laidler used a mode of speech training previously found to be effective with autistic children.

influence or exaggerated interpretation by the trainers. The apes seem to be genuinely communicating with their questioners.

Lexigrams and keyboards

Keen to avoid the danger of influencing or misinterpreting replies when communicating through sign language, some researchers have tried to teach apes to communicate using physical media. Early experiments involved teaching chimps to use lexigrams – colored pieces of plastic, or plastic pieces with abstract symbols on them, representing particular nouns, verbs, and other word forms. The chimps placed these in specific meaningful arrangements either to respond to questions or to formulate their own.

This method of communication has become more sophisticated in recent years, as shown by the training of Panbanisha, a teenage female pygmy chimpanzee (*Pan paniscus*) at Georgia State University in Atlanta. By mid-1999, she had acquired a vocabulary of 3,000 words and could construct complex sentences using a remarkable

method of communication. After first learning sign language, Panbanisha was given a keyboard containing 400 symbol-marked buttons, each representing a specific word or abstract concept (such as "good" and "give me"). As she types these buttons, the words that they represent appear on a computer screen, and are spoken by a computer voice synthesizer. Panbanisha is now so accustomed to symbols that she has even begun to draw some of them on the floor using chalk, and to teach her young son, Nyota, her reading and "speaking" skills.

The same system is also being used by an orangutan at Atlanta Zoo, who took advantage of it during a heatwave – and showed a sense of humor – to comment, "I want to buy a pool."

Artistic apes

Some apes express themselves through art, a medium favored by such ape artists as Congo, a celebrated chimpanzee painter who became a television star during the 1950s. Congo began with pencil drawings, and was closely studied throughout his two-year artistic period by British

Djakarta Jim (above) of Topeka Zoo in Kansas won a painting competition for young people at the age of three. Nonja (left), a female orangutan in Vienna Zoo, expresses herself using felt-tip pens.

anthropologist Dr. Desmond Morris. Morris swiftly realized that the abstract patterns that Congo produced during bouts of intense concentration were not random but possessed a personal, readily recognizable style.

Certain motifs were clearly favored, as they appeared time and again within his drawings. These included a radiating fan, which, as he became more experienced, was produced in a variety of different forms: sometimes split in two, or divided by a central spot, or even paired with a second, subsidiary fan. Moreover, like many human artists, Congo took violent exception to being interrupted while creating a drawing, and was also very decisive about when a drawing was complete, refusing to add a single additional line once he had finished working on it.

Congo subsequently took up painting, too, and eventually attracted such widespread public attention that an exhibition of his output, together with that of a finger-painting chimp from Baltimore Zoo called Betsy, was held at the Institute of Contemporary Arts galleries in Mayfair, London. Many of their works were eagerly purchased by aficionados of modern art, and attracted genuine praise from such celebrated human artists as Salvador Dali, Pablo Picasso, and Joan Miró.

Zoologists were also intrigued by Congo's work, whose scientific significance was fully explored by Morris in his book *The Biology of Art* (1962). It was also eloquently described in a *New York Times* article by the zoologist Professor Julian Huxley: "These paintings are of considerable interest because they tell us something of the way in which art may have evolved … In fact, we are witnessing the springs of art. The results show conclusively that chimpanzees do have artistic potentials which can be brought to light by providing suitable opportunities."

Interestingly, the ability to communicate through art does not seem to be restricted to the great apes. Certain monkeys have also proven themselves skilled practitioners with pigment and pencil. These include a South American capuchin monkey called Frederica at Dartmoor Wildlife Park in Devon, England. She began by tracing with a finger in condensation on the windows of her home and scratching patterns on the floor with a stone. By the early 1990s, however, she had progressed to creating full-color sketches using crayons provided by her keeper, Stephen Eddy.

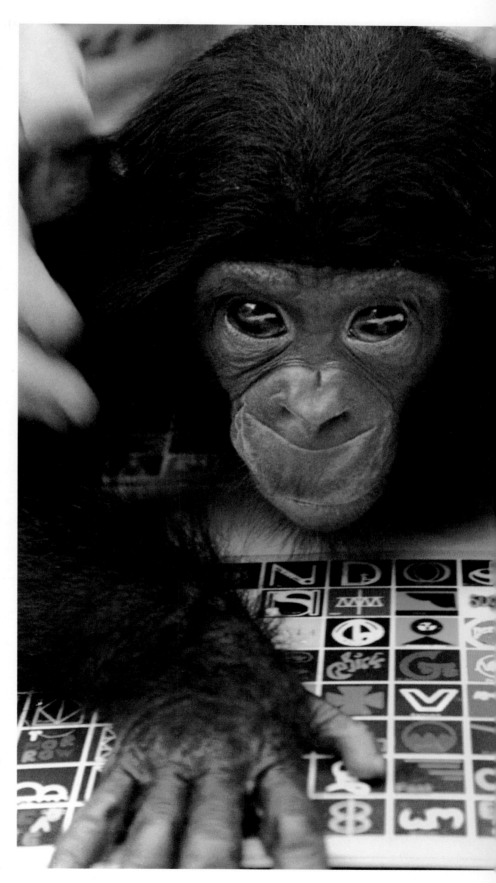

One-year-old Nyota is learning to communicate using lexigrams.

Cetacean Communication

Singing humpbacks, clicking sperm whales, and vocal dolphins are all adept undersea communicators.

The undersea world is not silent, as zoologists once believed. We now know that it is filled with a cacophony of sounds. Many of these are produced by whales, dolphins, and other cetaceans, and scientists are still unsure of the meaning of many of their exotic and mysterious calls.

Humpback songs

Its haunting "songs" make the male humpback whale (*Megaptera novaeangliae*) one of the world's most extraordinary communicators. The purpose of these songs, however, is unclear. Some researchers believe they are intended to attract females; others, that they are territorial and are used as a means of spacing the males apart during communal activity.

As first revealed in the 1960s by whale researchers and conservationists Roger and Katherine Payne, the fundamental component of each song is a "unit," which is equivalent to a note in a human song. These units are grouped into short repeating sequences dubbed "phrases," which

Male humpback whales are among the most vocal species of the undersea world, singing long and complex songs often for many hours at a time.

in turn are grouped into longer sequences termed "themes"; a single song can contain as many as ten themes. Humpback songs are complex constructions, but what makes them even more distinctive among animal vocalizations is their length. Comprising a continuous vocal outpouring known as a song pattern, a single song can be repeated over and over without a pause for up to 22 hours at a time.

All of the humpbacks within a given geographical area sing the same song, but the song varies markedly between different regions. Humpbacks in the North Atlantic, for example, sing a very different song from those in the North Pacific. Even within a given region, however, the song does not remain

the same indefinitely. A change can occur in one component of the song, such as swapping the order of two themes, or omitting one theme, or adding a new one. This change will be adopted by all of the whales so that they all sing the new, updated version. This gradual evolution of the song occurs continuously, each component changing after a couple of months or so. As a result, after about eight years the original song will have been transformed into a completely new one.

Several major aspects of humpback singing, however, remain unclear. Why, for example, does the song change at all? How do all of the humpbacks in the region learn each new version of it so quickly? And how is it remembered during

Unlike the humpback, the sperm whale does not sing. Instead it communicates through a series of clicks and pauses.

ANIMAL PROFILE

Out With the Old, In With the New

A new discovery has shown that humpbacks are not averse to abandoning a traditional song in favor of a totally new one introduced from elsewhere. Sydney University researcher Dr. Michael Noad and his team analyzed more than 1,000 hours of whale song. In 2000, they revealed that less than two years after the migration in 1996 of some humpbacks from the Indian Ocean off Western Australia into the Pacific Ocean around Queensland in east Australia, all 112 of the male humpbacks native to Queensland's seas had swapped over to the visitors' song, a cultural revolution in terms of the normal evolution of humpback songs.

the long period between the breeding and migration seasons, when this remarkable vocal manifestation ceases entirely?

Equally intriguing is the presence of rhyme-like phrases in songs containing many themes, and their absence in songs containing only a few themes. It has been suggested by Katherine Payne that these "rhymes" may assist the whales in remembering long, complex songs.

Cachalot codas

Far shorter but no less enigmatic than the humpback's songs, which are invariably solo performances, are the clicking duets performed by sperm whales, or cachalots (*Physeter macrocephalus*).

Each sperm whale apparently emits a series of clicks and pauses, or codas, which has been likened to Morse code. This vocalization is unique to the individual whale and lasts several seconds. In a duet, two whales emit their codas alternately, in a manner similar to a human conversation.

Some cetacean biologists consider that this phenomenon has a deeper significance than communicating territorial limits or attracting a mate. Moreover, as noted by marine biologist Dr. Bernd Wursig of Texas A&M University, the codas of certain populations of sperm whale have been found to possess distinct dialects.

Individuality or gang language?

When swimming together as a school, dolphins emit an amazing range of sounds, including squeaks, whistles, raspberries, clicks, barks, and groans. The clicks and other pulsed sounds were once believed to be used solely for echolocation, with only the more continuous sounds, such as whistles and squeaks, functioning as communication. This is no longer thought to be the case, however. Researchers now know that the whistles and squeaks vary between dolphins and appear to serve

as individual-specific identification messages, whereas some clicks and raspberries convey an individual's mood or emotional state.

Recent studies have revealed that there are also situations when individual identity is suppressed in favor of a collective identity, if such an action benefits all of the participating individuals. In 1999, University of Michigan dolphin researchers Dr. John Pepper and Dr. Rachel Smolker published their lengthy investigations of a trio of male bottlenose dolphins (*Tursiops truncatus*) inhabiting Shark Bay off Western Australia. The three had associated with each other for several years, a common phenomenon among male dolphins, enabling them to increase their likelihood of each mating with a female.

The researchers discovered that over the years since this dolphin trio had first formed, their individual whistles had become increasingly similar, eventually merging into a single group call emitted by all three. But why should this have happened? Pepper and Smolker believe that the group call is similar in human terms to a badge, emblem, or tattoo possessed by every member of a gang, which alerts a potential rival to an individual's gang membership, and thereby warns them that the individual is not to be trifled with.

Dolphins may modify their unique whistle if there are clear benefits for other members of the school.

Insect Language

see also:
- Ultraviolet Vision, p. 20
- Magnetoreception, p. 44
- Unexpected Vocalists, p. 154

The need to share with their fellow workers the location of rich sources of pollen and nectar has created a remarkably sophisticated system of communication among honeybees (*Apis mellifera*). When a honeybee returns to its hive after finding a flower-filled garden or meadow and collecting nectar and pollen there, it can describe the precise location of this food source to other workers in the hive so that they, too, can find these same flowers and bring back more nectar and pollen to the hive – but how?

Professor Karl von Frisch from Bavaria, Germany, spent more than two decades researching honeybee communication in order to answer this question. His two books *The Dancing Bees* (1956) and *The Dance Language and Orientation of Bees* (1967) chronicle his remarkable discoveries. They were of such profound significance in the field of animal behavior that his findings earned him the Nobel Prize for Medicine in 1973.

Extensive studies by Von Frisch and his team over time, using marked worker bees and special hives whose interior could be subtly observed by researchers without disturbing the bees, revealed that a returning worker bee communicates information about how to find food sources through various dances. Each dance, performed in a

Complex methods of communication are not, as many people believe, limited to vertebrates; there are many examples from the insect world too.

very special way, provides precise details regarding the location of the nectar or pollen source, its distance from the hive, and the quality of the nectar and pollen that can be found there.

Dancing around

If the source is 250 feet (80 m) or less from the hive, when a worker bee returns with nectar and pollen and enters the hive it performs a characteristic dance – known as the round dance – on a vertical honeycomb. Followed closely by three or four other workers, the bee walks a circle on the honeycomb, first in one direction and then in the other, again and again. The round dance tells these workers that the nectar or pollen source is close by. But the dance can tell them even more – by paying attention to more specific aspects of the dance, they learn important additional details about the source. The dance's length and the energy with which the bee performs it reveal the quality of the source – the greater the number of circuits paced out on the honeycomb and the more energetic the dance, the richer the source of nectar and pollen.

A waggle away

If the nectar or pollen source is more than 250 feet (80 m) from the hive, the returning worker performs a more complex dance, termed the waggle dance. This dance consists of walking a circuit comprising two facing crescents joined vertically in the middle by a straight portion. When the bee is executing this straight portion, it waggles its abdomen – hence the dance's name.

The slower the complete dance is executed, and the fewer the number of waggles performed by the dancing bee on the straight portion, the farther the nectar or pollen source is from the hive. Moreover,

Worker honeybees may travel considerable distances in their search for nectar to bring back to the queen in the hive.

Worker bees communicate with each other through sound and dance about sources of pollen and nectar and their quality. As they do so, they make the honeycomb vibrate, contributing to this exchange of information.

with this dance, not only its length and energy but also the precise orientation of the straight portion provides workers with information about the source.

The straight portion's orientation yields explicit details regarding the nectar or pollen source's location relative to the Sun (see box, below). Put simply, the angle between the perpendicular and the axis of the waggle dance's straight portion corresponds to the angle between the direction of the Sun and the direction of the nectar or pollen source.

Adding in sound

The instructions relayed to fellow worker bees are emphasized by vibrations caused when the bee dances on the honeycomb. Consequently, they are more effective when the bee is on an empty honeycomb than when it is on one filled with bee larvae, because the larvae tend to dampen the vibrations, thus reducing the effectiveness of the communication. As the bees dance, they buzz. These sounds are believed to provide additional information about the food source to the listening workers. Hence the dancing bee seemingly communicates not merely by dance, but by song *and* dance.

Intriguingly, there does not appear to be a dance to inform workers that a bee has failed to find food; in the language of the dancing bees, all news is good news.

Interpreting the Waggle Dance

Bee moves perpendicularly upward	Fly directly into the Sun
Bee moves perpendicularly downward	Fly directly away from the Sun
Bee moves upward and 30° to left of perpendicular	Fly into Sun and 30° to left of it
Bee moves downward, 30° to right of perpendicular	Fly away from Sun and 30° to right of it

Robot dancers

Von Frisch's findings were not universally accepted. After they were published, some researchers speculated that revealing the location of a source of pollen had nothing to do with the movement of the bee's dances at all, but depended on the flower odors trapped on the bee's body hair. It was claimed that if the worker bees could recognize these same scents in the wild, they would find the same pollen source. In 1989, however, a team of German and Danish scientists unveiled an extraordinary invention that has enabled researchers to test Von Frisch's hypothesis directly.

Their invention was a robot bee, programmed to be fluent in the complexities of the honeybee's language of dance and able to reproduce any component of it in the presence of real bees. Researchers could therefore test their reactions. In other words, if dancing really is the key to communicating information regarding nectar or pollen sources, researchers should now be capable of "talking" directly to bees and instructing them them through dance messages to seek out sources in specific locations. Sure enough, it has been found that a robot bee's dances can influence worker bees, inducing them to go out of their hive and search for sources of nectar and pollen in a particular direction.

Language by flashlight

Bees are not the only insects who seem able to say what they mean to their fellows. Fireflies, too, are skilled communicators.

Fireflies are not flies at all, but beetles, which are able to produce their own light — called bioluminescence — for the purpose of attracting a mate. Part of the underside of the abdomen of both male and female fireflies is transparent. Inside this portion, a compound called luciferin reacts with oxygen during a chemical process to create a substance called oxyluciferin. In this process, energy is released in the form of light.

Because no heat is produced, the firefly's method of light production is extremely energy-efficient, achieving a level of approximately 90 percent efficiency. (By contrast, mankind's artificial-light production processes, which yield hot light, have an energy efficiency of just 3 percent.)

Each species of firefly communicates its intention in a different manner. In one species, *Photinus pyralis*, for example, the male produces a half-second flash of light every 5.8 seconds, waiting between each flash for a female to reply by flashing her own light. When they see each other's flashes, the male and female move closer to one another, continuing to flash in order to maintain visual contact, until they meet up and mate.

In certain Asian and Pacific species of firefly, communal displays of availability take place. All the males in a given area congregate together in trees, and instead of flashing individually, they flash simultaneously — transforming the tree into what looks like a single enormous light bulb, flicking on and off. This eye-catching spectacle readily attracts the attention of all the females in the vicinity.

Unfortunately, the firefly's remarkable flashlight language can attract predators as well as potential partners. Female specimens of *Photuris* fireflies cunningly mimic the flashing patterns produced by the females of *Photinus* fireflies in order to lure unsuspecting male *Photinus* specimens. When these lustful males approach the *Photuris* females (wrongly assuming that they are female *Photinus*), these lethal females seize the hapless suitors and proceed to devour them.

The firefly attracts potential mates by flashing light from its abdomen.

Talking Birds

see also:
- Bird Migration, p.68
- Bird Parliaments, p.136
- Animal Herbalists, p.214

Do birds that talk
understand the true
meanings of the words they use,
or are they simply mimicking the voices
they hear around them?

Certain species of bird are able to pronounce human words with remarkable accuracy, despite possessing vocal systems fundamentally different from our own. Some gifted individual birds have acquired sizable vocabularies during their years of training. But are these birds literally reciting words parrot-fashion, or can some of these talented birds actually understand what they are saying and use their linguistic skills to communicate with us?

Mimicking mynahs and prolix parrots

Taken as a species, the most gifted avian mimic is the Indian hill mynah (*Gracula religiosa*). In captivity (yet not in the wild), this relative of the starling can accurately imitate an extraordinary range of sounds outside its species' typical repertoire, including snatches of songs from many other bird species, noises made by all manner of inanimate objects, and, most famously, words spoken by humans – all with extremely clear, distinct enunciation. Indeed, it is an Indian hill mynah called Rajah, owned by Colin Kerry of Toronto,

The Indian hill mynah is the most talented mimic in the animal kingdom.

Alex has been trained to talk using a system of visual prompts and rewards. For successfully saying the word "heart," he gets to keep the heart to play with.

Canada, who is still the only talking bird ever to utter successfully the "jaw-breaking" English word "antidisestablishmentarianism."

Possibly the most celebrated talking mynah of all, however, was Raffles, owned by the American explorer Carveth Wells. Before he died, at the age of eight in 1946, he had appeared many times on television, often whistling "The Star-Spangled Banner"; had entertained wounded armed servicemen during World War II in hospitals all over America; had helped to sell more than a million dollars' worth of war savings bonds; and had earned many thousands of dollars in film and television appearances.

Nevertheless, it is among the parrots that the greatest feats of human mimicry can be found. Some African gray parrots (*Psittacus erithacus*) have truly amazing linguistic abilities, able to faithfully reproduce every slightest intonation of the human voice and amass a prodigious vocabulary. In 1965, a female African gray called Prudle, originally owned by Lyn Logue of Seaford, Sussex, won the first of 13 consecutive titles in the "Best Talking Parrotlike Bird" class at London's National Cage and Aviary Bird Show. She retired undefeated in 1977. Prudle's unparalleled success is hardly surprising: She possessed a vocabulary of more than 800 words, and was even said to be able to create her own sentences.

But do such birds actually understand any of the words they are saying? Traditionally, scientists have doubted it, but there is at least one talking parrot that has made many skeptics think again – this is an extraordinary African gray called Alex.

Mimic or creditable conversationalist?

In 1977, ethologist Dr. Irene Pepperberg, now at the University of Arizona, bought a young cock African gray from a Chicago pet shop and began training him to speak words. She named him Alex, which is also an acronym for her research program – Avian Language Experiment. Whenever Alex correctly identified an object by speaking its name, instead of rewarding him with food Pepperberg gave him the object itself, to play with or destroy if he so wished. She was startled by how quickly and effectively he added words to his vocabulary.

However, it soon became evident that Alex was not just reciting words on cue, but was actively associating them with the objects that they represented, and was using his vocabulary to communicate with her. If, for instance, he is offered a selection of objects, each one having a different color (he can differentiate and name seven different colors), and is asked to name which one is blue (or red, etc.), Alex will duly name the object of that color. Moreover, if two objects of the same color are shown to him, and he is asked what is the same about them, Alex will say "color." Likewise, if he is shown two objects of different colors but the same size, he will answer "size." He will even teach himself words. Once, after seeing himself in a mirror, Alex asked Pepperberg what color he was, and when she told him he was gray he repeated the word "gray" over and over until he had memorized it.

Nocturnal tape recordings reveal that Alex sometimes mumbles words to himself at night, as if practicing them. He is readily able to construct sentences too, in order to ask for things he wants, including items that are not visible to him at the time. He can also count up to six, and is capable of correctly identifying how many objects are present if he is shown a small selection.

Pepperberg feels that Alex demonstrates the rudiments of language and possesses the intellectual capability of a three-year-old child. But like all small children, he is not averse to throwing tantrums, refusing to answer questions when he is bored, throwing objects shown to him onto the floor, and even deliberately answering questions incorrectly, or answering correctly only once Pepperberg has left the room.

Pepperberg believes that her work with Alex has more value than simply its potential to provide a unique insight into animal communication and intelligence. Her work may help those clinicians devising rehabilitation programs for brain-damaged humans. In addition, her methods have been used successfully to help the learning of children with developmental delay, and may be able to assist children with other learning problems.

Talking budgies

As many devoted owners confirm, budgerigars (*Melopsittacus undulatus*) can become skilled chatterboxes. As with parrots and mynahs, there have been some truly exceptional individuals — perhaps none more so than Puck. Owned by Camille Jordan of Petaluma, California, by February 1993 Puck had acquired a vocabulary estimated at 1,728 words.

Even more famous, however, was Sparkie, owned and trained by Mattie Williams, an English teacher from Newcastle-upon-Tyne. After winning a budgie-talking contest organized by the BBC in Britain in 1958, Sparkie became a media star, advertising bird seed and earning so much money that he had his own bank account and income tax number. At the height of his success, he could speak 531 different words and 383 sentences, and was able to recite eight complete nursery rhymes.

Several talking budgerigars have become so skilled at acquiring new words that they have become media stars, some even earning significant sums for their owners.

Unexpected Vocalists

see also:
- Ultrasonic Hearing, p. 22
- Infrasonic Messages, p. 25
- Insect Language, p. 148

The Bornean cave racer snake may use its cat-like cry as a means to disrupt the echolocation system of the birds called cave swiftlets on which it preys.

Some surprising creatures are vocally skilled, although the reasons for this ability are not always easy to determine.

Among the members of the animal world there are some unexpected and controversial communicators and vocalists whose talents are only just being discovered. Some of the more surprising among them include snakes, moths, and mice.

Snakes that meow and chime

Well known for their characteristic hiss, snakes have long been considered incapable of uttering other sounds. The sibilant hiss is produced by air being forced through the opening in the back of the throat – the glottis – into the trachea, and its pitch

is controlled by the width of the glottis. In reality, however, there are many reports of other, much more exotic noises being uttered by serpents belonging to several different species.

Some of these have been fully documented. The North American bull snake (*Pituophis melanoleucus*), for example, is well known among herpetologists for its ability to emit a very loud bovine grunt that can be heard up to 100 feet (30 m) away. This remarkable bellowing noise is made possible by a peculiarity of this snake's anatomy. The bull snake possesses an exceptionally well-developed epiglottis that greatly enhances the sound produced when air is being forced through the glottis.

An even more extraordinary serpentine vocalist was discovered as recently as 1980, during a scientific expedition to Borneo to explore the enormous Melinau limestone cave system in Sarawak's Gunung Mulu National Park. In the near-lightless depths of Clearwater Cave, the team suddenly heard an eerie, penetrating yowling sound directly ahead. When they shone their torches in the direction of this cry, which they described as sounding like the meowing of a cat, they were astonished to discover that it was emerging from the open mouth of a snake. The slender blue snake

squatting on the cave floor was a Bornean cave racer (*Elaphe taeniurae grabowskyi*). Despite being known to science, this snake had not previously been suspected of being capable of emitting such a bizarre and singularly unsnakelike sound.

Researchers consider it possible that the cry is a mechanism for luring its prey – small, fast-flying birds called cave swiftlets – near enough to the snake for it to strike out and snatch them from the air as they fly past. It may even be a ploy to disrupt the birds' echolocation mode of navigation; like bats, cave swiftlets emit high-pitched squeaks and then listen to their echoes in order to build up an aural picture of their surroundings.

In 1991, studies conducted by Dr. Bruce Young of Hollins College, Virginia, with king cobras (*Ophiophagus hannah*) suggest

The cobra, despite poorly developed hearing, has been proved capable of unexpected listening skills.

that although they have only vestigial ears, they are able to hear their characteristic, unusually deep, growl-like hisses. These are believed to be produced via pocket-like structures called diverticula extending from the trachea that seem to function as low-frequency resonance chambers. Clearly, there is still a lot to learn about the mechanisms and limits of snake vocalization, especially in view of the controversial claims that have been made for the abilities of certain species.

The African puff adder (*Bitis arietans*), for instance, has long been said to emit a sustained, bell-like chiming sound. In September 1929, Captain G. B. Ritchie, an experienced wildlife observer, noted in an article in the journal *East Africa*: "Puff adders calling their mates at breeding time emit a beautiful bell-like

The puff adder vocalizes as a means of attracting a mate. These sounds can be heard over considerable distances.

note, audible for about 200 yards [180 m]. Dr. G. Prentice, whose attention I drew to this matter, personally proved it."

At much the same time, Jan H. Koens of the Royal Empire Society claimed to have witnessed a 27-foot (8-m) -long python raise itself up and give voice to a deerlike bleat. And in a letter to *The Times*, Mrs. Duncan Carse of Crowthorne, Berkshire in England, revealed how, when an ordinary European grass snake (*Natrix natrix*) sleeping in her garden woke and spotted her with her dog nearby, it emitted "a clear birdlike call, obviously of alarm". This sound was so loud that her husband, working several yards away in his studio, came running out to see what he assumed was some kind of strange bird.

Can snakes hear?

What makes the discovery of overtly vocal snakes seem particularly surprising, at least initially, is that snakes are traditionally assumed to be deaf. If that is the case, why should they evolve mechanisms for emitting sounds? In reality, although in comparison with other terrestrial reptiles snakes have only very vestigial ears, they are well known for their ability to sense ground-borne vibrations through their lower jaw when resting their heads on the ground.

Experiments during the 1960s and 1970s, however, revealed that snakes were also sensitive to airborne vibrations within a frequency range of 100–500 Hz. In fact, within the 200–400 Hz range, their hearing was actually better than that of frogs, whose auditory powers are rather well developed.

A squeaking death's-head

Even more unlikely than a growling cobra is a squeaking moth, but such a creature does exist. The moth may use its remarkable vocal ability to communicate a deceptive message to certain fellow insects. The species in question is the death's-head hawkmoth (*Acherontia atropos*), named after the remarkable skull-like marking on its thorax. Reports of its ability to squeak date back at least three centuries, and it is now known that this strange sound occurs when the moth inhales air into its pharynx. This in turn causes the very rapid vibration of a stiffened flap in the throat known as the epipharynx.

This vibration consists of a pulsed sound made up of about 280 pulses per second for a period of approximately 80 milliseconds, followed by a brief pause of 20 milliseconds before the epipharynx is held upward, permitting the air to be blown out, thereby creating the squeak. The moth will

perform as many as six of these squeak cycles in a single second, but with the sound becoming shorter as the moth becomes tired. The squeak itself is, in any case, very brief – lasting no more than 40 milliseconds – and is very high pitched, with a frequency of approximately 6 kHz. This is above the upper hearing threshold for many adults, although children can usually detect it.

But why does the death's-head hawkmoth produce such an odd sound? A clue may lie in this species' well-documented fondness for honey: A death's-head can often be found inside beehives, sucking honey out of the storage cells with its short, stout proboscis. Despite the fact that its visits to hives are hardly beneficial to the bees, and also that it clearly looks nothing like a bee, this moth is usually permitted to enter unmolested. Consequently, some researchers believe that it gains immunity by mimicking the squeaking sound made by the queen bee. Certainly, the moth's squeak is produced deliberately, as it has been observed purposefully raising its body when squeaking, thereby ensuring that the sound is communicated through the air to all of the bees nearby. The

Often seen in and around beehives and known to eat honey, the death's-head hawkmoth may use its ability to squeak to imitate the queen bee.

squeak may be a form of password, needed in order to enter the hive safely.

Singing mice

One of the most unexpected radio stars of the 20th century was a mouse, and not an ordinary one. Named Minnie, she was a singing mouse, and duly entertained listeners on a Detroit radio station on December 15, 1936. According to her audience, she sounded like a robin or a tone-deaf canary. In May 1937, there was even a transatlantic radio contest for singing mice, attracting entrants from localities as widely separated as London, Toronto, and Illinois. Many accounts of singing mice are on file, but the explanation for their vocal talents remains unclear. The most popular theory is that the sounds they produce are nothing more than the vocal by-products of a respiratory infection. However, the wheezing, short-of-breath noises usually associated with such conditions are different from the outpourings described by naturalists who have personally listened to these musical mice.

According to Samuel Lockwood, for a considerable time a caged female specimen " ... carolled almost incessantly, except when she slept. Day and night she rollicked in tiny song, her best performances being usually at night ... it was a low, very low, sweet voice ... She had two especially notable performances. I called these roles – one, the 'wheel song,' because it was usually sung

ANIMAL PROFILE

The Tiger's Paralyzing Roar

Closing in on its prey, the roaring tiger momentarily paralyzes it with fear, gaining an extra second or two in which to pounce. Scientists have just discovered how it does this. A tiger's roar has an infrasonic component, comprising growls at frequencies of 18 Hz or less—below the lower audible threshold for humans and other mammals. We cannot hear them, but we can feel their vibrations. This combination of audible roar and infrasonic blast paralyzes the tiger's prey.

while in the revolving cylinder, and the other the 'grand role.' A remarkable fact in the latter is the scope of the little creature's musical powers. Her soft, clear voice falls an octave with all the precision possible; then, at its wind up, it rises again into a very quick trill on C sharp and D."

Such a remarkably canary-like song is far removed from what we would expect from a sick mouse. So, too, is the performance of another singing mouse, this one documented by W. S. Berridge in his book *Animal Curiosities* (1922): " ... a specimen kept by a lady as a pet was able to run up an octave when singing ... it would often finish its vocal performance with a trill. When thus engaged it would vibrate and inflate its throat in the manner of a bird in song, and usually assume an upright posture upon its hind feet."

Bearing in mind that it is now known that mice communicate extensively with one another using ultrasonic squeaks in order to avoid being "overheard" and hence detected by predators, it may simply be that singing mice are nothing more than specimens with unusually deep voices, enabling us to hear their vocalizations.

The sight of clearly fit and healthy mice singing would appear to disprove the theory that these sounds result from respiratory problems.

CHAPTER EIGHT

LIVING TOGETHER

Just as no man is an island, so no animal is entirely independent – in every ecosystem animals are constantly interacting with each other, as well as with the local plants, fungi, and other life forms. These interactions can take many forms – positive, negative, active, passive, intimate, casual – but they sometimes involve truly bizarre, mysterious, and highly complex mechanisms that scientists are still attempting to explain.

Symbiosis

see also:
● Multiple Senses, p.40
● Parasitism, p.165
● Animal Herbalists, p.214

Literally translated as "living together," symbiosis is the mutually beneficial association of different types of organisms. Many extraordinary examples of symbiosis are on record from the animal kingdom.

Cleaning partnerships

Some remarkable symbiotic relationships have arisen because various predatory animals need help to rid themselves of troublesome external parasites (ectoparasites), and therefore resist attacking certain vulnerable creatures that are willing to consume these parasites. One of the most striking examples features the Nile crocodile (*Crocodylus niloticus*), which lies with its deadly jaws wide open while a small species of wader – aptly known as the crocodile bird (*Pluvianus aegyptius*) – steps inside its jaws. The little bird moves all over its mouth and body, with total impunity, deftly extracting leeches and other parasites, as well as slivers of meat caught between the crocodile's teeth.

Even more intimate cleaning associations have developed in the sea, with at least 45 species of fishes acting as cleaners to larger fishes. The most notable of these is a small slender species of striped fish called the cleaner wrasse (*Labroides dimidiatus*), which is regularly visited by a wide range of larger species to have irritating ectoparasites removed from between their scales or from their gills. Finding a cleaner wrasse is not difficult, since in order to attract its clients the wrasse performs an unusual dance, in which it swims vertically with its head pointing downward and sways its body from side to side. Once its clients arrive, they form a line, taking their turn to be cleaned by the wrasse. In the case of a very large client (even a carnivorous one), the wrasse will even be permitted to swim unharmed inside the client's mouth or gill chambers.

Intriguingly, this close association is shadowed by a sinister duplicate, featuring a deceitful species of blenny suitably dubbed the false cleaner (*Aspidontus taeniatus*), which has evolved a similar striped appearance and beckoning dance. When a client approaches the false cleaner, however, instead of cleaning it, this imposter swiftly bites a chunk out of the unfortunate client's fins.

Finding another creature to rid it of irksome parasites or unwanted attention, in return for food or protection, is a strategy adopted by many creatures.

Protective cover

Some deep-sea hermit crabs do not bother to seek shells in which to live. Instead, they merely keep their soft, vulnerable body hidden amid an array of sea anemones, which afford them protection from outside assailants.

There are some species of crab that actually carry sea anemones around in their claws, using them almost as weapons by thrusting them like

The cleaner wrasse rids a great number of different species, including the lizardfish, of parasites on the gills and scales. This wrasse's reputation as a cleaner has spawned a deadly imitator: the false cleaner looks very much like it and mimics its dance to lure prey.

The sponge crab, as its name suggests, uses a sponge as camouflage; in time the sponge grows all over the crab's body, effectively masking it from would-be attackers.

fiery torches at any would-be aggressor that ventures too close.

The sponge crab (*Dromia vulgaris*), by contrast, chooses camouflage as an effective survival mechanism. It achieves this by placing a sponge on top of its body. The sponge gradually grows all over it, so that the crab becomes cunningly disguised as a sponge, and therefore avoids predation by crab eaters. The sponge gains the benefit of being carried along by the crab, which increases the flow of water through the sponge, providing it with more nutrients and also a regularly changing and varied diet for consumption.

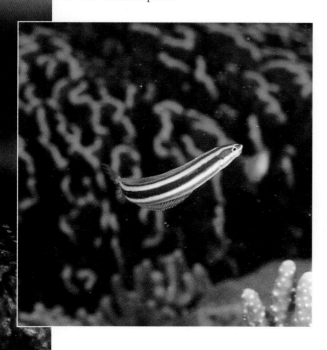

Netting a symbiotic secret

Also called thaliaceans, salps are small free-swimming marine creatures with gelatinous, semitransparent bodies that move around by means of jet propulsion, drawing in water through an aperture at one end of the body, and then forcing it out through another aperture at the opposite end. The water drawn in is also used for feeding, because while inside the body it is strained through a baglike net of mucus, which traps any tiny algae present. The salp feeds on the algae.

Normally, this method of filter-feeding works very efficiently. Sometimes, however, the seas in which salps live experience algal blooms – sudden, vast increases in numbers of algae – creating a veritable algal soup that can poison many aquatic life forms. The salps' survival is threatened because their mucus net can become totally clogged by this excessive algal mass, rendering them incapable of sieving and, therefore, feeding. In 1997, however, a team of South African biologists led by Dr. Renzo Perissinotto, studying Thompson's salp (*Salpa thompsoni*), a 6-inch- (15-cm) long Antarctic species, uncovered a remarkable secret. When its mucus net becomes clogged, this salp is rescued by a tiny copepod crustacean called *Rhincalanus gigas*, which enters the salp's body cavity and feeds on the algae coating its net. In this way the net is freed and the salp can begin to use it efficiently again.

This would seem to be a true symbiotic relationship, because both partners benefit; by devouring the algae clogging the salp's net the crustacean gains a rich meal, and the salp in turn regains the use of its net. However, it is only a

ANIMAL PROFILE

Edible Earwax

Relatives of the starlings, oxpeckers are renowned for eating ticks and other undesirable ectoparasites that live on the hides of large African ungulates, such as buffalo, antelopes, rhinoceroses, domestic cattle, and zebras. In 1997, Cambridge University zoologist Dr. Paul Weeks revealed that these birds actually provide a further, hitherto-unsuspected benefit to their mammalian hosts.

Oxpeckers are often seen entering the ears of ungulates, but it was assumed that they do so merely to seek out ectoparasites. When Weeks compared a herd of cattle from which oxpeckers were deliberately deterred by Weeks's assistant with one that was regularly attended by oxpeckers, however, he was amazed to discover that within a matter of weeks, the ears of the oxpecker-free cattle became totally clogged with earwax. Clearly, therefore, the oxpeckers were eating not only ear-dwelling ectoparasites but also earwax, thereby preventing it from accumulating. The nutritional qualities (if any) of earwax for the oxpeckers, however, is still a matter of some debate among scientists.

temporary partnership: Once the algal bloom comes to an end and conditions in the water return to normal, the relationship comes to an end.

A taste of honey

Perhaps the most amazing example of animal symbiosis features a small relative of the woodpeckers known as the honeyguide (*Indicator indicator*), and a large, fierce badgerlike mammal called the ratel, or honey badger (*Mellivora capensis*). Adept at locating beehives but preferring not to attempt breaking into them in order to obtain wax from the honeycombs inside, the honeyguide instead employs the services of the powerful, honey-loving ratel.

When it spots a hive, the honeyguide utters a special cry that alerts any ratel within hearing range to the presence of a hive in the vicinity. The ratel follows the direction of the honeyguide's cry as the bird hops from tree to tree, leading its partner ever nearer to the hive. As soon as the ratel sees it, this formidable creature loses no time in tearing the hive apart with its strong claws to reach the honey within. It is protected from the stings of the infuriated bees by its extremely dense fur and tough skin. Once the ratel has eaten all that it wants and has left, and the bees have calmed down, the honeyguide is able to eat whatever honeycomb wax remains.

Human mimics

Kenya's Boran people can also follow the honeyguide's cry, and do the ratel's job of ripping the hive open. Indeed, some attract a honeyguide on purpose, using a call of their own (or imitating a ratel's growls), so that it will lead them to a hive.

When the honeyguide finds a beehive, it turns to the badgerlike ratel, whose thick fur can withstand bee stings, to draw the bees' attention before eating any beeswax in the hive.

The remora is protected by the shark and gets food from it, in return helping to groom the shark.

Dangerous Friends

see also:
- Multiple Senses, p.40
- Symbiosis, p.160
- Social Organization, p.174

Associating with a creature known to be deadly to most other species may not seem like a good idea, but some creatures find these symbiotic relationships work well.

Some relatively defenseless animals trade their services to more dangerous creatures in exchange for protection from potential attackers, as in the cleaning–based association between voracious sharks and the extraordinary remora.

The remora is a relative of the perch which habitually attaches itself to the belly of a shark using a specialized, corrugated, suckerlike structure on top of its head; this in fact develops from its dorsal fin. The remora is thus carried like a hitchhiker as the shark swims through the sea. Any chunks of meat that fall from the carcass of one of the shark's victims are eaten by the remora. Moreover, by being attached to such a dangerous and feared marine predator as a shark, the remora is effectively protected from any would-be attacker.

In return for food and protection, when not feeding on the shark's meal scraps, the remora swims all over the shark's body, eating any parasites and dead tissue that it finds on the latter's skin. Nor is this a unique relationship: Some species of remora attach themselves not to sharks but to other large fishes or marine turtles instead.

The hermit crab benefits from the presence of sea anemones which can sting potential prey. The anemone gains food and nutrients from the relationship.

The anemone protects the clownfish from predators. In return, the clownfish feeds the anemone and lures potential prey.

The Portuguese man-of-war (*Physalia physalis*) is famous for its long, vertical "curtain" of deadly tentacles that trail down through the water as it sails with its large bell floating on the sea's surface. Anything that makes contact with this lethal curtain − with one notable exception − is killed by its tentacles' potent stinging cells.

A small species of blue-and-white fish called the horse mackerel (*Trachurus trachurus*) spends a lot of time swimming among the man-of-war's tentacles, without suffering any ill effects, because it can withstand ten times the dose of venom that would kill other fishes of the same size. Therefore it is effectively protected from the attention of any would-be predators. But what does the man-of-war obtain from this partnership? Studies suggest that the horse mackerel functions as an eye-catching lure, attracting larger fishes which hope to devour it. Instead they find themselves fatally stung by the man-of-war's tentacles and then consumed by it.

A similar association exists between large sea anemones and the small clownfishes or anemone fishes that swim safely among their tentacles. These small fish are protected by the anemone. In return, they supply the anemone with scraps of food and lure predators toward their tentacles.

Lizards form a significant part of the diet of cliff-nesting gulls on a number of the islands of the eastern Mediterranean. However, one species, the common wall lizard (*Podarcis muralis*), is not preyed upon by the gulls. This is because it feeds on the many species of parasitic insect that commonly infest these seabirds' nests during the hot summer. Without the help of the wall lizard, the insects would weaken and infect the nestlings.

Crabby coexistences

Hermit crabs are famous for seeking out empty seashells in which to live. However, they are also well known for attaching one or more sea anemones to their sequestered shells. The sea anemones serve as stinging shields against the unwelcome advances of potential predators. And in return, the sea anemones feed upon any scraps of food from the crab's meals that drift their way.

As an added bonus, as the crab is perpetually on the move in search of bigger, better shells to inhabit, the sea anemones are exposed to a greater variety of nutrients than they would encounter if they remained in one site.

Parasitism

see also:
- Extreme Endurance, p.110
- Animal Hypnotists, p.122
- Anting, p.222

Macaque monkeys groom each other to remove fleas.

Several species choose to rely on others for many of their vital life functions, including feeding and rearing their young.

In the realm of fiction, vampires live on the blood of their victims. In real life, parasites live off other animals. The only partner to derive any benefit in a parasitic association is the parasite, the uninvited guest, and its presence is often highly detrimental to the host.

Ectoparasites are usually found on their hosts' outer body surface. Many are insects, including fleas, lice, and certain highly specialized dipterans, or true flies. Fleas parasitize both mammals and birds, and have several distinctive specializations for efficient parasitism. They suck the blood of their hosts through specially modified piercing mouthparts. Their bodies are streamlined, lacking wings, showy antennae, and other projecting structures. They are also flat and hard, so they can move easily and effectively between the hairs or feathers of their hosts without being squashed by scratching paws, beaks, or fingers.

Lice are much more sedentary, clutching onto their host's skin with strong gripping claws. They have flattened bodies that rebuff attempts by the host to dislodge them. Mallophagans, or biting lice, usually parasitize birds, and use their jaws to scrape skin and chew feathers, though some do ingest blood. Sucking lice feed exclusively on blood, live on mammals, and include the human louse (*Pediculus humanus*).

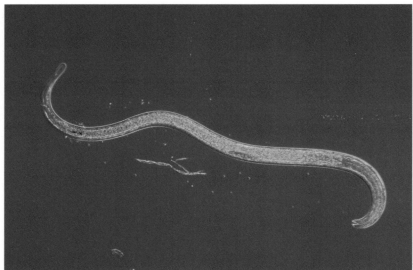

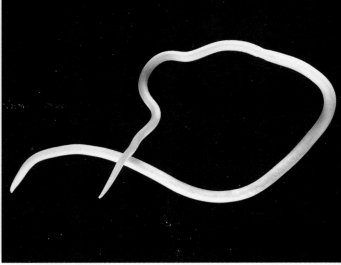

The Life Cycle of a Parasite

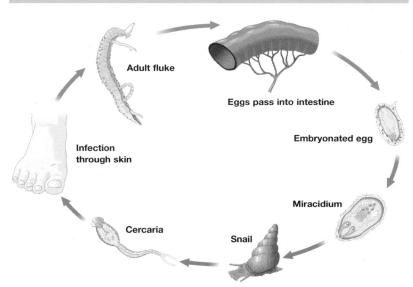

Adult fluke

Eggs pass into intestine

Infection through skin

Embryonated egg

Cercaria

Miracidium

Snail

The life cycle of the blood parasite *Schistosoma mansoni* has four main stages, during which it makes use of two hosts. Fertilized eggs enter the human host's blood and are transported to the intestine, where they bore through the intestinal wall and exit the body in the feces. If the feces enter water, the eggs hatch into tiny free-swimming larvae called miracidia. Each of these swims around until it finds

a snail. Penetrating the snail's body, it transforms into a highly mobile long-tailed larva known as a cercaria, which leaves the snail and swims away. When it makes contact with human skin, usually in polluted water, it enters the host's blood by penetrating the skin. This carries it to the lungs, liver, and intestinal veins, by which time it is an adult fluke. The life cycle then begins again.

Living inside the living

Some parasites live inside their hosts' bodies — these are endoparasites, the most significant of which are the digenean flukes, the tapeworms, and some nematodes. These internal parasites have a complex life cycle in which they move between two and sometimes as many as four hosts. The host that harbors the parasite's adult stage is termed the primary host, and the others, intermediary hosts.

Notable digeneans include the liver fluke (*Fasciola hepatica*), which can consume 0.007 fluid ounces (0.2 ml) of blood a day and is responsible for liver rot in sheep and cattle; and the Chinese liver fluke (*Opisthorchis sinensis*), which includes two intermediary hosts — a snail and a fish — as well as the human primary host in its life cycle.

Whereas at various stages of a digenean's life cycle it actively seeks its hosts, the life cycle of tapeworms tends to be passive. Also, whereas flukes have guts, tapeworms have none, so they must absorb their nutrients directly through their body surface from the intestine of their primary host (normally a vertebrate).

A typical species, such as the pork tapeworm (*Taenia solium*), consists of an anterior region known as the scolex, armed with suckers and sometimes hooks, too, for attachment to its host's internal intestinal wall, and a long body called a strobila, composed of numerous similar segments called proglottids. These contain fertilized eggs,

Roundworms (far left) are found in fresh water. The parasitic nematode, or roundworm (above), lives in the guts of several animals on which humans feed, including the pig.

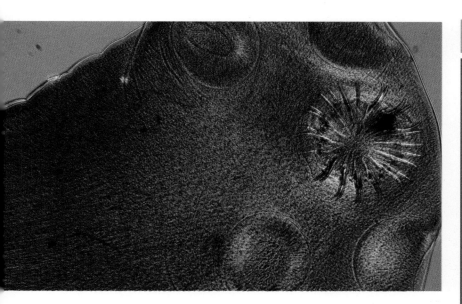

The pork tapeworm can exceed 20 feet (6 m) in length, while the beef tapeworm (above) can measure more than 80 feet (25 m), three times as long as the human intestine.

which break off when mature (but are replaced by new proglottids), to be excreted by the host when defecating. If any feces containing shed proglottids are eaten by a mammal, the tapeworm eggs hatch, releasing larvae. These bore into this intermediary host's intestinal wall and are transported by the host's blood system until they reach striated muscle. There, each develops into a cyst. These remain in the host's muscle until eaten by a human, when each cyst transforms into an adult tapeworm.

Tapeworms can grow to enormous lengths. The broad (fish) tapeworm (*Diphyllobothrium latum*), inhabiting the intestine of fishes and sometimes humans, is 33–43 feet (10–13 m) long, but some specimens have attained a length of 66 feet (20 m).

Bloodsucking parasites

The most infamous parasitic nematodes are the intestinal *Ascaris lumbricoides*, measuring up to 18 inches (45 cm); the subcutaneous Guinea worm (*Dracunculus medinensis*), whose females are up to 4 feet (120 cm) long (but only 0.05 inches/1 mm thick); and the smaller bloodsucking intestinal hookworms. *Ascaris* infects more than 25 percent of the world's human population. A single female can produce up to 200,000 eggs every day of her adult life. Eggs pass out of the human host in feces, and inside these eggs the *Ascaris* larvae develop. If any eggs are eaten, perhaps in contaminated food, the larvae hatch in the new host's intestine, then migrate all over the body, causing tissue or organ damage, then return to the intestine to mature.

Bloodsucking hookworms parasitize 700 million people worldwide, and are responsible for a daily blood loss equivalent to the total blood supply of more than a million people.

ANIMAL PROFILE

Symbion pandora

Many new species of parasite are discovered every year, but none is as significant from a classification standpoint as *Symbion pandora*. Its discoverer, Copenhagen University zoologist Prof. Reinhardt Kristensen, realized that *S. pandora* is unique. Its structure and biological makeup mean that it is fundamentally different from all other animal species known to science. Consequently, when formally documenting the species in December 1995, Kristensen created a totally new division of the animal kingdom, or phylum, called Cycliophora.

This microscopic ectoparasite was found living on the mouthparts of the Norwegian lobster (*Nephrops norvegicus*). The availability of food and oxygen varies according to where the parasite attaches to the mouth, so there is strong competition among the parasites for the best sites. *S. pandora* has an extremely complex life cycle involving several different stages.

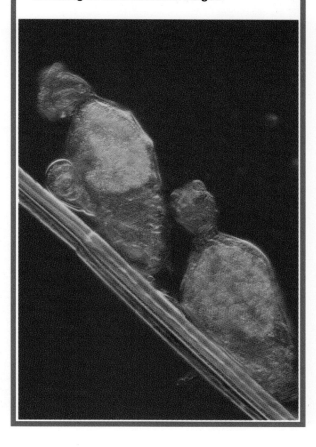

Parasites in Control

see also:
● Dangerous Friends, p.163
● Parasitism, p.165
● Brood Parasitism, p.170

A parasitized pond snail may have its genetic makeup altered, causing it to grow faster to make it a better host for its parasites.

Not content with simply parasitizing a host, some species can exert an influence over the life, makeup, and characteristics of the host.

Many parasites adopt devious methods in order to retain their parasitic lifestyle, and some recent studies have exposed some exceptionally sophisticated means. In January 1998, for example, scientists at Vrije University in Amsterdam, the Netherlands, revealed that specimens of the freshwater snail *Lymnaea stagnalis* parasitized by the digenean fluke *Trichobilharzia ocellata* develop an aversion to sex. In place of sexual activity, they grow more quickly, which allows their parasites to thrive. But how does *T. ocellata* manage to make its host change its behavior? The team found that levels of certain types of messenger RNA (a nucleic acid) responsible for producing proteins that influence snail behavior were much higher in parasitized snails than in nonparasitized snails. In other words, *T. ocellata* was directly affecting the genetic functioning of *Lymnaea*.

Footless cockle

Also in 1998, Otago University researchers Dr. Frederic Thomas and Dr. Robert Poulin showed that the digenean *Curtuteria australis* is cunning, too. One of its intermediary hosts is the cockle *Austrovenus stutchburyi*, and infection by the encysting larva of *C. australis* causes the cockle's foot to be shorter than normal. This in turn means that it cannot dig down through the sand to hide itself from predatory birds, particularly

The presence of extra legs on a frog can be caused by a parasite that disrupts limb formation at the tadpole stage of the frog's life.

ANIMAL PROFILE

A Parasitic Tongue

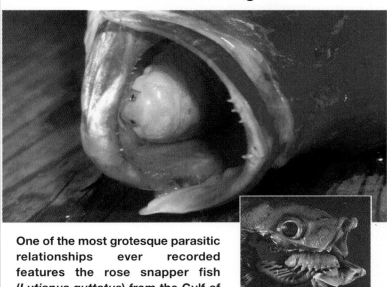

SIDE VIEW

One of the most grotesque parasitic relationships ever recorded features the rose snapper fish (*Lutjanus guttatus*) from the Gulf of California and a marine isopod crustacean called *Cymothoa exigua*, which is related to woodlice. When one of these ectoparasitic crustaceans encounters a rose snapper, it enters the fish's mouth and steadily devours its tongue. Once it has done this, the crustacean uses hooks on its underside to attach itself to the floor of the fish's mouth, and thereafter serves as a replacement tongue.

oystercatchers, so parasitized cockles are more readily discovered and eaten by these birds. This is bad for the cockles, but good for *C. australis*, because oystercatchers are the next intermediary host in its life cycle. Consequently, by giving cockles bad feet, *C. australis* is increasing its own chance of being successfully transferred to its next host.

Multilegged frogs

Sometimes parasites can have very dramatic effects upon their hosts. Bees, homopteran bugs, and other insects hosting tiny endoparasitic insects known as strepsipterans or stylopids often experience alterations of their secondary sexual characteristics and are said to have been stylopized. Female hosts can even be rendered sterile by the stylopids.

Even more grotesque are cases of multilegged frogs, with six or more limbs. Biologist Dr. Stanley Sessions of New York's Hartwick College found that the bases of these frogs' extra legs were packed with masses of encysted digenean larvae called metacercariae. He believes that these cysts may disrupt limb development in tadpoles, splitting the limb buds into several sections, each of which grows a limb, resulting in frogs with extra legs.

Sex-reversed crabs

Most bizarre of all, however, is the parasitic copepod crustacean *Sacculina carcini*. Although its larvae are free-swimming and closely resemble those of typical, nonparasitic copepods, the adult bears no resemblance to any type of crustacean. Losing its limbs, gut, and segmentation, its body transforms into a shapeless saclike structure, which pierces the body of a crab, then sends rootlike branches throughout the crab's body and limbs.

Bearing this bizarre parasitic copepod's amorphous body on its own undersurface, the crab is thus said to be sacculinized. After it has been invaded it often undergoes a degree of sex reversal. This may be caused by the modification of its gonads, or the release of inhibiting compounds, by the now strangely plantlike *Sacculina*, or by a combination of the two.

Brood Parasitism

see also:
● Bird Migration, p.68
● Symbiosis, p.160
● Insect Language, p.148

A fledgling cuckoo pushes the eggs of its host out of the nest, thereby eliminating competition for food and attention from its foster parent, a reed warbler (inset).

Also termed nest parasitism, brood parasitism is the exploitation by a parasitic species of the parenting behavior of a host species, so that the parasite's offspring are reared by the host species. Although this results in great energy savings for the parasite, which is freed from the task of tending its own offspring, the relationship is often detrimental to the host's own offspring.

Cuckoo in the nest

Perhaps the most famous brood parasites belong to the cuckoo family, especially the European cuckoo (*Cuculus canorus*), which lays its eggs in other birds' nests so that the other birds are left with the task of rearing the cuckoo fledglings. Parasitizing a wide range of small songbird species, the female cuckoo selects a suitable nest and waits until its owners have laid their eggs in it. As soon as the nest is left

Coercing another species into raising their young is a strategy adopted by many creatures, particularly birds and insects.

unguarded by its owners, the cuckoo removes one of the eggs and lays an egg of her own in it, then flies off to find another nest in which to lay an egg. The process is complete within seconds.

The cuckoo's egg looks so like the eggs of the nest's owners that when they return, they rarely realize that the substitution has been made, and so

Although the black-headed duck finds someone else's nest in which to lay its eggs, the fledglings are self-sufficient from the time of hatching.

proceed to incubate the entire clutch. Usually, however, the first egg to hatch is the cuckoo egg, and the young cuckoo energetically demands to be fed by its unsuspecting foster parents. Whenever the parent birds are away from the nest, the young cuckoo loses no time in getting rid of its rivals, one by one. It achieves this by maneuvering itself under one of the parent birds' eggs (or fledglings, if they have hatched), lifting it up onto its concave back between its wings, then tipping it over the side of the nest. It repeats this murderous action until eventually the cuckoo is the only youngster left in the nest. From then on, its foster parents devote all their time to rearing the cuckoo and, even though it soon becomes considerably bigger than they are, they remain convinced that it is their own. Once it is old enough to fend for itself, the cuckoo flies away, and never returns to the nest.

Some species of parasitic cuckoo, such as koels and *Clamator* cuckoos, do not have a hollow back when young and do not evict their rival nestlings

The young of the shiny cowbird parasitize the nest of the rufous-collared sparrow.

from the nest, remaining content instead to share their foster parents' attention.

Other avian examples of brood parasites are the African whydahs, which parasitize the nests of weaver finches such as waxbills. Some American cowbirds are also parasitic. The South American black-headed duck (*Heteronetta atricapilla*) lays its eggs in the nests of other ducks (as well as in those of wholly unrelated species of water bird such as herons and ibises), but its young hatch and fend for themselves, so they do not need rearing by their foster parents.

Cowbird parasitism

One of the most complex examples of brood parasitism features the giant cowbird (*Scaphidura oryzivora*). These natives of Central and South America generally parasitize other birds in the same family, the icterids. They particularly favor the huge, pendulous, colonial nests of the chestnut-headed oropendola (*Psarocolius cassini*). However, the precise nature of the relationship between them depends on the location of the hosts' nests.

In certain nests, the oropendolas do not discriminate between their own eggs and those of the cowbird, nor do they display aggression toward the cowbird. And the cowbird makes no attempt to lay its eggs secretly in these oropendolas' nests. It will evict a female oropendola to lay its own eggs there. In this instance, the eggs laid by the cowbird are numerous and different in appearance from those of the oropendolas. Yet they are not rejected.

Other oropendolas, however, are aggressive toward the cowbird and will reject the egg if they notice its presence. Because of this the cowbird will lay only a single egg in the nest and does so secretly, while the oropendolas are away. A cowbird egg laid in such circumstances could blend in unnoticed with the oropendola's own eggs. The reason for these two very different scenarios has recently been revealed.

Researchers discovered that when the oropendolas are not aggressive toward the cowbird and readily rear its young with their own, the young cowbirds are serving a useful purpose. They devour botflies that would otherwise lay parasitic eggs in the nests, and even groom their young oropendola nest-mates, removing any botfly larvae that may have evaded detection. In this case, therefore, the association between cowbird and oropendola is more symbiotic than parasitic, because both partners benefit.

Conversely, where the oropendolas are aggressive to the cowbird and can tell their own eggs from those of the cowbird, the researchers invariably found that these particular oropendola nests were situated close to bee or wasp nests: botflies avoid areas containing bee or wasp nests. In this scenario, therefore, since there are no botflies to eliminate, the young cowbird serves no useful purpose for the oropendola. The association here is truly parasitic, with only the cowbird benefiting (as long as it can fool the oropendolas into rearing its young, that is).

Insect parasites

Nest parasitism in insects is most common among the social insects – ants, bees, wasps, and termites,

for example – and is sometimes referred to as inquilinism. This term has been defined in a number of different ways. In its loosest sense, it involves one animal species (the inquiline) living in the home of another (the host), either on a casual or habitual basis, and eating some of its food, but without bringing either harm or benefit to the host. Some entomologists use the term to cover only cases in which the inquiline is a parasite that is dependent upon an insect host throughout its entire life cycle. More commonly, however, the term is used to describe associations in which the inquiline is a parasite that habitually inhabits the nest of a social insect species for part of its life cycle, usually to the detriment of the host: this is the definition of inquilinism used in this book.

A large blue mystery

The large blue butterfly (*Maculinea arion*) has one of the most unusual life cycles of any butterfly because its caterpillars are reared by ants. In June, the adult female butterfly lays her eggs on wild thyme, usually near a colony of red ants (often *Myrmica scabrinoides* or *M. laevonoides*). When they hatch later that month, the caterpillars begin feeding on the thyme's flowers and continue to feed on them for the next three weeks. During this period, each caterpillar molts three times. Following the third molt the caterpillar loses interest in the thyme flowers and wanders around in a random fashion until it is found by a red ant.

As soon as the ant sees the caterpillar, it runs up to it and strokes a gland on the caterpillar's flank. This gland secretes a drop of sweet syrupy liquid that the ant drinks. Once it has taken its fill of this syrup, the ant picks up the caterpillar and carries it inside its nest, where the caterpillar stays for the remainder of the year. During this period, the ants diligently feed their own larvae to the caterpillar, so that the caterpillar grows larger, and in exchange they regularly milk it for its syrup. Throughout the winter, the caterpillar sleeps, but once it wakes up it continues to mature until early spring, by which time it has become sluggish. At this point, it transforms into the resting pupal or chrysalis stage, and subsequently undergoes a dramatic metamorphosis, emerging from the chrysalis in early June as a fully formed adult butterfly. Only then does it leave the ants' nest, crawling outside to expand its wings before flying away.

Cuckoo bees

These insects are so named because they lay their eggs inside the nests of other bees, leaving them to be reared by their unsuspecting hosts. While their

The larva of the large blue butterfly is "adopted" by an ant and spends several months inside the ant's nest in an inquilinic relationship.

The female cuckoo bee is so similar in appearance to a bumblebee that her presence in the hive is often undetected.

hosts are true bees, living socially, rearing their larvae in hives, and collecting pollen from flowers to bring back to the hives, cuckoo bees are solitary species that do not build hives and do not collect pollen. This is why females do not have pollen baskets on their legs.

One of the most familiar species of cuckoo bee is *Psithyrus rupestris*, which parasitizes the red-tailed bumblebee (*Bombus lapidarius*). It looks so much like this species that a female *P. rupestris* cuckoo bee can usually enter a *B. lapidarius* hive without attracting attention from its genuine inhabitants. Even if challenged, she is larger than them and has such a thick exoskeleton that she can withstand any stings she may receive. Once inside and accepted by the bumblebee workers, she swiftly lays her eggs and leaves them to be fed and reared by her hosts.

To ensure that her offspring do not face undue competition from the hive's own offspring, the cuckoo bee searches for the hive's queen – the only reproductive female in the hive – and either kills her or eats all her eggs before leaving. The inevitable outcome of this devastating action is that the only unhatched eggs now left in the hive are those of the cuckoo bee, which thereafter receive all of the attention that the hive's bumblebee workers would have lavished on their own larvae.

Consequently, whereas the host ants do at least gain some benefit from sacrificing a proportion of their own larvae as food for the large blue caterpillar – namely, the tasty syrup secreted by the caterpillar – the host bumblebees receive no benefit at all from rearing the cuckoo bee's larvae. On the contrary, if the adult cuckoo bee kills the hive's queen, the eventual result is the demise of the entire hive, because no further bumblebee eggs will be laid and hatched there.

Tadpoles Reared by Ants?

Zoologists have long been puzzled by the frequent appearances of an Ecuador frog called *Lithodytes lineatus* near the nests of leafcutter ants. In 1997, research by the Ecuador-based naturalists Morley Read and Francisco Sornoza revealed an extraordinary chain of events.

After noticing some of these frogs hopping inside one such nest, they dug into the nest and discovered a chamber 3 feet (1 m) underground, partly filled with water. The water contained numerous tadpoles. Moreover, as they watched, they were amazed to see a column of ants climb down to this chamber and drop yellow-colored material into the water. This was instantly eaten by the tadpoles. Were the ants actively feeding the tadpoles, or was the behavior the scientists saw just an aberrant instance? If it was atypical behavior, why didn't the ants attack the tadpoles as they would do with any other species intruding into their nest?

It may well be that this is a newly disclosed, highly novel case of inquilinism, featuring the young of a vertebrate species – rather than, as is more usual, another invertebrate species – being reared by the workers of a social insect. Further research is needed before this behavior can be fully explained and understood.

Social Organization

see also:
● Electromagnetic Enigmas, p.58
● Insect Language, p.148
● Dangerous Friends, p.163

Many insects, such as bees, termites, and ants, spend their whole lives in an organized colony where their role and function are preordained.

Although they are all female, worker bees are smaller than the queen, do not reproduce, and live for only a short time.

Many species live in colonies, in which each individual has a specific role to play. Although all the individuals in the colony are physically separate, their roles are so interdependent that without them all the colony would not thrive. The most dramatic examples of this kind of social organization occur in the insect world, but in recent years some extraordinary cases outside the insect world have also been verified.

Hives of social activity

Hymenopteran insects comprise bees, wasps, and ants, and include many socially organized, or eusocial, species. Within a hive or nest at least three functional castes exist – the queen, the workers, and the drones – and each has a particular role to play. In general, the most distinctive caste is the queen, an exceptionally large female – the largest

individual in the entire nest – whose sole function is to reproduce, and who can live for several years. The most common caste is the worker caste, made up of numerous females, all hatched from fertilized eggs laid by the queen. Workers are devoted to maintaining the nest, feeding the queen, and rearing her countless offspring, the vast majority of which become more workers. The third caste comprises the drones, the only males in the nest, which emerge from unfertilized eggs laid by the queen. Therefore, they have only half the normal number of chromosomes of the workers and queen. The drones are fed by the workers and do no work in the hive. Their only function is to mate with the queen. Once they have done this they die, or are ejected from the nest by the workers so that they starve to death.

Scientists have long wondered how these castes arise. The most-studied eusocial hymenopteran is the honeybee (*Apis mellifera*). In this species, the queen lays most of her eggs (up to 2,000 every day of her three- to-five-year life) inside ordinary hexagonal honeycomb cells within the nest, but she also lays a few inside special cone-shaped cells separated from the hexagonal ones. All larvae

A termite queen can live for 15 to 25 years and may lay more than 30,000 eggs every day, making a lifetime total of more than 270 million eggs.

hatching from the queen's eggs, regardless of where they were laid, are fed by the workers for the first few days on a proteinlike substance called royal jelly, obtained from the workers' salivary glands.

After a few days, however, the workers stop feeding this rich nutrient to those larvae in the hexagonal cells, and supply them with pollen and nectar instead. These larvae mature into nonreproducing workers if female, and into drones if male. But those few larvae laid in the cone-shaped cells continue to receive royal jelly from the workers. These larvae, which are all female, transform into queens. One of them will eventually replace the nest's present queen, who will either be killed or fly away, taking with her a swarm of workers to establish a new nest elsewhere. So, too, will any of the new queen's royal siblings that survive (often, however, the first mature queen to come out from her conical chamber promptly kills all of the others before they have time to emerge).

In ant colonies, a fourth caste – the soldier – is sometimes present. The soldiers are nonreproducing females who are bigger than the workers and equipped with large heads and formidable jaws that protect the nest from attack. Worker ants are usually wingless, nonreproducing females, but toward the end of the year some nests produce many winged,

ANIMAL PROFILE

A Eusocial Shrimp

The world's first-known species of eusocial marine animal, the tiny shrimp *Synalpheus regalis,* was described in 1996. Each colony of this crustacean has a breeding queen and up to 300 nonreproducing females. The smaller ones serve as workers, raising the queen's offspring and maintaining the colony; the larger ones are soldiers, defending the colony from aggressors.

The naked mole rat is the first mammal known to have a eusocial lifestyle. Each mole rat in a colony has a specific function. The colony consists of interconnected tunnels and chambers containing 70-250 individuals.

reproducing females, and other nests produce winged males. These winged individuals all fly from their nests within a given area in swarms on the same day, dictated by climate, in order to mate with one another and ensure crossbreeding.

Termite queens and kings

The other major order of eusocial insects are the isopterans or termites, and their social situation features some interesting differences from that of the bees, wasps, and ants. Most noticeably, each nest has not only a queen but also a king. The king is larger than other males in the nest, is a permanent member of it, and mates with the queen frequently during their life together, spanning many years. The soldiers are also large, some with sizable heads and biting jaws with which to attack invaders, others with smaller pointed heads capable of squirting repellent liquid.

The biggest individual of all, however, is the queen, instantly recognizable when mature due to her grossly enlarged body, which can measure up to 5½ inches (14 cm) long in some species. This prevents her from moving. Her whole life is devoted to eating, and laying eggs.

The workers of primitive species are juveniles that never mature, whereas in more advanced species they make up a distinct caste. Termite workers and soldiers can be female or male, but

they are all wingless. Only the young kings and queens have wings, enabling them to pair up for short mating flights and then disperse to found new colonies, after which their wings break off.

A social rodent

Aptly named, the desert-dwelling naked mole rat (*Heterocephalus glaber*) of eastern Africa is virtually hairless, almost blind, and lives entirely underground in colonies, each comprising a large central nest and countless tunnels. The most remarkable characteristic of this bizarre rodent, however, is its eusocial lifestyle, which closely parallels that of the social insects.

Each colony is headed by a queen mole rat – the only female in the colony who reproduces. The youngest mole rats serve as workers, bringing food to the nest and digging tunnels. Older, larger mole rats act as soldiers, protecting the nest. The biggest, most mature mole rats, however, neither work nor act as soldiers. If they are male (which most are), they mate with the queen. If they are female, they either leave the nest to establish colonies of their own, each becoming the queen of a new nest, or remain in the old nest and act as nurses to the ruling queen's offspring. When she eventually dies, one of these senior females will take her place.

Genetic studies of naked mole rats have shown that each colony is virtually a clone. That is, all of its members are almost identical genetically due to the extreme degree of inbreeding that takes place within this essentially closed system.

**The Portuguese man-of-war develops
from a single polyp into a collection of
interdependent organisms functioning as
organs, each with a specialist role to play.**

A "superorganism"

Outwardly, the Portuguese man-of-war
(*Physalia physalis*) looks like a true jellyfish
but, although it is distantly related to these
animals, it is actually a siphonophore.
These species are truly remarkable. Each
"individual" siphonophore is not a single
organism; instead, it is best thought of as a
superorganism, since it is actually an entire
colony of organisms. That is, every organ
or part of the siphonophore is an organism
in its own right.

The Portuguese man-of-war's large
floating bell (as well as the swimming bells
in the related and similar-looking
siphonophore *Stephalia*), each of its long
stinging tentacles, its reproductive organs,
and its feeding organs are all modified
individuals that collectively add up to the
complete Portuguese man-of-war.

This amazing superorganism is an
extreme example of polymorphism, a
condition whereby individuals within the
same species exhibit a range of different
external forms. Each superorganism begins
as a single polyp, which becomes the float
but also gives rise to a series of budding
zones. These in turn generate more polyps
and, instead of detaching to become
independent entities, they remain attached
to the float and transform into various parts
of the organism.

Some of the polyps become tentacles,
and lack mouths; they are called
dactylozooids. Other polyps become the
feeding organs, each possessing a mouth and
usually a branched feeding tentacle as well;
they are gastrozooids. And some polyps
become the reproductive organs, often
lacking mouths but possessing branches; they
are gonozooids. In certain siphonophore
species, a colony also contains some
modified medusae, which remain attached
and transform into reproductive organs,
called gonophores. Food engulfed and
digested by the gastrozooids is transported
into all of the colony members through
interconnecting gastrovascular cavities.

CHAPTER NINE

THOUGHT POWER

*We consider the concepts of
self-recognition, the ability to dream, the
capacity to create and use tools,
and even alleged psychic capabilities
to be uniquely human.
In reality, however, every one of them
exists in the the animal kingdom, too,
and in an extraordinary variety of forms,
from apes and even birds who fashion
sticks into tools, to creatures who recognize
themselves in mirrors, and even dogs
and cats who seem able
to see into the future.*

Self-Awareness

see also:
- Primate Sign Language, p.140
- Cetacean Communication, p.144
- Tool-Using Animals, p.186

When cats see themselves in the mirror, they think that they are looking at another cat and do not realize that they are seeing their own reflection.

Human beings can recognize themselves in mirrors, but other animals can't – or so it was once believed.

Human beings are often said to be different from other animals because we have the ability to know ourselves. There appear to be stages in self-awareness – some animals appear to have a sort of group consciousness, but no individual self-consciousness. This self-knowledge, or self-awareness, means that we are able to form a concept of ourselves and our own thoughts. These cognitive abilities allow human beings to take into account the minds and experiences of others.

Look at me, look at you

One simple illustration of this self-awareness is that, from the age of two, we humans can recognize our own reflection in a mirror. Before the age of two, babies believe that they are looking at another baby rather than at themselves. Scientists once assumed that this self-recognition was one of the crucial factors that made humans human.

When most other animals see their own reflection, like human infants they mistakenly believe that they are seeing another individual of their own species, rather than themselves. Modern research, however, now suggests that certain species of animal may be more self-aware than scientists originally believed.

In 1969, the field of animal psychology was revolutionized by a simple yet very significant experiment called the mirror test, devised by

Tulane University animal behaviorist Dr. Gordon Gallup Jr. and carried out with chimpanzees at the university's Delta Regional Primate Research Center. First, Dr. Gallup gave the chimps a full-length mirror and was intrigued to discover that after the first few days of touching the mirror and looking behind it, believing that they were gazing at other chimps rather than at their own reflections, their behavior changed.

They began using the mirror to view parts of their own bodies that they would normally be unable to see, such as their faces and the inside of their mouths. Did this mean that they had now realized they were looking at themselves and were they thus exhibiting self-recognition?

Bad hair day

To test this theory, Gallup anesthetized some of the chimps, and while they were asleep he applied red dye to one eyebrow ridge and to the upper half of the opposite ear. When they awoke, the chimps showed no preference for touching these areas – until they saw themselves in the mirror, whereupon they spontaneously touched the marks while looking at their reflections. This indicated that they did indeed recognize themselves in the mirror. As a control, Gallup repeated the marking experiments with chimps that had not had any prior mirror experience. When these chimps awoke and looked in the mirror, they attempted to touch the marks on the reflected chimps, not on themselves – showing that these chimps did not recognize themselves in the mirror.

Gallup then conducted this experiment with a wide range of other animals, including a pair of rhesus monkeys (*Macaca mulatta*) who had been continually exposed to a mirror for 17 years with no apparent increase in self-recognition. But, except for humans and chimps, the only species to show self-recognition were the pygmy chimpanzee or bonobo (*Pan paniscus*), and the orangutan (*Pongo pygmaeus*).

Gorilla looks

Even the gorilla (*Gorilla gorilla*) failed the mirror test – with the exception of the "talking" gorilla Koko, who was adept at communicating with humans using sign language. Koko not only wiped the marks off her eyebrow and her ear while looking in

The chimp is humankind's closest living relative. It seems that chimps may show signs of self-awareness.

Gorillas are social animals who live in groups. They do not make eye contact because that is considered to be a form of aggression.

the mirror, but when asked what she saw in the mirror, made signs indicating, "Me, Koko," having apparently recognized herself.

Gallup suggests that gorillas generally fail the mirror test because, as a species, they avoid eye contact with one another and so avoid eye contact with the "other" gorilla they see in the mirror. As for Koko, her decidedly humanlike response may be due to the fact that she has been raised in a human environment and communicates with humans.

Thus it seems likely (though some researchers are still unconvinced) that chimps and orangutans do exhibit self-recognition. But whether they also possess self-awareness is another matter. The great problem facing any attempt to determine this is not being able to see into an animal's mind in order to know precisely what it is thinking. At present, therefore, to quote Gallup's own view: "I think most people working in this area would agree that the jury is still out on whether great apes can attribute mental states to others."

Project Delphis

What about dolphins? Based at Sea Life Park in Honolulu, Hawaii, and initiated in 1985 by Don White and pioneer dolphin advocate Dexter Cate, Project Delphis is a long-term conservation effort and scientific research program investigating and assessing the way these animals think. One of its most compelling studies, conducted by Dr. Kenneth Marten and Suchi Psarakos and published in 1995, was an investigation of self-recognition in the bottlenose dolphin (*Tursiops truncatus*).

Mirror images

A special underwater mirror was used, as well as underwater video screens offering both real-time self-view and playback film of the dolphins swimming in the viewing laboratory where the research was taking place. The researchers then employed a modified version of Gallup's mark and mirror test to see if the dolphins would recognize themselves in the mirror.

The researchers found that four of the five dolphins tested apparently examined their marks in the mirror, and that most of the mirror-mode television tests designed to distinguish self-examination from social behavior indicated self-examination. Hence Marten and Psarakos believe their results are consistent with the hypothesis that the dolphins were using the mirror to look at themselves – and thus that these marine mammals do indeed exhibit self-recognition.

ANIMAL PROFILE

Self-recognition in Monkeys?

The cotton-top tamarin monkey (*Saguinus oedipus*) of South America is named after the distinctive tuft of white hair on top of its head. After exposing some specimens to a mirror for a few days, animal psychology researcher Prof. Marc Hauser from Harvard University dyed their white tufts with various bright colors. Before this was done, the monkeys showed little interest in either their hair tufts or the mirror. Yet afterward, they touched their hair while peering into the mirror for long periods. Conversely, the control tamarins, which had no previous mirror experience, made no attempt to touch their hair after it had been dyed when they saw themselves in a mirror. So does this small nonanthropoid primate also possess self-recognition? At present, no one is really sure.

Animal Dreams

see also:
- Self-Awareness, p.180
- Animal Humor, p.198
- Animal Grief and Mourning, p.201

Do animals dream? New research provides evidence that they do – but is there any way to find out why they dream, and what they dream about?

Scientists once believed that only humans had dreams. New research offers evidence that virtually all mammals, as well as some birds and even a few reptiles, experience the kinds of sleep cycles in which humans usually have their dreams. Humans usually dream during the type of sleep known as REM (rapid eye movement) sleep, and it appears that animals experience REM sleep too.

Perchance to dream

There is still controversy regarding the actual function of dreaming. The most widely accepted view is that its purpose is to sort out the varied events and emotions experienced by the dreamer during the day, filing away important new information gained and discarding unimportant data. If this theory is true, we would expect the brain to be noticeably active, despite the fact that the dreamer is asleep. And sure enough, physiological monitoring of human sleepers has shown that during REM sleep, blood flow and brain temperature increase, and sudden changes in blood pressure and heart rate occur – all indicating significant brain activity.

Sleep research has shown that, in adult humans, 25 percent or less of the amount of time spent sleeping is taken up by REM sleep. Certain animals spend more time in REM sleep. Some opossums spend up to seven hours each day engaged in this type of sleep. Moreover, the younger the animal (including humans), the greater the amount of REM sleep exhibited, with newborn kittens spending as much as 90 percent of their first ten days engaged in REM sleep.

Anyone who has seen a sleeping dog or cat quiver, growl, and twitch its legs in half-formed running movements can have little doubt that they do indeed dream. And although we can currently offer little more than speculation as to the subjects of their dreams, their outward actions suggest that they, like us, are reliving in dream form – albeit rather more animatedly than we tend to – recent events in their lives.

Not everyone, however, believes that this is the only purpose of dreaming. In *The Animal Mind*

Sleeping cats and dogs spend about 36 percent of their total sleep time in REM sleep, much more than humans do. Does that mean they dream more?

REM Sleep

Human beings experience dreams most commonly during a type of sleep characterized by rapid eye movements and a particular pattern of electroencephalogram (EEG) and referred to as REM sleep. Periods of REM sleep, each lasting 5-30 minutes, alternate with periods of non-REM sleep (lasting 70-90 minutes). These cycles normally occur four to five times every night.

REM SLEEP EEG

NON-REM SLEEP EEG

(1994), Princeton University evolutionary biologist Prof. James L. Gould and Carol G. Gould opine that, by itself, this function seems insufficiently important for dreaming to have evolved by natural selection. Animal dream researcher Dr. Michel Jouvet has proposed that, especially in younger animals, dreaming may function almost as a form of virtual reality, in which these creatures rehearse and expand, via the totally safe, harmless medium of dreams, their skills in hunting, or in escaping from predators.

But new evidence suggests that animals do indeed dream of previous events. In January, 2001, neurobiologists Dr. Kenway Louie and Dr. Matthew Wilson from Massachusetts Institute of Technology published in the journal *Neuron* some very thought-provoking results obtained from monitoring rats during REM sleep. They had trained the rats to run around a circular track in order to gain a reward of food. While the rats ran around the track, the scientists monitored the activity in a brain region called the hippocampus. Then they monitored over 40 periods of REM

Most animals spend more time in REM sleep than human beings do, and the young tend to experience more REM sleep than adults do.

activity when the rats were sleeping and, in about half of them, the same pattern of brain activity that was present when they had been running around the track was recorded – strongly indicating that the rats were dreaming about doing this. Indeed, they could even pinpoint from the precise electrical pattern occurring in a sleeping rat's hippocampus at a given moment where that rat would be on the track if it had actually been running along it.

One other intriguing idea about dreaming in animals that has been aired is that actions such as leg twitches and growling when an animal is sleeping are not due to dreaming at all, but quite the opposite. In other words, these actions are due merely to uncontrolled muscular spasms, and have actually induced the dreaming (rather than the other way around) by stimulating the brain to weave a story in response to receiving impulses from the animal's twitching legs and throat muscles.

Dreaming down under

Early research with the Australian echidna, or spiny anteater (*Tachyglossus aculeatus*), seemed to indicate that this creature did not undergo REM sleep at all, making it an anomaly among mammals. In 1997, however, a new study by Dr. J. Siegel and co-workers from California's Sepulveda VA Medical Center revealed that the echidna does have only one sleep state, but that this single state is midway between non-REM sleep and REM sleep, thereby suggesting that echidnas may dream after all.

And when they tested the only other type of living monotreme – the duck-billed platypus (*Ornithorhynchus anatinus*) – they discovered that this species exhibits more REM sleep than any

The echidna, a primitive egg-laying mammal (monotreme), has an equally primitive and unusual sleep state.

other adult mammal in the world, spending more than eight hours per day in REM sleep (equivalent to 60.1 percent of its total sleep time).

The fact that monotremes (which are very primitive) dream suggests that REM sleep may have evolved as far back as the reptiles, explaining why REM sleep occurs in both mammals and birds, which are independently descended from reptiles. In fact, in humans dreaming originates in a primitive area of the brain dubbed the reptile brain, since it is derived directly from reptiles.

ANIMAL PROFILE

Singing in Their Sleep

In 2001, Chicago University researchers Dr. Amish Dave and Dr. Daniel Margoliash revealed that zebra finches (*Poephila guttata*) actually practice their singing while asleep. After monitoring the specific brain patterns occurring when a zebra finch is singing, the scientists found that this same pattern also occurs in its brain while it is asleep. Moreover, sometimes it is slightly modified, as if the finch were improving its song during its sleep.

Tool-Using Animals

see also:
- Primate Sign Language, p.140
- Cetacean Communication, p.144
- Talking Birds, p.151

Termite hills (left) and other insect nests (right) provide a tasty supper for a chimp with the right tools. A stick allows the chimp to access hard-to-reach places.

Nature provides some animals with a veritable tool chest, letting them fish with feathers, probe with twigs, and crack things open with stones.

It was once thought that humans were the only animals with the mental capacity and manual dexterity required to design, make, and use tools. But we now know that an extraordinarily diverse range of other creatures are also adept, long-standing users and manufacturers of tools.

Primate tool operators

As defined by Jane Goodall in 1970, tool using in the strictest scientific sense is the use of an external object as a functional extension of the body to attain an immediate goal. Not surprisingly, our closest relatives, the chimpanzees, are extremely proficient tool users, manufacturers, and designers. Perhaps their most famous tool-using behavior is shown in termite fishing, the name given to these apes' skillful gathering of tasty insects from termite and ant hills. After using their powerful fingers to push holes into the walls of a termite (or ant) hill, chimps in Okorobiko, Central Africa, meticulously shape twigs by snapping them into smaller, more manageable sticks and stripping them of any protruding pieces of bark or stalk until they have produced short, smooth probes. They then carefully

insert these probes into the holes made by their fingers and gently pull them out again. After eating all of the insects covering the stick they reinsert it into the hill to gather more.

An interesting variation on termite fishing is practiced by chimps living in Senegal's Mount Assirik. They use large sticks (instead of their own fingers) to force holes into termite nests, making openings that are big enough to enable the chimps to reach inside with their hands and scoop out the insects directly. Other well-documented examples of tool-using techniques among chimps include using sticks to dig up edible roots, employing stones as tools for cracking open the tough shells of certain nuts, and using leaves as sponges to soak up water from hollow tree trunks for drinking or cleaning themselves.

The famous "talking" pygmy chimpanzee, Kanzi, at Georgia State University learned how to make sharp-edged stone flakes for cutting string that was tying up a box containing food. And Charles Darwin's classic work *The Descent of Man* (1871) contains a mention of how he once saw an orangutan use a stick as a lever.

Non-anthropoid primates have also been known to use tools. A captive South American titi monkey was seen using pieces of straw to pry cockroaches out of crevices to eat. Baboons employ sticks as probes to ferret out insects hiding in hard-to-reach places, and they also use stones for squashing scorpions. Similarly, South American capuchin monkeys are adept at breaking open nuts with stones, using sticks to obtain food beyond their arms' reach, and hurling branches like weapons at potential attackers.

But is such tool using in other animals merely instinctive, accidental, or imitative (cultural exchange)? Or could it be a valid indication of intelligent innovation?

There is still a great deal of controversy concerning these questions. Most researchers, however, are content to accept a compromise view. The consensus is that even if tool using in these and other nonhuman animals is probably largely innate, initially accidental, or even the result of cultural exchange, and thus not in itself a sign of intelligence, it surely sets the stage for genuinely intelligent behavior involving true innovation.

Chimpanzees use stones to crack open the nuts that they feed on (left). They also use leaves to soak up water from tree trunks so that they can drink it (right).

Sea otters open mollusk shells with large flat stones as they float on their backs.

Skilled sea otters

After spending some time diving underwater in search of mollusks, crabs, and sea urchins, the sea otter (*Enhydra lutris*) ascends again and floats upon its back, using its broad hairy chest as a dining table on which it arranges not only its collected prey but also the tools with which to eat it. These tools consist of large flat stones that the sea otter gathers while procuring its prey, which it uses as anvils on which to hammer open the shells of bivalves and other shelled sea creatures. It will also use such stones to break open or knock off mollusks that it finds clinging to rocks. Intriguingly, if it finds a particularly good stone for these purposes, instead of discarding it after a single use, the resourceful sea otter tucks it in its armpit when diving in search of its next meal. This saves it from looking for a fresh stone on each dive.

Tool using in sea otters occurs only in areas where the shells of prey are normally too tough to crack with just their jaws. In regions where these shells are weak enough for the otters to open on their own, only young otters whose jaws have not yet reached their full strength need the assistance of the stones.

Feathered tool users

Mammals are by no means the only skilled tool users in the animal kingdom. One of the classic examples of tool using involves the Galapagos woodpecker finch (*Cactospiza* − or *Camarhynchus* − *pallida*). Its beak is not always long enough to reach

ANIMAL PROFILE

Sponges, Snouts, and Tool-using Dolphins

In 1997, Michigan University researcher Dr. Rachel Smolker and co-researchers were studying dolphins in Western Australia's Shark Bay when they saw several dolphins "wearing" large conical sponges on their heads, holding them in place by inserting their beaks inside the sponges. Since these odd "hats" may reduce the dolphins' swimming efficiency, and possibly interfere with their echolocation abilities too, why were they wearing sponges? The scientists believe that the sponges help protect the dolphins' faces and sensitive beaks as they probe for food on the seabed, where they may accidentally disturb sea snakes or stingrays.

inside crevices in tree bark to seek out the insect grubs on which it feeds, so it sometimes employs a tool for this purpose. Flying off to a nearby cactus bush, the finch either picks up a shed cactus spine from the ground or snaps one from the cactus itself, then flies back to the tree, holding the spine in its beak.

Sometimes, just like the termite-fishing chimps, a woodpecker finch actually takes the time and trouble to modify the spine, trimming it until it is just the right length for the job. Then the finch carefully inserts the spine into a crack or crevice in the tree's bark, until an insect is flushed out, whereupon the finch drops the spine and seizes the insect in its beak. Afterward, it either retrieves the fallen spine to use again or flies off to find another one.

Curiously, not all woodpecker finches are tool users; it seems that a finch will behave in this way only if it has previously seen another finch do so. If it hasn't, it remains content simply to probe the tree bark with its beak. This does not seem, therefore, to be innate behavior, but rather the product of cultural exchange (though spine trimming does suggest innovation).

Hard eggs to crack

Another well-known avian tool user is the Egyptian vulture (*Neophron percnopterus*). This species loves to eat eggs but, when faced with the extremely tough shells of ostrich eggs, it turns to tool using in order to obtain the tasty yolk. Standing in front of an ostrich egg, the Egyptian vulture picks up a large, heavy stone in its beak, extends its neck up as high as possible, then hurls the stone down with all its force onto the egg. Although this is a somewhat haphazard process, since the vulture's aim is far from accurate, the ostrich egg usually succumbs after six to twelve blows with a stone. So important are such tools to this species when dealing with ostrich eggs that an Egyptian vulture will fly up to 3 miles (5 km) carrying a suitable stone in its beak.

Avian artisans

One of the world's many clever birds, the male satin bowerbird (*Ptilonorhynchus violaceus*) uses a tool to enhance its renowned artistic ability as a highly skilled painter. After building an elaborate bower of twigs in which to display itself to prospective mates during the breeding season, the male paints it with its favorite color – blue – using as its brush and paint a stick daubed with the blue juice from crushed berries, affixed to the stick with the bird's own saliva.

Using a cactus spine, the woodpecker finch pries insects out of their holes.

The Egyptian vulture uses large stones to crack open the hard shells of ostrich eggs.

The male satin bowerbird decorates its nest with glass and other objects before painting it blue with berry juice, using a stick held in its beak.

Cunning fly-fisher

One bird that very memorably employs a tool to assist it in obtaining food is the green heron (*Butorides virescens*). The heron drops a fly or some other insect (occasionally even a feather) onto the surface of a pond as a lure, then waits motionless nearby until a fish ascends toward the lure. At this point, the heron strikes down with lightning speed, seizing or even spearing the fish with its beak. So adept is this fly-fisherman that if it has no luck in a certain spot, it will pick up its insect lure and try again elsewhere.

Bearing in mind that they are commonly deemed to be the world's cleverest birds, it is hardly surprising that crows are accomplished tool users. In January, 1996, ornithologist Dr. Gavin Hunt of Massey University, New Zealand, documented in

The green heron waits motionless for a fish to approach its lure.

ANIMAL PROFILE

When Is Tool Using Not Tool Using?

Song thrushes (*Turdus philomelos*) are often claimed to be tool users because they employ stones as anvils on which to break open the tough shells of the snails they eat. Sometimes they even drop the snails down onto the stones from the air. Strictly speaking, however, this is not tool using because these stone "anvils" are not extensions of the birds' bodies. Only if the birds picked up the stones and hit the snail shells with them (rather than the reverse) could this be classed as tool using.

Nature his observations of tool-using crows on the Pacific island of New Caledonia, east of Australia. In actions that recall those of the woodpecker finch, the birds break off pieces of hook-shaped twig, trim any extraneous projections until a hook is produced, then use these as tools for reaching insects lurking inside dead wood. Some crows also remove chunks from well-tapered leaves, producing harpoonlike tools with barbs facing away from the pointed tip.

Cleverer still are crows in Sendai, Japan, that use cars as nutcracking tools. They deliberately drop walnuts in front of moving cars, wait for the vehicles to drive over them, then swoop down to pick the tasty kernels out of the smashed nuts.

The bearded vulture, or lammergeier (*Gypaetus barbatus*), drops heavy animal bones onto rocks in order to crack them open and get at the marrow inside.

Sometimes they even perch on traffic lights and wait for the lights to change to red, then fly down to the stationary cars and place their walnuts in front of the tires before the lights change to green, and the moving cars crush them. The crows then sensibly wait for the lights to change back to red before collecting the kernels.

Wily wasps and well-armed octopuses

Tool using is even known among invertebrates. After a female digger wasp (*Ammophila* spp.) has paralyzed a caterpillar and laid her egg in it (from which a wasp grub will later hatch and feed on the hapless caterpillar), she buries its still-living but immobile body in her underground nest, filling the hole with sand. To ensure that the sand cannot be penetrated by some other creature hoping to reach the caterpillar and devour it, she picks up a large stone and pounds it against the sand until the ground is firm and well packed.

Another insect tool user is the weaver ant (*Oecophylla smaragdina*), which makes nests by rolling up leaves and then gluing the sides together with silk. Although it is the adult ants that do this, only the larvae produce silk, so how is the process of leaf gluing achieved? In fact, the adults carry larvae in their jaws and squeeze them gently so that the larvae secrete a drop of silk on one end of the leaf edges. The ants then carry the larvae along the entire length of the leaf edges, squeezing as they go, using the larvae like living bottles of glue, until the edges of the leaves are stuck together from end to end.

Still more intriguing is the way in which young blanket octopuses (*Tremoctopus violaceus*) defend themselves. They carry around broken tentacles from the Portuguese man-of-war (*Physalia physalis*) between the suckers of their four longest (dorsal) arms, ensuring that any potential predator risks being stung. Some hermit crabs go even further, using entire, living sea anemones as tools to ward off predators. They carry these stinging sea creatures in their claws and thrust them aggressively at any would-be attacker.

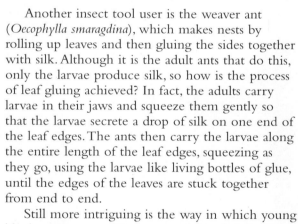

The weaver ant makes its nest by sticking leaves together with a glue made from the silk of its own larvae, which it holds in its mouth.

Psychic Animals

see also:
● Psi-Trailing, p. 85
● Animal Grief and Mourning, p. 201
● Animal Fidelity, p. 205

Reports abound of animals that seem able to read their owners' minds and even to sense when danger lies ahead – but are these pets really psychic?

From the earliest times to the present day, people have claimed to possess or to have experienced some form of psychic ability, such as telepathy or precognition. As yet, however, there is still no scientific confirmation that these abilities actually exist. Nevertheless, such claims are not confined to humans – there are many reports of allegedly psychic animals that are even more perplexing and extraordinary than any human phenomenon.

Ready and waiting

Dogs that Know When Their Owners Are Coming Home (1999), by biologist Dr. Rupert Sheldrake, not only surveys but also investigates a range of reputedly psychic talents exhibited by animals. Among them is the apparent ability of some pets, especially dogs, to sense when their owner is coming home, long before there are any detectable visual, aural, olfactory, or other accepted sensory stimuli. One dog that Dr. Sheldrake studied in great detail was a terrier called Jaytee, owned by Pam Smart of Ramsbottom, Lancashire, in England.

Pam's father noticed that each day, at about 4:30 P.M., Jaytee would sit by the window, waiting for Pam to return home. The father didn't think anything of this, however, until Pam lost her job, and began coming back at all different times. Jaytee would still go and sit by the window, waiting for her. Yet, remarkably, the time when Jaytee got up and went to the window seemed to match the time when Pam set off for home from where she had been – no matter where that was or what time she set off. Sheldrake had Jaytee's actions videoed and timed by a film crew who were themselves unaware of when Pam would be leaving for home and hence could not influence the dog in any way.

The tapes revealed that Jaytee's reactions usually began up to 10 minutes before Pam even began her return journey. No matter how far away Pam was or what time she left, Jaytee seemed to sense she would soon be on her way. Consequently, Sheldrake speculated that Jaytee may have somehow been detecting Pam's thoughts of leaving before she actually departed.

In 1995, Jaytee also passed a London *Daily Mail* test of his skill, in which Pam and reporter Stephen Oldfield drove to a destination without telling her father where it was or when they would come

Jaytee, a terrier owned by Pam Smart, always seemed to know when Pam was on her way home, and would wait by the window for her to arrive.

dog, Rusty, would bark, jump onto the sofa, peer out of the window for a short time, then jump off again and run to the front door, where he would remain until Elizabeth finally arrived.

Remembering an old friend

A case featuring very different animals but a similar outcome occurred at Dudley Zoo, England, one morning in June, 1937. The zoo was awaiting a very famous visitor – the actor Sabu, star of the film *Elephant Boy*, who wanted to see two elephants there, Yuvaranee and Maharanee. Sabu had worked with them as a child in Mysore, India, and had not seen them in several years. Remarkably, however, when he arrived at the zoo, both elephants began trumpeting excitedly long before he reached their enclosure.

Dr. Sheldrake believes that pets and their owners may be linked together by a kind of flexible energy field, which he terms a morphic field – analogous to an elastic band that can stretch over a great distance without breaking when pet and owner are separated, and which can also contract, bringing pet and owner closer together. It seems that animals are very sensitive to this field, thereby enabling pets to determine when their owners are returning home.

Ringing out a mystery

Another very remarkable but frequently cited claim relating to psychic animals is that some pets know when the telephone is about to ring and will go to the phone, or sound the alert in some other way, before it actually begins ringing. This has happened many times in the household of Keith and Linda Ralph from Bury in Lancashire, England. At least a minute before the telephone rings, their pet British bulldog, Carrie, and her son, Bruno, prick up their ears, cock their heads to one side, saunter over to the telephone table, and wait until it rings.

Even more extraordinary are cases in which the pet seems to know who is calling *before* the phone is answered. Every time that Marie McCurrach's son phoned her at their home in Ipswich, Suffolk, England, his labrador would rush to the phone and begin barking, before Mrs. McCurrach had time to pick it up. What made this so remarkable is that her son was in the Merchant Navy, and therefore phoned at all times, and from different places, some as far away as South Africa. Yet his dog always ran to the phone when he called, and never when anyone else did. During the phone call, Mrs. McCurrach would place the receiver to the dog's ear, enabling her son to talk to him, and the dog would bark in reply.

The actor Sabu was recognized by two elephants long before he arrived at their enclosure.

back. When they did return, the journey took 20 minutes. Once inside they asked her father when Jaytee had gotten up to wait at the window. Pam's father replied that it had been 20 minutes ago.

The same scenario was played out for ten years at the home of sisters Sue and Elizabeth Bryan, of Crawley, West Sussex, in England. Elizabeth was a flight attendant, whose time of arrival back home varied randomly from day to day. Sometimes she was away for a few days at a time. Yet whenever her plane landed at Gatwick Airport, at home her pet

Godzilla always knew when her owner, David Waite, would telephone.

ANIMAL PROFILE

Telepathic Cats?

In 1973, Dr. J. Bigu del Blanco and Dr. Cesar Romero-Sierra from Queen's University in Kingston, Ontario, proposed a way animal telepathy might work. Measurements of microwave emissions from human and rabbit subjects had revealed levels above the background levels expected from any radiating warm body. Moreover, the extra emissions fluctuated in proportion to oscillating states of stress. The researchers suggested that this may explain how cats sometimes seem to know when other cats are stressed, even when they are beyond normal visual and aural contact. Perhaps they may literally be tuning into each other's emotions by radio.

Similarly, David Waite's cat, Godzilla, always ran to the phone and sat by it if David was the caller, even though he was working in different parts of the world and phoned home in Oxfordshire, England, at various times. Could it be, as suggested by Dr. Sheldrake, that these pets are telepathic, tuning into their owner's intention to telephone home, thus explaining why they become alert just before the phone actually rings or is answered?

Telepathic requests

Morphic fields linking pets to owners may also explain cases in which a pet, especially a lost or distressed one, has seemingly contacted its owners telepathically, guiding them to it.

One incident in Lancashire, England, featured a cat called Solitaire and her owner, Martha Lees. One day, Solitaire vanished and, despite a thorough search, Martha was unable to find her. Two days later, Martha experienced a compulsive urge to go out and look for Solitaire again. As she walked, she felt as if she were being deliberately guided, and after ten minutes she found herself ringing a doorbell. She didn't know the house, but she explained to the occupant that she somehow felt it was important for her to look in his backyard for her missing cat. When she went into the garden, she heard a faint meow, and discovered that Solitaire had wedged herself inside a mound of garden rubbish. Martha remains convinced that Solitaire had telepathically led her there in order to be found.

Sensing disaster and death

No less weird are the many reports on file of pets that seem able to sense impending disaster or death. Keith Ralph's bulldog, Carrie, mentioned earlier, once saved him from a possible mugging. She is not normally afraid of people, yet one evening in 1988, while walking with Keith, she suddenly halted, then began pulling her lead violently in the opposite direction. Since both ways ultimately led to where he wanted to go, Keith followed the direction that Carrie seemed to prefer, which took them up a hill overlooking the path that Keith would otherwise have walked along. Glancing down onto that path, Keith was horrified to see three men there, lying in wait, armed with baseball bats. Keith hurried home, thankful that he had followed Carrie's instincts.

Elliott, a cocker spaniel, normally took little if any notice when his owner, Chris Houghton, left each morning to travel by train from their home in Haslemere, Surrey, to her office in London. On the morning of December 12, 1988, however, Elliott

Winston Churchill's cat (below) seemed to know when his spirit was gone, ending his vigil in the sick room just before Churchill died.

became distraught when she was about to leave. Eventually, he calmed down, so Chris left for the train station, but she had missed her usual train. When she finally arrived at work, she was horrified but amazed to learn that the train she normally took had crashed en route at Clapham, killing 36 people – the worst train crash in British history. Was it just a coincidence that Elliott's abnormal behavior had delayed her so that she had missed that train?

On July 17, 1977, England's *Sunday Express* newspaper published a letter from Mrs. B. N. Harris of Harrogate, Yorkshire, concerning a very intriguing World War II incident: "During the wartime evacuation from London, we were housed in Tiverton Road, Exeter – the straight road out into the country. In the early evening before the tragic raid which so devastated the city, there was an unbelievable exodus of cats padding in a gentle stream past our windows toward Tiverton. Knowing nothing about cats, we watched in great surprise, wondering why. Before morning – sadly we knew."

Many similar reports of animals leaving areas just before bombing raids and other violent acts are also on record from all around the world – as are accounts of pets reacting to the death of their owner even if they were not present at the time.

One of the most famous incidents, recounted by Dennis Bardens in *Psychic Animals* (1987), concerns a naval officer from Harwich, assigned to mine-sweeping duties in the North Sea during World War I. Whenever he set out on an expedition, his wife and his dog, an airedale, would see him off. The airedale never showed any distress at such partings. One night, however, for no apparent reason, the Airedale behaved very differently, howling at his owner and even tugging his trousers and coat to keep him from boarding the ship. Finally, the officer did board, and set out on the expedition – from which he never returned. His ship sank, and he drowned. At the moment of his death, his airedale back home suddenly began howling inconsolably.

Bardens also recalled a traditional rural English belief, that just before a person dies their soul leaves their body – which makes a report about a cat belonging to Sir Winston Churchill of particular interest. During Churchill's final illness, his cat stayed beside him day and night – until just before Churchill's death, when the cat suddenly got up and left. Perhaps the cat detected changes in his dying owner's temperature, respiration, or heartbeat. Or could it be that he somehow sensed that the great man's soul was gone, and that the person he had loved was no longer there?

Perhaps the last word on the subject should go to Giessen University researcher Dr. Ute Pleimes, who has recorded over 800 cases of pets warning their owners of impending disaster: "I have seen enough to convince me that animals do have a special psychic power to sense danger before it happens. We are fools to ignore them."

CHAPTER TEN

ANIMAL EMOTIONS

*Scientists once thought that
animals – even those that were relatively
advanced, such as other mammals –
were devoid of true emotions; they believed
them to be little more than living automata.
The remarkable cases presented in this chapter,
however, show that this supposition is
not correct. It is abundantly clear that happiness,
sadness, loyalty, compassion, concern for
unrelated species, and even respect
for the dead can no longer be
considered to be uniquely human
attributes after all.*

Animal Humor

see also:
● Infrasonic Messages, p.25
● Primate Sign Language, p.140
● Psychic Animals, p.192

Animals may not feel emotions in the same way as humans do, but they undoubtedly show happiness and pleasure.

Happiness and joy are emotions not solely displayed by humans, as anyone who has ever kept a pet dog or cat or watched wild otters or young monkeys at play could confirm. What these animals are feeling may not be comparable to what humans feel in similar circumstances, but there are close similarities, and never more so than when joy has given rise to clearly intentional displays of outright humor.

The joy of reunion

In humans, joy can be induced in many ways, but one of the most effective is a reunion between close relatives or friends, especially if the reunion is unexpected. Differing interpretations of animal behavior, and the risk of anthropomorphism, make exact correlations in the animal world difficult to cite. However, African elephants rejoining their herd after a separation exhibit wild displays of joy.

Rushing toward one another and spinning around as they meet, they flap their ears, fill the air with trumpeting and with thunderous infrasound, urinate and defecate with abandon, entwine their trunks, and weep. Joyce Poole of the Amboseli Elephant Research Project in Kenya has little doubt that this is not an unemotional proclamation to other creatures that the herd is now united once more, but a genuine expression of joy at meeting up again with family or friends.

Many young animals seem to enjoy playing, but its purpose is not clear; it may be a way of honing skills they will need as adults, or simply for fun.

One of the most unequivocal cases of animal joy involves a pygmy chimpanzee called Kanzi. Kanzi had been taught to communicate using lexigrams by primate researcher Dr. Sue Savage–Rumbaugh at Georgia State University's primate communication laboratory, and had become very proficient. One day, Savage–Rumbaugh informed Kanzi via the lexigrams that she had a surprise for him: His

A reunion of separated elephants is an occasion for an obvious display of joy as the animals trumpet, flap ears, and link trunks.

ANIMAL PROFILE

A Fishy Kind of Kissing

A freshwater fish native to southeast Asia, the kissing gourami (*Helostoma temmincki*) is well named. Place two of these fishes in an aquarium, and they soon line up to face one another, swaying backward and forward for a time, and then swim right up to each other until their noticeably large, rubbery lips touch. Once this happens, the two gouramis remain locked for a time in what looks just like a passionate kiss, their thick lips pressed firmly together, before eventually separating and swimming away. Scientists have long speculated over the purpose of this curious kissing behavior. Some believe that it is a bona fide expression of affection, displayed between potential mates. Others, however, feel that it signifies the exact opposite emotion – aggression. They suggest that when "'kissing," the gouramis are actually engaging in a bout of mouth-wrestling, an injury-avoiding test of strength – comparable to arm-wrestling in humans – in order to determine which of the two kissing fish is the stronger.

stepmother, Matata, who had been away from him for some time, had now come back to the laboratory and was waiting for him. Kanzi's expressive face plainly showed that he was initially stunned by this news, but then he ran swiftly to the door and gestured urgently to Savage-Rumbaugh to open it. As soon as Kanzi and Matata saw one another, they let out a series of ear-splitting screams, raced up to the wire door separating them, and pushed their hands through the wire in an eager attempt to touch each other. When Savage-Rumbaugh opened the door, Kanzi leapt into Matata's arms, and for five minutes they remained hugging and screaming continually, in obvious delight at their unexpected reunion.

Playing the fool?

Play in animals has always been something of an enigma to animal behaviorists. Some forms, especially those indulged in by young animals, have been explained by researchers as processes by which they learn adult skills, as when kittens stalk leaves or pounce upon balls of string. Yet play is very costly in terms of the energy expended, and sometimes even puts those animals involved in danger if they are less attentive than normal to what is happening in their immediate surroundings. Moreover, on many occasions play seems to provide no useful function at all, other than amusement for those participating in it.

How else can the bizarre behavior of crows living near the famous onion domes of Moscow's Kremlin be explained? These buildings' domes are magnificently gilded, or they were, until the local hooded crow population incorporated them into a novel game. They would alight on the apex of a dome, and then slide down it, plummeting off the end into the air, only to fly up to the apex and slide down again. The problem was that their sharp claws were scratching off swathes of gold leaf, inciting worried officials to install crow-scaring devices to ward off the feathered tobogganists.

Equally frivolous, and evidently fun-filled in the eyes of its protagonists, are the many cases of deliberate teasing instigated by an individual of one species against one of another species. Stately swans are prone to suffering the indignity of having their tail feathers tweaked by fun-loving dabchicks (*Podiceps ruficollis*) that dive underwater before the swans can retaliate. A dolphin that shared its tank with a small fish living in a crevice was often seen teasing the fish by placing a piece of tasty squid by the crevice's opening, only to snatch it away again as soon as the fish emerged to take it. And the pet magpie of zoologist Prof. Miriam Rothschild delighted in imitating the quacking of ducks, as this unfailingly brought her pet dogs racing outside in the vain hope of finding some fowl to chase.

The sounds of happiness

There are also many aural clues to animal happiness, with some creatures producing special sounds associated with the state of being happy. One of the most familiar examples is purring in cats, both domestic and large. Less well known is that contented gorillas in family groups often sing.

Animal Grief & Mourning

see also:
● Primate Sign Language, p.140
● Social Organization, p.174
● Psychic Animals, p.192

They may look different from humans, but a wide range of other animals from greylag geese to elephants outwardly express grief and react to death, especially of relatives or long-standing companions, in ways that are extraordinarily similar to human responses.

The sorrow of family bereavement

Humankind's nearest relatives, the apes and monkeys, experience grief when confronted with the death of a close relative, but what is startling is how profound such sorrow can be. Dr. Jane Goodall recorded one moving case during her research into the behavior of wild chimpanzees.

In 1972, while Goodall was studying a chimp community in Tanzania's Gombe National Park, its elderly matriarch, Flo, died. Flo had been in the company of her 8½-year-old son, Flint, who, unlike most adult chimps, had always remained with his mother rather than becoming independent. Flint initially appeared bemused by her death, sitting alongside her throughout the first day, sometimes inspecting her body, grooming her, and even pulling her hand toward him, hoping that she would groom him in return. When evening came, he constructed a nest for himself in a tree. Here he passed the night, the first that he had spent alone.

Animals of many different species sometimes seem to respond to adverse life events by undergoing a period best described as mourning.

Although distracted for a time the next day by his brother's chimp group, it was not long before Flint returned to the place where Flo had died, and sat there, staring. Later, he climbed a tree to visit a nest where he and Flo had slept a week earlier, then he climbed down again, and continued staring.

As the days passed, it was evident that Flint was sinking into a state of deep depression, showing no interest in anything or any other chimp in his community, and not eating, just lying huddled on the ground. His eyes had sunk back into their sockets, and when he did move it was with the shambling gait of an old chimp. Three weeks after Flo's death, Flint returned to the place where she had died, and lay down there, staring out vacantly. Shortly afterward, he died – of grief, in Goodall's

Greylag geese have long-term mating partnerships, and are known to grieve if their partner dies.

opinion. In view of how very closely Flint's behavior mirrored the grieving of a bereaved human, it would be difficult to draw any other conclusion.

While wildlife producer George Page was filming a group of Japanese macaques for a TV documentary, one of them gave birth to a stillborn infant. Instead of abandoning it, its mother carried the body with her. And each night, after climbing a tree with it in her arms, she would utter a series of heart-rending screams. Not until three full days and nights of mourning had passed did she finally place her baby's body on the ground and leave it.

Nor are grief and mourning confined to primates. While studying baboons in Kenya, Michigan University behaviorist Dr. Barbara Smuts witnessed four baboons chasing an infant impala. Despite its mother's attempts to protect it, one of the baboons seized the impala, killing it, and eating it in front of its mother. After the baboons left, she remained there, staring motionless at her calf's remains. When Smuts revisited the site several hours later, and again the following morning, the female impala was still there, and was still gazing fixedly at her dead calf. Later that day, she finally departed, but she had ignored the world to pay homage to her dead calf, for more than a day.

Birds, especially species that mate for life, exhibit unmistakable signs of grief when their partner dies. As noted by eminent animal behaviorist Prof. Konrad Lorenz, a greylag goose that has lost its partner shows all the symptoms that John Bowlby has described in young human children in his book *Infant Grief*. The eyes sink into their sockets, and the individual literally droops and hangs its head. Nor is it unknown among swans, which mate for life, for the bereaved survivor of a long-standing pair to stop eating and die a short time afterward.

Grieving for departed friends

Emotional responses have also been documented in animals confronted by the death of an animal friend.

In the 1960s, animal rescuers Ken and Mary Jones of Cornwall, England, received a young seal for care, one of many coated with oil

from a tanker spill. Naming him Simon, they nursed him back to health. While he was with them they received another seal, a female dubbed Sally, who had been blinded by the oil. Simon and Sally became friends, with Simon acting as Sally's eyes. A year later Simon died. Sally was distraught, lying next to Simon's body and refusing to move from the spot. Sally rejected all enticements to eat, and in less than a week she, too, had died, not from physical illness, but, it seemed, from grief.

The same fate almost befell a female donkey named Julie. Julie had spent many years in the company of Leonardo, an Icelandic pony. Finally, Leonardo had to be put to sleep. Julie was taken to a field some distance from the shed she shared with Leonardo, while Leonardo was euthanized in the shed. When his body had been removed, Julie was released, and galloped across the field to the shed. After standing inside for a time, looking down at the spot where he had been lying, Julie came out of the shed again, raised her muzzle skyward, and let out an agonized scream. After that, she stopped eating, and seemed destined to join Leonardo in death, until fate intervened. A Shetland pony was introduced as a new companion, and Julie and the pony became friends. Julie's appetite returned, and several years later the two could still be seen together.

Animal "funerals"

Traditional folklore throughout the world tells of animals attending funerals for members of their own kind, and also contains stories of creatures

ANIMAL PROFILE

Are Animal Tears Emotional?

EYE DETAIL

Elephants that have been separated from relatives weep floods of tears when reunited. And they are "true" tears, secreted from their lachrymal glands. Such tears are normally for lubrication purposes, but they are also allegedly wept at times of grief or fear. Young elephants orphaned when their mothers were killed by poachers for their tusks are known to wake screaming in the night, their eyes full of tears. And in their book *When Elephants Weep* (1994), animal behaviorists Dr. Jeffrey Masson and Dr. Susan McCarthy include several reports of captive elephants weeping when ill treated by their human masters.

When researching their book *Crying, the Mystery of Tears* (1985), Minnesota-based biochemist Dr. William Frey and journalist Muriel Langseth received many letters from dog owners claiming that their pets had wept emotional tears. Among the more thought-provoking examples are an Irish setter that cried when the family cat died, a Boston terrier that hid under the table and sobbed tears whenever his owner scolded him, and several reports of Mexican hairless dogs weeping if upset.

burying their dead. Some wildlife observers claim that such events sometimes occur in real life, too. Elephants are known for standing around a dead member of their herd in a solemn, almost ritualistic manner, with their heads pointing away from the body, and adult females have been seen placing leaves or branches over the body of a dead calf.

Badgers are said to bury their dead, and naturalist Brian Vesey-Fitzgerald reported an adult female's bizarre behavior. After emitting a macabre scream at her sett's entrance, she dug a large hole nearby. Then, assisted by an adult male, she pulled the dead body of another male out of her sett, deposited it in the hole, and covered it with soil. After this, the two went their separate ways. Skeptics suggest that badgers are merely hiding corpses to eat later. Yet dead rabbits, too, have been found in warren tunnels that are otherwise sealed off, and rabbits do not eat each other.

Most bizarre of all, however, are reports of alleged bee mourners. These are honeybee swarms that have massed at the funeral of their beekeeper. A case in July 1994 featured beekeeper Margaret Bell. She kept her bees 7 miles (11 km) from the town in Shropshire, England, where she lived. Nonetheless, on the day of the funeral a swarm settled on the corner of the street opposite her house. Skeptics, argue that the appearance of a swarm at a funeral is simply coincidence.

Honeybees have been said to swarm at the funeral of their keeper, on one occasion reputedly traveling some miles in order to be present nearby.

Animal Fidelity

see also:
● Psi-Trailing, p.85
● Psychic Animals, p.192
● Animal Grief & Mourning, p.201

Dogs are well known for their loyalty to their human masters, even after death. Other pets are also capable of devoted behavior.

An ornamental fountain featuring a statue of Bobby stands in Edinburgh's Candlemaker Row, near Greyfriars, where he kept his 14-year vigil.

The bonds of loyalty and fidelity forged between a pet animal and its owner (and often between a wild animal and an adoptive human, too) can be strong and long lasting. So much so, in fact, that such bonds sometimes even persist after the death of the pet's owner.

Dogged devotion

Undoubtedly the most famous examples of such tenacious fidelity can be found among canines. The most celebrated of these is probably a Skye terrier dubbed "Greyfriars Bobby." Owned by John Gray, an elderly shepherd nicknamed Auld Jock, Bobby was two years old in 1858 when he traveled with Jock to Edinburgh, Scotland. There, Jock fell ill and died. He was buried in Edinburgh's Greyfriars churchyard, with Bobby in attendance. Afterward,

A statue immortalizes an akita, who waited at the station for his master every evening for ten years.

Bobby refused to abandon his dead master, and faithfully returned to sleep on Jock's grave every night for the next 14 years, until he, too, died.

Bobby's poignant story attracted enormous attention both in Scotland and overseas: The children of Edinburgh even saved their pennies to buy him a collar, so that he would not be rounded up and killed as a stray. Bobby was eventually granted the Freedom of the City of Edinburgh, the only dog ever to receive such an honor. His remains, buried with special permission alongside his master, are marked by his own gravestone, still commemorating a bond of loyal devotion so strong that not even death could break it.

Waiting at the station

Similar canine case histories have been recorded elsewhere in the world. Equally famous in Japan, for example, is the statue outside Tokyo's Shibuya Railway Station of a large akita called Hachi-Ko.

Hachi-Ko was owned by Dr. Ueno, a lecturer at Tokyo's Imperial University. Each evening when Dr. Ueno returned home by train, Hachi-Ko would meet him at Shibuya Station. Tragically, however, one evening in 1925, when Hachi-Ko was three years old, he waited in vain: Dr. Ueno had died earlier that day from a heart attack while still at the university.

Nevertheless, the following evening Hachi-Ko went faithfully back to the station and, although he was soon given a new home and became increasingly crippled by arthritis as he aged, he continued to go to the station every single evening for the next 10 years. Eventually he died, still waiting loyally for the master who would never return. Hachi-Ko's death at the age of 12 was marked in Japan by a National Day of Mourning, and his breed was formally declared a living monument.

Similarly, as recently as 1997, a guide dog named Canelo was still a daily visitor to the hospital in Cadiz, southern Spain, where his blind master had died seven years earlier.

Loyalty rewarded

Some animals are so devoted to their owners that they risk their own lives in order to stay by an owner's side. When an ambulance arrived at the home of Reuben Richards in Bolton, England, the

14-year-old Beauty stayed curled up close to her dead master for two weeks, with neither food nor drink, until rescued by Nigel Butterworth.

ANIMAL PROFILE

Does an Elephant Ever Forget?

The loyalty and recognition shown by elephants to the remains of their dead relatives is memorable and mystifying. Elephant researcher Cynthia Moss has revealed that an elephant herd will make a detour to investigate unearthed elephant skeletons and run their trunks along the contours of the bones (particularly the skulls and tusks), fondle them, smell them, even carry them for some distance before finally dropping them again. One seven-year-old elephant in a herd came upon the jaw of his dead mother, brought by Moss into the camp in the hope of uncovering its age. Long after the herd had moved on, this elephant remained there, touching and turning over his mother's jaw with his trunk and feet. Did he recognize it as his mother's? If so, what were the thoughts passing through his mind?

paramedics found that he had been dead for at least two weeks. Still by his side was his 14-year-old mongrel, Beauty. Ambulance crew member Nigel Butterworth assumed the dog was dead, too. Yet even after two weeks' starvation, she was alive, but emaciated and weak. Although she ate and drank, she remained weak for several days. Now she is fully recovered and lives with Butterworth.

How did they know?

Even more remarkable are cases in which a pet has not merely visited the grave of its deceased owner repeatedly, but has also first located a grave that it has never been to before.

In 1975, while the family of Philip Friedman was attending his funeral in Brooklyn, New York, Friedman's pet German shepherd, King, escaped from the house and could not be found anywhere. Three weeks later, however, a family member happened to mention King's disappearance to the groundskeeper of the cemetery where Friedman was buried. He was amazed to learn from the groundskeeper that at 2 o'clock each day for the past three weeks, a German shepherd had come

into the cemetery and had lain down on Friedman's grave, howling softly. It was, of course, King. How he knew where his master was buried is a mystery.

Homing cats?

This homing ability is not only a canine trait. In 1974, the elderly owner of a cat called Moggie was admitted to a hospital in Oxfordshire, England, and a friend, Mrs. Bridget Wastie of Charlbury, agreed to look after Moggie until her owner came out again. Moggie's owner, however, died in the hospital, and the next day Moggie vanished. Two days later, Mrs. Wastie and her mother journeyed to the funeral of Moggie's owner in a village 15 miles (24 km) away. As her coffin was being lowered into its grave, the two women were astonished to see Moggie sitting on a gravestone nearby, solemnly watching the proceedings. The cat had never been to this village before (let alone to the precise grave where her owner would be buried), but somehow she had homed in to her deceased owner, seemingly bridging the chasm of death that now separated them.

Following the death of his master, the U.S. general George Patton, in January 1946, his dog, Willy, showed his devotion by spending days lying listlessly by the general's personal belongings at his home in Bad Nauheim, Germany

Animal Rescuers

see also:
● Multiple Senses, p. 40
● Whale Strandings, p. 50
● Cetacean Communication, p. 144

Stories abound of the altruistic behavior of one species toward another, often with no gain for itself.

Bottlenose dolphins may act as guides to help stranded whales (inset) back out to sea.

Altruistic behavior benefits another animal (the recipient) at the expense of the animal exhibiting that behavior (the donor). Such behavior is mostly limited to cases in which the recipient is related to the donor. Examples include parents risking their lives to save their offspring, as when birds lure predators away from their nests; non-reproducing females helping to rear a sibling's offspring, which occurs in many mammal and bird species; and members of a herd attempting to assist one of their company, as when elephants try to lift a fallen colleague to its feet. This form of altruism is known as kin altruism. In reciprocal altruism, by contrast, a donor offers assistance to a recipient in the hope that it will in turn be assisted by the recipient at some point in the future.

The stimulus for kin altruism can be explained by natural selection: The recipient possesses a proportion of its donor's genes, and so by helping the recipient to survive, and go on to reproduce, the donor is ensuring the perpetuation of some of its own genes. Reciprocal altruism is a riskier concept, since the recipient may fail to return the favor to the donor. Thus, it would be natural to expect that, as with kin altruism, some genetic affinity should exist between donor and recipient for reciprocal altruism to function effectively.

There are, however, many extraordinary cases of apparent altruism featuring entirely unrelated individuals as donor and recipient. Moreover, in these cases there is clearly little if any prospect that the donor's altruism will ever be reciprocated by the recipient. So why does such behavior occur? Is it possible that these animals are exhibiting a trait traditionally deemed to be uniquely human, which is perhaps best described as selfless compassion?

THE STUFF OF LEGEND

Stories of dolphins coming to the rescue of human beings date from the days of the ancient Greeks. One of these involved Arion, musician at the court of the King of Corinth, who traveled to Sicily to enter a singing contest. He won the contest and set sail for home with his prize of a small fortune. The sailors on board, however, decided to kill him and keep the treasure for themselves, so they threw him overboard. But his beautiful singing had attracted the attention of a school of dolphins who carried him on their backs safely to Corinth.

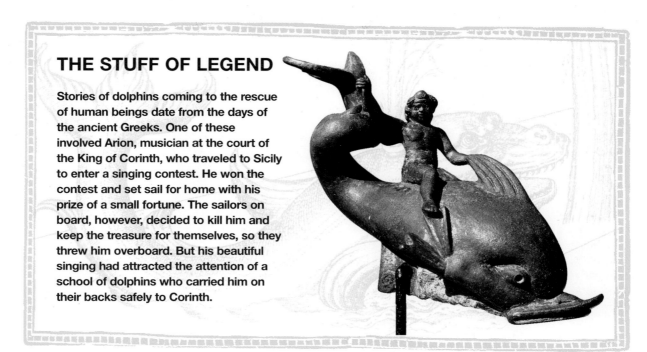

Dolphins to the rescue

Epimelesis is the rescue of one animal by another. There are numerous cases of epimelesis in which the boundary between dispassionate reciprocal altruism and genuine compassion appears blurred. Some of these involve wild animals, especially dolphins. Dolphins are famous for coming to the assistance of others belonging to their own species, but have also been known to rescue individuals of different species, including humans.

Dolphins were on hand in September 1983 when a team of human rescuers was trying to rescue a pod of 80 pilot whales stranded on New Zealand's Tokerau Beach. Herds or pods of pilot whales regularly become stranded, possibly due to a region's geomagnetic forces confusing the whales' navigational systems. Human rescuers frequently free the whales and guide them back out to sea. On this occasion, they received some unexpected assistance from a school of dolphins that had been swimming nearby.

Although the humans had successfully freed most of the whales, they seemed unable to navigate back out to sea. The dolphins came right up to the shore edge, swam among the disoriented whales, and began leading them out into the open sea, continuing to guide them until all of the rescued whales were well away from the shore. Back in 1978, a similar event had occurred in New Zealand's Whangarei Harbor, with human observers in a helicopter monitoring a pod of released pilot whales as they were led for several miles out to the safety of the open sea by their dolphin rescuers.

Even more difficult to explain as unemotional reciprocal altruism are confirmed cases in which dolphins have come to the aid of human swimmers. In July 1996, British diver Martin Richardson and his friends were swimming with some dolphins in the Red Sea when Richardson became separated from the others and was attacked by a shark, which bit him several times. During Richardson's recovery in an Egyptian hospital, his friends told him that he owed his life to the dolphins. They had formed a protective circle around him and had scared away the shark, keeping it at bay until his friends arrived in a boat to rescue him.

A few months later, film-maker Bertrand Loyer revealed that he had experienced a similar rescue while filming in Tahiti's Rangiroa atoll. He had been following a bottlenose dolphin underwater when a 10-foot (3 m)-long white-tipped shark swam headlong toward him. But when the shark was less than a few feet away, it suddenly turned to one side, and Loyer noticed two bottlenoses swimming down toward him. They proceeded to tease the shark, swimming around it so that it couldn't move, before briefly departing, only to return with a third bottlenose. This third dolphin in turn departed, but came back with two more bottlenoses and a spinner dolphin. Challenged now by six dolphins weaving around it and whacking it with a tail, the shark sank into the depths, enabling Loyer to rise to the surface, followed by his rescuers.

On April 17, 1997, an exhausted Doris Svorinic was lifted to the surface of the shark-infested sea off Garvies Beach near Durban, South Africa, by a

Dolphins are one of the species most commonly associated with helping humans – as well as other marine animals – in distress.

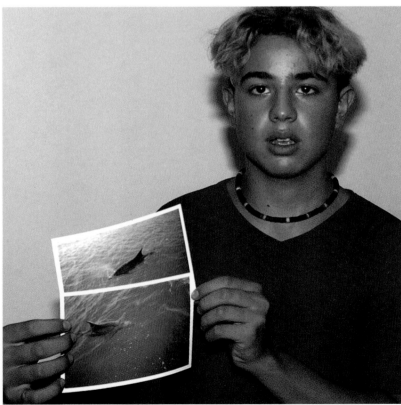

Teenager Davide Cece was rescued by a dolphin known as Filippo when he fell from a boat off the Italian coast.

team of five dolphins, who carried her back to shore. But perhaps most poignant of all is the report of a dolphin that carried the drowned body of Egyptian swimmer Sami Antar through the sea until it encountered some fishermen 135 miles (217 km) northeast of Cairo, whereupon it deposited Antar's body on the beach close to them before swimming away.

This may have been an example of displaced maternal behavior. There are several cases of female dolphins carrying a stillborn offspring for days, sometimes even after it had begun to decompose, before abandoning it. Dolphin expert Mark Simmonds has suggested that dolphins may rescue humans from sharks because they deem humans to be natural allies against a common shark enemy. It may be that they save humans from drowning because they consider human divers to be part of their own tribe. If that is true, perhaps this behavior should be thought of not as reciprocal altruism but as kin altruism instead. Or is it truly an example of compassion between species?

On January 31, 1999, swimmer Charlene Camburn became lost and chilled while swimming with her family off the coast of Lincolnshire. Suddenly, a herd of mammals appeared and swam all around her; they were not dolphins but seals. By surrounding her, they prevented her from drifting further astray, enabling two lifeboat crews to find her. Simon Foster, curator of marine mammals at the Scarborough Sea Life Centre, later stated that this was the first instance of seals protecting a human swimmer that he had ever encountered. He suggested that their action may have been accidental. The seals' inquisitive nature may have caused them to swim close to her and give the impression of protecting her. Camburn, though, has no doubt that they purposefully saved her.

Caring cows and heroic hippos

Sea creatures aren't the only ones to have rescued a human in dramatic circumstances. In August 1996, farmer Donald Mottram of Carmarthen, in south Wales, was so badly gored by a bull in a field containing his herd of cows that he was left unconscious for over an hour. When he awoke, he discovered that his cows had come to his rescue, safeguarding him from the threatening bull by forming a protective circle around him.

One of the most remarkable sequences of animal photos ever published appeared in *African Wildlife* in 1971. They depict an extraordinary episode of heroic endeavor and tragedy. Taken by wildlife photographer D. D. Reucassel in the Kruger National Park, they began with the sudden emergence from a waterhole of a large crocodile, which seized one of the impalas drinking there and tried to drag the antelope underwater. Before it could do so, however, a hippopotamus appeared and charged at the crocodile with such force that the startled reptile dropped the impala and sank back into the water. Then, to Reucassel's amazement, and recorded by his still-clicking camera, the hippo gently picked up the wounded impala in its jaws and stood it upright on its legs. The impala was too gravely injured, however, and soon collapsed. Yet instead of abandoning it, the hippo lifted its head onto its snout and seemed to breathe into the dying impala's mouth, as if attempting to resuscitate it. It was in vain. The hippo, however, remained by the impala's body for at least a quarter of an hour before departing.

Gored by a bull, Donald Mottram was protected for more than an hour by his herd of cows.

CHAPTER ELEVEN

ANIMALS AS HEALERS

One of the most incredible facets of animal behavior is their capacity for self-healing. Like humans, animals appear to treat themselves with all manner of medicinal plants. Also like humans, they are known to abuse certain substances – the sight of birds drunk on fermented fruit is not uncommon. Some healing techniques, such as fire-bathing by birds, are amazing enigmas. And the therapeutic effects of animals on humans, including benefits for sick or disabled children who swim with dolphins, remain nearly as mystifying as they are marvelous.

Animal Herbalists

see also:
● Refined Taste, p.31
● Parasitism, p.165
● Brood Parasitism, p.170

Mammals and birds may make use of the therapeutic qualities of plants, in much the same way as humans do.

A chimpanzee prepares aloe leaves to apply to the skin on the underside of its foot. The plant contains a soothing gel.

Zoologists have recently been startled to discover that a surprising number of animals actively use medicinal plants and other therapeutic substances for a wide range of purposes, including regulating fertility and inducing labor.

Primate pharmacologists

Perhaps the most famous example of an animal herbalist is the common chimpanzee (*Pan troglodytes*). Those living in Tanzania's Gombe National Park are often seen pulling leaves off any of three species of *Aspilia*, a genus of bushy plant related to the sunflower. Instead of simply chewing the leaves, the apes roll them around their mouths for a while, rather like humans sucking medicinal pills, before swallowing them whole.

Humans living in this area do precisely the same with *Aspilia* leaves (which taste far too unpleasant to chew, anyway), as they are effective in killing harmful bacteria and fungi because they contain thiarubine A, a powerful antibiotic. They also rid the intestinal tract of parasitic nematodes. In addition, scientists believe that these leaves act as a stimulant for the chimps, since they tend to eat them first thing in the morning, just as humans often drink coffee or tea shortly after waking to benefit from the stimulating effect of caffeine.

Another herbal remedy employed by Tanzanian chimps is the bitter-tasting pith of the aptly named bitterleaf shrub (*Vernonia amygdalina*). This is popularly used by native tribes to counter both parasites and stomach pains, and has been proven to help the recovery of sick chimps.

Dr. Joan Garey from New York's Mount Sinai School of Medicine has also observed these chimps eating leaves from certain *Ziziphus* (jujub) and *Combretum* species, which are used by the local women to induce abortions. Consequently, in a paper presented at the annual meeting of the American Society of Primatologists in 1997, Garey speculated that the chimps may use these plants deliberately for the same purpose, as a means of reducing the size of the local chimp population if it has become too large.

Certain African monkeys are accomplished herbalists, too. Baboons, for instance, cure parasitic infections caused by *Schistosoma* flukes by eating the fruit of the *Balanites* tree. They also eat leaves from the Sodom apple (*Solanum incanum*) to halt bouts of diarrhea. And the leaves of the candelabra tree (*Cassia*) are much sought after by menstruating baboons to bring relief from menstrual cramps.

Comparable medicinal feats have been recorded among vervet (green) monkeys, Zanzibar red colobuses, and various Madagascan lemurs. As discovered during the late 1990s by Dr. Thomas Struhsaker and fellow researchers from North Carolina's Duke University, the Zanzibar red

Menstruating baboons chew the leaves of the candelabra tree. The leaves are believed to have analgesic properties, bringing relief from pain and cramps.

colobus (*Colobus kirkii*) eats charcoal in the wild, making it the only primate species other than humans to do so. The reason for its daily – and very enthusiastic – charcoal intake (which it obtains by stealing charcoal from human charcoal burners) is that the substance is effective in removing harmful toxins such as phenols from the protein-rich leaves of the mango (*Mangifera indica*) and almond (*Terminalia catappa*) upon which it feeds. These substances would otherwise have a harmful effect on the functioning of the monkey's digestive system.

In the New World, female woolly spider monkeys (*Brachyteles arachnoides*) from Brazil appear to intentionally consume certain plants that affect fertility. Wisconsin University primatologist Dr. K. Strier has noted that once a female monkey has given birth, she seeks out certain leaves that contain isoflavonoids, estrogen-like compounds that reduce fertility. Conversely, when ready to have offspring, females appear to eat more of a particular legume nicknamed the monkey ear, which produces a steroid believed to enhance fertility. Researchers are still not sure whether this is just a coincidence or a deliberate choice.

Even more remarkable, studies in the 1990s by zoologist Dr. K. Glander of Duke University suggest that females of South America's mantled howler monkey (*Alouatta palliata*) may be actively employing pharmacological methods to determine the sex of their offspring. Glander noticed that the sex of a given female's offspring seemed to be directly related to the plants she had been eating at the time of mating. And the plants in turn controlled the electrical conditions

present in the female's reproductive tract, either attracting or repelling those sperm carrying the male sex (Y) chromosome, which are believed to possess different electrical charges from those sperm carrying the female sex (X) chromosome.

Medicine and birds

Birds are experienced herbalists, too. Eagles and various other birds of prey keep parasitic insects out of their nests by adding aromatic leaves that act as efficient insecticides. Macaws in South America are adept at neutralizing the toxins present in their diet simply by eating kaolin from riverbank clay before beginning to look for food. This medicinal technique is also practiced by humans in the area: The local Indians eat kaolin since it enables them to consume with relative impunity the wild potatoes whose poisons would otherwise give them severe gastric problems.

During an outbreak of malaria in Calcutta during 1998, Dr. Sudhim Sengupta and fellow scientists at Calcutta's Center for Nature Conservation and Human

Green-winged macaws and scarlet macaws eat the riverbank soil for the kaolin it contains. This neutralizes potentially harmful substances in their food.

The mantled howler monkey may be using plants to influence the gender of its offspring.

Survival were surprised to witness house sparrows lining their nests with (and also eating) leaves from the paradise flower tree (*Caesalpina pulcherrima*), a species whose leaves are rich in the anti-malarial drug quinine. Confirming that their choice of leaves was deliberate, the sparrows swiftly gathered fresh leaves of this same species when the scientists removed those already lining their nests. Moreover, before the malaria outbreak, these birds had been using leaves from the neem tree (*Azadirachta indica*) for nest lining. These contain high concentrations of insect-repellent compounds, which are of great benefit to birds
rearing

The leaves of the paradise flower tree are a good source of quinine, which sparrows have been seen to eat during an outbreak of malaria.

After spending almost a year observing the unchanging daily feeding ritual of this particular animal, ecologist H. T. Dublin was puzzled one day when the elephant wandered much farther afield than usual, not feeding until she came upon a small tree belonging to a species related to borage that she had never been seen by Dublin to include in her diet before. Watched by Dublin, the elephant almost entirely devoured the tree, until only its stump remained.

Four days later, she gave birth to a healthy calf, and investigations by Dublin revealed that tea made from the leaves and bark of this particular species of tree seemed to induce uterine contractions, since it was often drunk by Kenyan women specifically to induce labor or abortion.

ANIMAL PROFILE

Vitamin D and Rabbit Ears

Even rabbits have a therapeutic trick or two – in their case, behind the ears. Mammals need vitamin D – which works with calcium to make healthy bones – in order to prevent such problems as fractures, as well as to keep diseases such as rickets at bay. It is well known that in mammals this vitamin is synthesized when the skin is exposed to sunlight. As noted by John Downer in *SuperNatural* (1999), rabbits put this principle to good medicinal use when they wash behind their ears with their paws. The oil on the outer surface of the rabbits' extra-long ears contains a chemical that transforms into vitamin D when there is enough sunlight. And when rabbits lick their paws after washing behind their ears, they transfer this vitamin supply to their mouths and, therefore, into their digestive system.

Elephants may eat the bark of the red seringa tree to induce labor.

nestlings, who are vulnerable to diseases spread by insects and to nest-dwelling parasitic insects.

Similarly, in 2000 Dr. Helga Gwinner and a team of researchers from the Ornithological Unit of Germany's Max Planck Society revealed that starlings (*Sturnus vulgaris*) lined their nests with herbs that ward off or kill nest parasites, such as fleas, lice, and mites. Experiments in which some nestlings were reared in nests lacking these herbs (and in which parasites therefore thrived) showed that these nestlings were anemic; nestlings reared in herb-lined nests were heavier and had stronger immune systems, as confirmed by the presence of greater quantities of infection-fighting cells in their blood.

An elephantine labor

One of the most extraordinary recent case histories featuring what would seem to be a bona fide example of an animal herbalist concerned a pregnant female elephant in Kenya's Tsavo Park.

Animal Intoxication

see also:
- Extreme Endurance, p.110
- Animal Humor, p.198
- Animal Herbalists, p.214

Many members of the animal kingdom have been known to overindulge in the consumption of alcohol and other toxins.

Humans are not the only animals to abuse certain herbal and other botanical derivatives (notably alcohol), and to suffer from a variety of unfortunate behavioral consequences afterward.

Falling for fruit

The overenthusiastic consumption of fermented apples and other fruit results in the frequently reported spectacle of flocks of heavily inebriated birds. They become unable to fly – and sometimes even to stand – as their brains and sensory systems struggle to overcome the intoxicating effects of these potent juices. In November 1997, a flock of cedar waxwings (*Bombycilla cedrorum*) indulged heavily in the fermented berries on a tree in a shopping area of Iowa City. They became so drunk that 40 were later found unconscious on the ground beneath the tree, with another 30 perching on its branches in an unsteady fashion. Several more had died after flying headlong into nearby shop windows.

Cedar waxwings eat the berries of the mountain ash. These birds have been recorded as becoming drunk on the juice of fermented apples.

Nor are intoxicated birds the only winged inebriates. While conducting a butterfly survey in 1994, S. A. Senadhi from the Society for Environmental Education in Sri Lanka encountered a considerable number of drunken butterflies on and around a berry-yielding plant known as the elephant's trunk (*Heliotropium indicum*). Dew on the berries had fermented, yielding a highly intoxicating brew that rendered the sampling butterflies incapable of flying and therefore unable to leave the plant for several days. Those that had attempted to depart had succeeded only in damaging their wings; others, however, were exceedingly unsteady and could not be incited to move away, even when disturbed by human observers.

Some species of butterfly drink the fermented dew of certain plants and become incapable of flying away from the plant, sometimes for days.

Trouble brewing

Inevitably, perhaps, some mammals are not satisfied with nature's own alcoholic offerings, but go in search of more refined – and potent – manmade versions. In parts of India, wild elephants are greatly feared due to their violent searches for distilled alcohol, and even more so for their ferocious drunken rampages afterward. At Christmas 1997 a herd of approximately 25 elephants charged down from the Himalayan foothills and invaded the

Bangladeshi village of Dighakon, seemingly for the express purpose of raiding the village's liquor supply, the Gara tribe's distillery. After guzzling its yield, the elephants demolished the entire village, flattening every hut and forcing the homeless villagers to flee for their lives.

Similarly, for several years the Customs and Excise Department's laboratory in New Delhi, India, was regularly raided by a troop of seven alcoholic monkeys eagerly seeking bottles of illegal, confiscated moonshine and medicinal alcohol. The monkeys trashed the laboratory afterward, despite vain attempts by security guards to prevent them from entering.

Webs of corruption

Those who believe that stimulants and other addictive drugs have no harmful effects should perhaps look at the corrupting influence that these substances have on the web-spinning abilities of the common house spider. In 1995 a team of NASA scientists did just this, giving spiders various familiar drugs. Spiders fed on caffeine almost entirely lost their web-spinning ability, and were capable only of stringing together a few threads at random. Those fed on marijuana fared a little better, starting off quite efficiently, but losing concentration halfway through and producing only a partially complete web. Fittingly, those specimens

Elephants in India are renowned for their drunken binges and have been known to destroy whole villages in the course of a spree.

WEB DESIGN

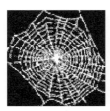
Normal Web

Marijuana

Benzedrine

Caffeine

Chloral Hydrate

When spiders are fed various drugs and stimulants, their ability to weave webs is reduced. Both the speed with which the web is finished and the design of the web are affected.

ANIMAL PROFILE

A Sobering Discovery

Many birds that consume fermented fruit duly suffer from the after-effects of alcohol abuse. Starlings (*Sturnus vulgaris*), however, seem immune to them, remaining surprisingly sober. The secret behind this phenomenon was revealed during the late 1990s by researchers Dr. Ghassem Hakimi and Dr. Roland Prinzinger at Frankfurt University in Germany.

They discovered that starlings were able to metabolize alcohol at an exceptional speed, due to the rate of activity of the alcohol-splitting enzyme alcoholdehydrogenase, which is 14 times greater in starlings than in humans. This means that the birds can indulge themselves on fermented fruit without getting drunk, since the alcohol is broken down quickly.

fed on "speed" (benzedrine) did indeed produce their webs very quickly, but without much planning, so that the result was very haphazard and full of holes. As for those fed on chloral hydrate, an ingredient in sleeping pills, very little in the way of webs was produced for the simple reason that the spiders fell asleep early in their weaving.

Scientists are hoping to use the results of this web-building experiment to devise a computer model to predict the toxicity of new medicines.

The catnip response

It is well known that many (but not all) domestic cats, and even some wild species, including lions, pumas, and bobcats, react in a bizarre manner in the presence of the plant known as catnip or catmint (*Nepeta cataria*). The cat enters a frenzied state of ecstasy outwardly recalling a drug "trip."

After first sniffing the plant, the cat begins, with ever-increasing fervor, to lick, bite (but not eat), and rub itself against the plant, purring or growling loudly as it rolls animatedly all over it. It also jumps up into the air as the minutes pass and the "trip" intensifies. After about ten minutes, however, this extraordinary behavior comes to an end, and the cat reverts to normal, without apparently suffering any lingering or harmful effects.

But what is responsible for the catnip's drug-like influence on cats? The answer would appear to be a compound called nepetalactone, present in the plant's leaves and stem. Researchers once thought that it exerted this effect because it was a feline aphrodisiac, since the rolling behavior of cats when in its presence is similar to that of female cats in heat. However, as revealed by Dr. Desmond Morris in his encyclopedic *Cat World* (1997), cats of both sexes respond in this same manner when exposed to catnip, as do neutered or spayed cats.

Instead, catnip seems to function as an ecstasy-inducing drug. And it is not alone in this respect. Certain other plants, notably valerian (*Valeriana officinalis*), have this same intense effect on cats. Ironically, however, when catnip (or valerian) extract is given to the animals internally, it no longer acts as a stimulant, but rather as a tranquilizer, having a very soothing effect upon the feline nervous system. Indeed, circus trainers sometimes use this herbal influence to keep big cats placid when performing in the ring.

The catnip response is not learned but is genetically inherited. Just under 50 percent of cats do not exhibit it. Of those that do, the response does not show itself until the cat is three months old; before then, it avoids catnip.

Anting

see also:
- Exotic Senses, p.38
- Hibernation, p.100
- Parasitism, p.165

Ritual "bathing" using ants, and even smoke and fire, is among the strangest and most controversial activities undertaken by birds.

Although the bizarre activity known as anting has been reported for many years and has even been formally observed in recent times by scientists, it is among the most mystifying behavioral phenomena on record, and its functions remain hotly debated. During anting, birds either rub ants against their skin or make the tiny insects crawl all over them.

More than 250 species of bird have been recorded anting. The vast majority of these are passerines (perching birds), but also included are various gallinaceous species, such as pheasants and turkeys. Parrots, woodpeckers, and even the great horned owl (*Bubo virginianus*) are on record as practicing anting.

There are two major categories of anting: direct and indirect. Direct anting is the commonest form, and is most frequently observed among starlings, babblers, tanagers, and weaver birds. In direct anting, the bird picks up a living ant in its beak and wipes it under the flight feathers on each of its extended wings, usually beginning with the left, and – strangely – often devoting more anting time to its left wing than to its right. A different ant is used for each wing, the bird eating or discarding the old one before picking up a new one. During this process, the bird quivers and shakes, and some researchers believe that it derives a pleasurable, even autoerotic, sensation from feeling the formic acid secreted by the ant against its skin. Curiously, some individual birds seem almost addicted to anting, whereas others of the same species hardly ever perform this ritual. Researchers are not sure why this is so.

Indirect anting, also called ant-bathing, is most often recorded among crows (especially jays), thrushes, and waxbills. The bird sits near a colony of ants, extends its wings into a throng of these insects, and allows them to crawl up its wings and

Birds are reported to derive visible pleasure from the process of anting.

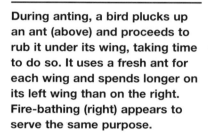

During anting, a bird plucks up an ant (above) and proceeds to rub it under its wing, taking time to do so. It uses a fresh ant for each wing and spends longer on its left wing than on the right. Fire-bathing (right) appears to serve the same purpose.

onto its body and head. Once again, the bird visibly trembles and shivers during this procedure, apparently deriving pleasure from it.

At least 25 different species of ant are documented as having been used by birds in anting. Occasionally other insects are used, too. And, in 1997, Pat Morris of High Wycombe in Buckinghamshire, England, reported seeing a robin performing direct anting using a small arthropod rather than an insect, identified by ornithologist Chris Mead as a millipede.

Why do birds ant?

Many theories have been proposed to explain anting, though none has been universally accepted so far. One theory is that its function is to eliminate ectoparasites from the bird's skin (by utilizing the insecticidal properties of the formic acid released by the ant). Another suggestion is that it offers the bird solace from the pain induced by its feathers' growth and replacement. Certain researchers believe it provides a means for the bird to tone its feathers (though why, if this is true, it should prefer to tone the feathers of its left wing

more than its right remains unresolved). Others claim that it is just a way of inducing pleasurable sensations. It has even been suggested that anting is a means of removing unpleasant liquids from the body of the ants before the bird eats them.

Bathed in smoke and fire

Smoke-bathing is very similar in appearance and effect to anting, but the birds use smoke rather than ants. Most commonly, one or more starlings or crows perch at the top of a chimney that is belching out smoke, with their wings extended over the smoke, quivering in the same manner as recorded with birds who are anting. They will even try to pluck a plume of smoke out of the cloud issuing from the chimney, and place it under each of their wings in turn. As with true anting, again they show a marked preference for their left wing.

A much more dramatic version of smoke-bathing is fire-bathing, in which a bird actually extends its wings over burning straw. Birds have even been known to ant with a lighted cigarette end. In his fascinating book *Phoenix Re-Born* (1959) – the definitive treatment of anting, and smoke-

The explanations on offer include those usually put forward to explain anting. In addition, however, self-anointing may be a means for the hedgehog to fool potential predators by disguising its body odor, or it may have a currently undefined function linked to mating or pre-mating. The latter theory has been put forward because hedgehogs self-anoint only during the breeding season.

In 1998, reptiles were shown to carry out anting. Carleton University researcher Dr. Dean McCurdy and his Acadia University colleague Dr. Thomas Herman reported seeing a North American wood turtle (*Clemmys insculpta*) – actually a species of freshwater tortoise – bathing on top of an ant mound. The turtle permitted the ants to crawl all over its body, with no apparent ill effects. The Canadian researchers speculated that this activity may be beneficial to all concerned: the turtle, because it would free itself of parasites such as leeches and gain some protection against future infestation from the formic acid that the ants secreted onto its skin; and the ants, because they would feed on the leeches.

The closest mammalian equivalent to anting is self-anointing, undertaken by hedgehogs using saliva impregnated with a strong scent.

and fire-bathing – zoologist Dr. Maurice Burton reported that one of his pets, a tame rook called Niger, enthusiastically fire-bathed over some burning straw. He performed characteristic anting movements with wild excitement, and snatched at the flames with his beak, yet deftly avoided burning his feathers or injuring himself in any way. Struck by the familiarity of this extraordinary scene, Burton speculated that similar sights long ago may have inspired the phoenix legend. As with anting, the function of such bizarre behavior remains, for the time being, unclear.

Mammalian and reptilian "anting"

Anting has recently been shown to be carried out by species other than birds. Self-anointing, which is performed by hedgehogs, is a mammalian equivalent of anting. Upon encountering an object with a strong scent, a hedgehog will continually lick it until it has built up a sizable amount of saliva in its mouth. It then throws its head on its side, twists its body, and uses its tongue to place this salivary froth either onto its back or its flank.

It repeats this entire procedure several times, until it has coated much of its spiny body in saliva. As with anting, during this process (which can last more than 20 minutes) the hedgehog enters a visibly ecstatic state, seemingly deriving considerable pleasure from it.

ANIMAL PROFILE

Lemurs

Although commonly considered to be an exclusively avian activity, anting has recently been observed in lemurs. In 1999, Christopher Birkinshaw from the Madagascar Research and Conservation Program reported watching on several occasions a female black lemur (*Eulemur macao*) pick up and bite a millipede, then rub its injured body over her fur. Because the wounded millipede would secrete a range of toxic liquids, this activity may serve to protect the lemur from unwanted parasites.

Therapeutic Animals

see also:
- Psychic Animals, p.192
- Animal Fidelity, p.205
- Dolphin Healing, p.229

The phenomenon of pets assisting in the recovery of hospitalized patients is both well known and widely investigated. Their mere presence seems to exert a soothing, benevolent effect upon their owners. Pets can help reduce high blood pressure, depression, and several other debilitating conditions. Less well known or understood, however, is the fact that some pets also display the extraordinary ability to sense impending epileptic seizures or diabetic comas in their owners, often long before the latter are aware that such an emergency is imminent.

Sensing impending illnesses

In January 1992, Reina Berner, executive director of the Epilepsy Institute in New York, organized a television program dealing with fully verified medical cases featuring epilepsy-prescient dogs and their owners. One case presented in the program involved Seattle veterinary surgeon Elizabeth Rudy, who has epilepsy, and Sally, her pet golden retriever. Whenever Elizabeth is about to have a seizure at home, Sally promptly comes up to her and sits in front of her, staring at her, whining, and licking her hands.

Moreover, Sally accompanies Elizabeth everywhere outdoors, and whenever she senses that her owner is about to have a seizure, Sally immediately stops walking and puts her ears down. This recognizable warning sign permits Elizabeth to prepare herself for the seizure. She can sit down in a safe place and thereby prevent herself from being harmed when the seizure occurs. If, for example, it happened while she was crossing the street in front of traffic, she might be hurt.

Indeed, fear of injuring themselves during a seizure has led some people with epilepsy to become virtually housebound. One such person was a woman named Vicki, who rarely ventured out until she realized that her dog, Harley, could sense when she was about to have an attack. Now, as soon as he senses this, Harley begins to bark frantically, disobeying all commands until Vicki sits down. Vicki is now so secure that Harley will always warn her in time for her to take precautionary measures when she has a seizure that she can finally go for walks outside her apartment. Thanks to Harley, Vicki is starting to rediscover the world.

Not only does having a pet improve health, in some cases pets seem to have given lifesaving warnings to their owners.

Tony Brown-Griffin's collie, Rupert (above), has been trained as a Seizure Alert Dog. He can sense when she is going to have an epileptic fit, as can Chad (left), Richard Beale's golden retriever.

George (right), a schnauzer, proved that dogs can be trained to detect the presence of cancerous cells in the skin, alerting doctor and patient to unsuspected carcinomas.

In the spring of 1993, the *Veterinary Record* in London published the findings of a survey carried out by Andrew Edney, which drew upon accounts obtained from 37 epileptic dog owners. The survey revealed that although none of the dogs involved had ever received any formal training in sensing epileptic seizures in their owners, 21 of them frequently displayed characteristically restless, apprehensive behavior immediately before the onset of such an attack. And once a seizure had begun, 25 of the dogs had tried to attract attention for their owners.

Using these findings, by 1997 a charity called Support Dogs, based in Sheffield, England, had trained a number of pets to recognize impending epileptic seizures in their owners and to respond in a manner that provides them with an unequivocal warning. One dog that was instrumental in the establishment of this pioneering training program was Rupert, a pet border collie belonging to Tony Brown-Griffin, from Tunbridge Wells, Kent, in England, who has epilepsy. Rupert can not only tell when Tony is about to have a seizure, but can actually distinguish between different types of seizure. Consequently, if he senses that Tony will shortly have an absence seizure, some three to five minutes before it takes place Rupert stops whatever he is doing and comes to sit at her feet. And up to 45 minutes before Tony experiences a grand mal seizure, Rupert begins to bark in a distinctive, urgent manner.

How do they do it?

The British Epilepsy Association believes that epilepsy-prescient dogs such as these are sensing two very subtle clues to impending epilepsy attacks. One is a high-pitched sound emitted by epileptics up to half an hour before an attack takes place, which is thought to be linked to the abnormal electrical impulses in the brain that occur prior to a seizure. The other is an exceedingly faint odor emitted by epileptics at about the same time as the sound, whose origin is as yet unexplained.

Both clues cannot be detected by humans, but can be discerned by the dogs' more acute senses of hearing and smell.

Detecting diabetes

Equally astonishing, and significant, is the ability of some pets to recognize when their diabetic owners are about to slip into a coma due to hypoglycemia, a sudden fall in their blood sugar level. Once again, such pets are able to warn their owners in good time; the owner can then take steps to prevent the coma by having a sugary snack or a soft drink in order to elevate their blood sugar to a safe level. One of the problems associated with hypoglycemia is that at the stage immediately prior to slipping into a coma, diabetics are usually confused, because the brain is starved of glucose. For this reason, they are often unaware of the danger; this makes a pet that can alert them to it so valuable.

As yet, it is not known precisely how pets can sense an impending diabetic coma in their owners. Small pets that are being held by their owners when a coma is about to begin may well be responding to temperature changes. These often occur at this time, causing diabetics to become pale, with clammy perspiration on their hands and face.

Cancer-sniffing dogs

In the course of some bibliographical research during the early 1990s, Dr. Armand Cognetta, a dermatologist based in Florida, was surprised to discover in the medical literature a number of confirmed cases in which patients had been found to possess hitherto-unsuspected skin cancers that were detected after their pet dogs (usually for several months before the diagnosis) had been compulsively sniffing the area of skin containing

ANIMAL PROFILE

Helper Dogs

Dogs can be trained to play life-saving roles in the lives of their owners. In addition to alerting an owner to an imminent epileptic seizure or diabetic coma, some species can be trained to respond to the phone. This border collie can pick up the telephone receiver for its disabled owner.

the malignancy. Indeed, in each case it had been the behavior of the dog that had finally prompted the owner to seek medical advice in order to find out why their pet was acting so strangely.

Anxious to test this remarkable ability for himself, Cognetta enlisted the help of a retired police dog handler, Duane Pickel, and his dog, George, a schnauzer. After Cognetta had trained him to recognize cancers by smell using stored melanoma samples, George was able to walk up to a patient with a melanoma, and, after sniffing him to detect the melanoma's presence, accurately place his paw on the growth. On one occasion, however, George repeated his performance with a man called James Garafolo, placing his paw upon one particular mole, even though it was supposedly benign. Taking no chances, Garafolo promptly had the mole removed, and when it was examined it was found to contain potentially lethal cancer cells, whose presence had not previously been suspected.

For the good of your health

Far from being unproven hearsay, the fact that keeping a pet is good for you is supported by results obtained from medical research. For

"Pet therapy," whereby pets are used to speed the recovery of hospital patients, is practiced in about 100 hospitals in the United States, including the Loma Linda University Medical Center in California.

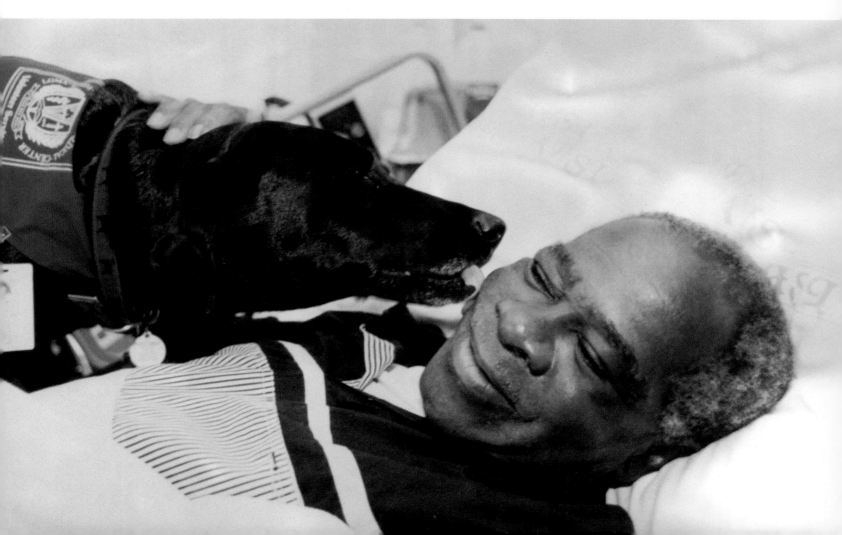

ANIMAL PROFILE

Therapeutic Snakes

One of the most unusual examples of the healing powers of animals features Leeds teenager Daniel Kelby and his pet snakes, Frosty, Fang, and Khan. Belonging to a harmless, North American species called the corn snake, this trio is used to being handled by Daniel. This proved vital to his recovery when he suffered traumatic injuries in May 1999 after falling 45 feet (15 m) through a roof skylight while playing with friends. After coming out of a 12-day coma, he was unable to coordinate movements in his left hand and arm, until he asked his occupational therapist, Sara Hewston, if he could see his snakes. She agreed, and the snakes were brought in to the hospital. Once Daniel started handling them, everyone was surprised to discover that his coordination rapidly began to improve. This improvement was reflected in his rehabilitation exercises, and continued after he returned home, where he regularly plays with his snakes using his injured arm and hand. Clearly, Daniel's physical coordination and mental motivation were both stimulated by his interaction with his animals, offering yet another instance of the unexpected therapeutic effects exerted by pets upon their owners.

instance, a study conducted during the early 1990s by researcher Warwick Anderson at the Baker Medical Research Institute in Prahran, Australia, involved questioning 5,741 patients attending a heart-disease risk clinic. The results revealed that the average cholesterol level of the 784 pet-owning patients was 2 percent lower than that of the non-pet owners. This in turn may lower the risk of heart attack by 4 percent. The pet owners also had lower blood levels of triglyceride fats and lower blood pressure.

In clinical terms, therefore, keeping a pet can be looked upon as being as efficient in reducing blood pressure as changing to a low-salt diet or reducing alcohol intake. Further studies in Australia revealed that cat owners visit their doctor 12 percent less frequently than non-cat owners, and an 8 percent reduction in visits to their doctor was recorded in dog owners in comparison with non-dog owners.

Clinical trials have proven that cat owners are less likely to visit the doctor than dog owners and visit much less than non-pet owners.

Dolphin Healing

see also:
- Ultrasonic Hearing, p. 22
- Animal Rescuers, p. 208
- Therapeutic Animals, p. 225

Swimming with dolphins has led to great progress in children with speech and other problems.

Some of the most dramatic, inspirational, and wholly perplexing cases of animals healing humans feature dolphins, as well as, in one case, shoals of tiny fishes.

One of the first centers to investigate swimming with dolphins as a method of therapeutic treatment was the Dolphin Research Center in Florida, run by Dr. David Nathanson, a psychologist. During the late 1980s, his studies into the effects of

In between sessions of speech therapy, Rebecca (above) plays with the dolphin Spunky. The methods used at this center in Key Largo, Florida, were pioneered by American neuropsychiatrist Dr. David Nathanson (right).

interaction between children with special needs and dolphins showed that the children's ability to communicate improved dramatically if they were motivated to succeed by the reward of swimming with the dolphins after a training session.

In January 1995, Key Largo's Dolphin–Human Therapy Center was opened to continue Nathanson's work, with encouraging results: 90 percent of the families who tried the therapy returned for more. In early July 1995, six-year-old

Daniel Ryder from Aberdeen, Scotland, arrived at the center, in the hope that its special mode of therapy would achieve a breakthrough where more traditional forms had failed. At the time, Daniel had hardly spoken; he said just a few half-formed words, plus "mama" and "dadda," and had been considered by his Scottish doctors to be "mentally handicapped with a touch of autism."

Within the first 15 minutes of speech therapy (which took place in the water with a bottlenose dolphin called Squirt), Daniel spontaneously and clearly spoke the word "yellow" when asked the color of a plastic ring. And when a pelican flew overhead, he pointed to it and said "bird." Daniel's parents were amazed, but for the center's staff it was just further proof of their aquatic helpers' ability to unlock the minds of their young human patients.

As the treatment progressed, each day Daniel greeted Squirt with a wave and a spoken "hello," and Squirt responded by shaking her head or a flipper. And at the end of each successful session,

Daniel's reward was a ride through the water in the arms of his therapist, Deena Hoagland, as she held on firmly to Squirt's dorsal fin.

Dr. Nathanson has a long waiting list of families seeking similar treatment for their children. He also has archives of records confirming that such results are achievable. The official line is more skeptical, however, with the American Psychological Association having refused to endorse the center's therapy until it has seen more research. Nevertheless, some health insurance companies cover the cost of this treatment.

Nathanson believes that the intense, unique sensory experience of such close contact with the dolphins pulls these withdrawn children out of themselves, increasing their self-confidence and encouraging them to explore the world outside their own minds. This reward, he believes, is ample motivation to induce them to communicate. Such contact also seems to trigger the increased secretion by patients' brains of endorphins, so-called happy hormones, which in turn lifts their mood, making them more receptive to communication therapy.

Even patients with physical rather than mental problems, including cancer and AIDS, appear to benefit from dolphin therapy. It has been suggested that in these cases, the pleasure elicited from swimming with dolphins somehow causes the production of a greater number of T-cells. These are vital in maintaining the human immune system, and thereby assist patients in fighting illnesses.

Giving birth with dolphins

In a related therapeutic practice, pregnant women give birth in water in the presence of dolphins. In the mid-1980s, Russian pioneer Igor Charkovsky suggested that women should swim and dive in the months before giving birth in water, and he oversaw several such births afterward. He claimed that the children could walk while still as young as four months, and stay underwater without breathing apparatus for longer than normal. He then extended this experiment by permitting one pregnant volunteer to swim with dolphins in the months before giving birth, and was amazed to discover that the dolphins seemed to recognize her baby boy when she returned with him several months after giving birth. Not only that, but the child actively reached out to the dolphins. Did he recognize them?

Charkovsky speculated that the dolphins may be using ultrasound to make telepathic contact with unborn human fetuses as their pregnant mothers swim. In July 1992, obstetrician Dr. Gowri Motha, a water birth specialist from London's Whipps Cross Hospital, and the French-born therapist Marie Hélène Roussel decided to test this hypothesis by organizing a scheme in which 12 women were to give birth alongside dolphins at Dolphin Reef in Eilat, Israel. They also hoped to learn whether the newborn children would be able to make telepathic contact with the dolphins. However, this plan was not well received, and although six of the 12 women did swim in the reef for several months of their pregnancy, they eventually gave birth – underwater – at Eilat's Yosef Tal Hospital.

Music of the dolphins

A different dolphin-mediated birth aid was used during the 1990s by British researcher Dr. Horace Dobbs. During a project in Scunthorpe, England, he achieved considerable success with new mothers suffering from postpartum depression by playing recordings of dolphin sounds to them. He has also obtained good results using this technique to treat other forms of depression.

ANIMAL PROFILE

Kangal's Fishy Dermatologist

Dolphins are not the only aquatic healers: The healing fishes of Kangal in Anatolia, Turkey, which are only 1-4 inches (2.5-10 cm) long, are also successful in easing human suffering. Their precise zoological identity has yet to be determined, but they seem to be relatives of the carp and are referred to as killifishes. There are three different types, each with a distinct dermatological function. They live in hot sulfurous pools and, each year since 1917, sufferers from psoriasis, a severe skin disorder, have been visiting these pools. For three weeks, they immerse themselves daily for two hours, hoping that the small aquatic inhabitants will heal them.

Once a patient is immersed, the killifishes swim around them and begin their remarkable therapy. One type nibbles away the white psoriasis scabs, the second cleans up the naked red sores, and the third removes any dead skin. Many patients subsequently report dramatic improvements in their skin's condition. In one case, long-standing sufferer Michael Shortt from Belfast, Northern Ireland, underwent a nine-day course of treatment at Kangal in the mid-1990s. When the treatment was over his psoriasis had largely vanished, leaving behind nothing more than a few pale pink marks.

Bibliography

In addition to the numerous scientific papers, magazine articles, and newspaper reports consulted during my preparation of this work, the following books were of particular value, and the works by **Jonathan Downer** are especially recommended.

Alcock, John *Animal Behavior: An Evolutionary Approach* Sinauer Associates, Sunderland, Mass., 6th ed., 1998

Ayensu, Edward S. and Philip Whitfield (eds.) *The Rhythms of Life* Marshall Editions, London, 1981

Baker, Robin (ed.) *The Mystery of Migration: The Story of Nature's Travellers Through the Cycle of the Seasons* Macdonald Futura, London, 1980

Balda, R. P., et al. (eds.) *Animal Cognition in Nature* Academic Press, New York, 1998

Bardens, Dennis *Psychic Animals: An Investigation of Their Secret Powers* Robert Hale, London, 1987

Bekoff, Marc (ed.) *The Smile of a Dolphin: Remarkable Accounts of Animal Emotions* Discovery Books/Cassell & Co, London, 2000

Bone, Q., et al. *Biology of Fishes* Stanley Thornes Ltd, Cheltenham, 2nd ed., 1995

Bright, Michael *Animal Language* British Broadcasting Corporation, London, 1984
——*Unlocking Nature's Secrets: Recent Discoveries From the Natural World* British Broadcasting Corporation, London, 1984
——*The Living World* Robson Books, London, 1987
——*Talking With Animals* Robson Books, London, 1998

Budiansky, Stephen *If A Lion Could Talk: How Animals Think* Weidenfeld & Nicolson, London, 1998

Burton, Maurice *The Sixth Sense of Animals* J. M. Dent & Sons, London, 1973
——*Just Like an Animal* J. M. Dent & Sons, London,1978

Burton, Maurice and Robert Burton *Inside the Animal World: An Encyclopedia of Animal Behaviour* Macmillan, London, London, 1977

Campbell, Bruce and Elisabeth Lack (eds.) *A Dictionary of Birds* T. & A. D. Poyser, Calton, 1985

Chapman, R. F. *The Insects: Structure and Function* Cambridge University Press, Cambridge, 4th ed., 1998

Cloudsley-Thompson, John L. *Predation and Defence Amongst Reptiles* R & A Publishing, Taunton, 1994
——*Biotic Interactions in Arid Lands* Springer-Verlag, New York, 1996
——*The Diversity of Amphibians and Reptiles* Springer-Verlag, New York, 1999

Cochrane, Amanda and Karena Callen *Dolphins and Their Power to Heal* Bloomsbury, London, 1992

Corliss, William R. *Strange Life* The Sourcebook Project, Glen Arm, 1975
——*Incredible Life: A Handbook of Biological Mysteries* The Sourcebook Project, Glen Arm, 1981
——*Science Frontiers: Some Anomalies and Curiosities of Nature* The Sourcebook Project, Glen Arm, 1994
——*Biological Anomalies: Mammals I* The Sourcebook Project, Glen Arm, 1995
——*Biological Anomalies: Mammals II* The Sourcebook Project, Glen Arm, 1996

Daan, Serge and Eberhard Gwinner (eds.) *Biological Clocks and Environmental Time* Guildford Press, New York, 1989

Davenport, John *Animal Life at Low Temperature* Chapman & Hall, London, 1992

Dingle, Hugh *Migration: The Biology of Life on the Move* Oxford University Press, Oxford, 1996

Dobbs, Horace *The Magic of Dolphins* Lutterworth Press, Guildford, 1984

Downer, John *Supersense: Perception in the Animal World*, BBC Books, London, 1988
——*Supernatural: The Unseen Powers of Animals* BBC Worldwide, London, 1999

Dugatkin, Lee A. *Cooperation Among Animals: An Evoltionary Perspective* Oxford University Press, Oxford, 1997

Elphick, Jonathan (ed.) *The Atlas of Bird Migration: Tracing the Great Journeys of the World's Birds* Random House, New York, 1995

Frey, William and Muriel Langseth *Crying, the Mystery of Tears* Harper & Row, New York, 1985

Graham, Bernie *Creature Comfort: Animals That Heal* Simon & Schuster, New York, 1999

Gullan, P. J. and P. S. Cranston *The Insects: An Outline of Entomology* Blackwell Science, London, 2nd ed., 2000

Hauser, Marc *Wild Minds: What Animals Really Think* Allen Lane/Penguin

Press, London, 2000

Hughes, Howard C. *Sensory Exotica: A World Beyond Human Experience* Massachusetts Institute of Technology, Cambridge, Mass., 1999

Laidler, Keith *The Talking Ape* Collins, London, 1980

Linden, Eugene *The Parrot's Lament* Souvenir Press, London, 1999

McElroy, Susan C. *Animals as Teachers and Healers* NewSage Press, New York, 1996

McFarland, David *Animal Behaviour* Prentice Hall, Harlow, 3rd ed., 1999

Masson, Jeffrey *Dogs Never Lie About Love: Reflections on the Emotional World of Dogs* Jonathan Cape, London, 1997

Masson, Jeffrey and Susan McCarthy *When Elephants Weep: The Emotional Lives of Animals* Jonathan Cape, London, 1994

Michell, John and Robert J. M. Rickard *Living Wonders: Mysteries and Curiosities of the Animal World* Thames & Hudson, London, 1982

Morris, Desmond *The Biology of Art: A Study of the Picture-Making Behaviour of the Great Apes and its Relationship to Human Art* Alfred A. Knopf, New York, 1962

——*Animals Days* Jonathan Cape, London, 1979

——*Animalwatching: A Field Guide to Animal Behaviour* Jonathan Cape, London, 1990

Page, George *The Singing Gorilla: Understanding Animal Intelligence* Headline, London, 1999

Papi. F. (ed.) *Animal Homing* Chapman and Hall, London, 1992

Parker, Eric *Oddities of Natural History* Seeley, Service, London, 1943

Parker, Sue Taylor, et al. (eds.) *Self-Awareness in Animals and Humans: Developmental Perspectives* Cambridge University Press, New York, 1995

Payne, Kathy *Silent Thunder: The Hidden Voice of Elephants* Weidenfeld & Nicolson, London, 1998

Pechenik, Jan A. *Biology of the Invertebrates* WCB, Chicago, 3rd ed., 1996

Perry, Nicolette *Symbiosis: Close Encounters of the Natural Kind* Blandford Press, Poole, 1983

Randall, David, et al. *Eckert Animal Physiology: Mechanisms and Adaptations* W.H. Freeman, New York, 4th ed., 1997

Savage-Rumbaugh, Sue and Roger Lewin *Kanzi: The Ape at the Brink of the Human Mind* John Wiley & Sons, New York, 1994

Schmidt-Nielsen, Knut *Animal Physiology: Adaptation and Environment* Cambridge University Press, Cambridge, 5th ed., 1997

Schul, Bill *The Psychic Power of Animals* Fawcett, Greenwich, Conn., 1977

Sheldrake, Rupert *Dogs That Know When Their Owners are Coming Home, and Other Unexplained Powers of Animals* Hutchinson, London, 1999

Shuker, Karl P. N. *Extraordinary Animals Worldwide* Robert Hale, London, 1991

——(Consultant) *Secrets of the Natural World* Reader's Digest, Pleasantville, 1993

——*The Unexplained* Carlton, London, 1996

——*Mysteries of Planet Earth* Carlton, London, 1999

——Chapter 6: A Sense of Disaster in Anna Grayson, et al. *The Earth* Macmillan, London, 2000

Sinclair, Sandra *How Animals See: Other Visions of Our World* Croom Helm, Beckenham, 1985

Skinner, Bob *Toad in the Hole: Source Material on the Entombed Toad Phenomenon* Fortean Times, London, 1986

Souder, William *A Plague of Frogs* Hyperion, New York, 2000

Sparks, John *The Discovery of Animal Behaviour* Collins, London, 1982

Sutton, John *Psychic Pets* Bloomsbury, London, 1997

Tributsch, Helmut *When the Snakes Awake: Animals and Earthquake Prediction* Massachusetts Institute of Technology, Cambridge, Mass., 1982

von Frisch, Karl *The Dancing Bees* Harcourt Brace Jovanovich, New York, 1956

——*The Dance Language and Orientation of Bees* Harvard University Press, Cambridge, Mass., 1967

Wigglesworth, Vincent B. *The Life of Insects* Mentor, New York, 1964

Wood, Gerald L. *Guinness Book of Pet Records* Guinness Superlatives, Enfield, Middlesex, 1984

Wylder, Joseph *Psychic Pets: The Secret World of Animals* J. M. Dent, London, 1980

Index

Acknowledgments

I wish to offer my most sincere thanks to my family for their constant encouragement and support during my preparation of this book; to the many friends, colleagues, and organizations who have so kindly provided me with data and information sources; to **Ellen Dupont**, **Frances Vargo**, and everyone at **Marshall Editions** and **Reader's Digest** for their greatly valued assistance in converting my work into the finished book you see before you; and to my agents **Sheila Watson** and **Amanda Little** of **Watson, Little Ltd** for creating the opportunity for me to enter into what has been a thoroughly fascinating and enjoyable writing project.

AL = Ardea, London Ltd; **BBC** = BBC Natural History Unit Picture Library; **BCC** = Bruce Coleman Collection; **FLPA** = Frank Lane Picture Agency; **FPL** = Fortean Picture Library; **FSP** = Frank Spooner Pictures; **MEPL** = Mary Evans Picture Library; **NHPA** = Natural History Photographic Agency; **NV** = Natural Visions; **OSF** = Oxford Scientific Films; **RF** = Rex Features; **WP** = Warren Photographic.

Key
b bottom; **c** center; **l** left; **r** right; **t** top

1 BCC/Bruce Coleman Inc; 2–3 Digital Vision; 8t NHPA/G.I. Bernard, 8b Digital Vision; 9l FLPA/E.&D. Hosking, 9c BCC /Kim Taylor, 9r WP/Kim Taylor; 10–11 BCC /Joe McDonald; 12b OSF/David Cotteridge; 13t AL/P.Morris, 13b WP/Kim Taylor; 14b OSF/David M. Dennis; 15 BCC/Kim Taylor; 17bl BCC/John Cancalosi; 17br OSF/G.I. Bernard; 18 NV/Peter Herring; 19t OSF/Max Gibbs, 19b OSF/Max Gibbs; 20bl NV/Heather Angel, 20br NV/Heather Angel; 21t OSF/David Tipling, 21b BCC/Jane Burton; 22c NHPA/Brian Hawkes; 22b OSF/John Brown; 23b BCC/Luis C. Marigo; 25b FLPA/Jurgen & Christine Sohns; 26–27 OSF/Okapia, 27t OSF/David Cotteridge; 28b Corbis/Anna Clopet; 29t OSF/G.I. Bernard, 29c WP/Jane Burton; 30l SF/Mantis Wildlife Films/Densye Cryne, 30r BCC/Jane Burton; 31b OSF/Animals Animals/Bates Littlehales; 32 WP/Jane Burton; 33t NV/Heather Angel, 33b NV/Heather Angel; 34b FLPA/D.P.Wilson; 35t BCC/Jane Burton, 35b WP/Jane Burton; 36t WP, 36b Dr. Jeannette Yen; 37 FLPA/David Hosking; 38b Science Photo Library/Martin Dohrn; 39t OSF/Kim Westerkov, 39b OSF/Michael Fogden; 41t BCC/Pacific Stock; 42–43 BCC/Pacific Stock; 44bl OSF/Kathie Atkinson, 44br OSF/Kjell B. Sandved; 45t OSF/David Thompson, 45b NHPA/Eric Soder; 46t BCC/Kim Taylor, 46b OSF/Rudie H. Kniter; 47b NHPA/G.I. Bernard; 48 BCC /Pacific Stock; 49tl NHPA/Stephen Krasemann, 49tc OSF/Survival Anglia/Nick Price, 49tr BCC/Kim Taylor, 49b FLPA/S. Maslowski; 50b NHPA/Dave Watts; 51t FLPA/Roger Tidman, 51b OSF/Animals Animals/Joe McDonald; 52b Corbis/Stephen Frink; 53t NHPA/Norbert Wu, 53b NHPA/B. Jones & M. Shimlock; 54t NV/Heather Angel; 54b BCC/Jane Burton; 55b FLPA/Silvestris; 56 BCC; 57 OSF/Animals Animals/Zig Leszczynski; 58–59b WP/Kim Taylor, 59b OSF/J.A.L. Cooke; 60t Ivan Mackerle, 60b NHPA/Nigel J. Dennis; 61b WP/Jane Burton; 62 Auscape/Jeff Foott; 63l OSF/Daniel Cox; 63r BBC/John Downer; 64b FLPA/Larry West; 65tl OSF/Alastair Shay;

65tr FLPA/F. Merlet, 65b NHPA/James Carmichael Jr.; 66–67 NHPA/Dr. Eckart Pott; 68 image 4 FLPA/John Watkins, 68bl OSF/Survival Anglia/Peter Hawkey; 69t BCC/Dr. Eckart Pott, 69b Photo by Dennis Coutts, Shetland; 70t NHPA/Stephen Krasemann; 71t OSF/Survival Anglia/Maurice Tibbles, 71b OSF/Survival Anglia/Jen & Des Bartlett; 72bl Corbis/Danny Lehman; 73t BCC/Kim Taylor, 73b FLPA/S. Charlie Brown; 74bl FLPA/Roger Wilmshurst; 75 WP/Kim Taylor; 76 BBC/Martha Holmes; 77bl BCC/Pacific Stock; 78t FLPA/W. Wisniewski, 78–79b FLPA/Silvestris, 79t MEPL, 79b Auscape/Wayne Lawler, 80b BCC/Pacific Stock; 81b NHPA/A.N.T.; 82b AL/Jim Zipp; 83 FLPA/S. Maslowski; 84tl FLPA/Derek Middleton, 84b OSF/Survival Anglia/Michael Pitts; 85b OSF/Alan & Sandy Carey; 86t FLPA/Gerard Lacz, 86bl FSP/Springer; 86br FSP/Springer; 87t Mr. & Mrs. Murray, Aylesbury, 87b WP/Jane Burton; 88–89 WP/Kim Taylor; 90c BCC/Kim Taylor, 90b OSF/G.I. Bernard; 91t OSF/Mike Hill, 91b MEPL/Brenda Hartill; 93b Auscape/Kevin Deacon; 94 OSF/Okapia/Jeff Foott; 95t NHPA/Anthony Bannister, 95b WP/Jane Burton; 96b WP/Jane Burton; 97t BBC/John Cancalosi; 97b Corbis/Gallo Images; 98–99 WP/Mark Taylor; 100c WP/Kim Taylor, 100b BCC/Bruce Coleman Inc; 101b AL/Werner Curth; 102 BCC/Bruce Coleman Inc; 103 NHPA/John Shaw; 104–105 NHPA/Daniel Heuclin, 105l FLPA/ Fotonatura/J. van Arkel, 105r BBC; 106l OSF/Okapia/John Cancalosi; 107t NHPA/Daniel Heuclin, 107b OSF/Daniel J. Cox; 108 BBC/Alan James; 109 AL/François Gohier; 110b National Oceanic & Atmospheric Administration; 111t NHPA/Karl Switak. 111b OAR/NURP/College of William and Mary; 112 NHPA/Stephen Dalton; 113t NHPA/M.I. Walker, 113b BBC; 114bl FLPA/Chris Newton, 114bl FPL/Booth Museum; 116–117 OSF/Michael Sewell; 118bl OSF/Tony Martin, 118br OSF/Richard Packwood; 119t Photo by Dennis Coutts, Shetland, 119b OSF/Survival Anglia/Dr. F. Köster; 120b Auscape/Michael Maconachie; 121 Auscape/Greg Harold; 122–123 FLPA/Roger Tidman, 122b WP/Jane Burton; 123r BCC/Joe McDonald; 124r FLPA/Silvestris; 125c WP/Kim Taylor; 125b OSF/Animals Animals/Joe & Carol McDonald; 126t NHPA/Daniel Heuclin, 126b BBC/Rico & Ruiz; 127l BBC/John Downer, 127r Cindy Pollock, Silver Cloud Farms, Oregon; 128l OSF/Animals Animals/Raymond A. Mendez; 129t NHPA/Anthony Bannister, 129b Nature Photographers Ltd./N.A. Callow; 130t OSF/Satoshi Kuribesyashi, 130b WP/Kim Taylor; 131bl OSF/Mike Birkhead, 131br OSF/Mike Linley; 132t WP/Jane Burton, 132c WP/Jane Burton, 132b WP/Jane Burton; 133 FLPA/David Hosking; 134c FPL/Göttingen Zoological Museum, Germany; 134b FPL/Göttingen Zoological Museum, Germany; 135 MEPL; 136b BBC/Mike Wilkes; 137l FLPA/David Hosking, 137r WP/Mark Taylor; 138–139 WP; 142r Corbis/Bettmann; 143 RF/SIPA Press 144–145 AL/François Gohier; 146l SF/Howard Hall; 146–147 OSF/Harold Taylor, 147b Photo copyrighted by The Dolphin Institute, Honolulu, HI; 148b; WP/Kim Taylor; 149 OSF/Neil Bromhall; 150 OSF/Harold Taylor; 151b FLPA/E.&D. Hosking; 152 RF/Gerald Davis; 153 RF; 154b BBC/Phil Chapman; 155l NHPA/Daniel Heuclin, 155r NHPA/Daniel Heuclin; 156 WP/Kim Taylor; 157t OSF/Mahipal Singh, 157b BCC/M.P.L. Fogden; 158–159 WP/Bruce Coleman Collection; 160b NHPA/Norbert Wu;

161t AL/Ron and Valerie Taylor, 161b OSF/Peter Parks; 162t Corbis/Yann-Arthus Bertrand, 162b NHPA/Nigel Dennis; 163 BBC/Jeff Rotman; 164t NHPA/Yves Lanceau, 164b WP/Jane Burton; 165b FLPA/Silvestris; 166tl NV/Heather Angel, 166tr NHPA/Image Quest 3-D; 167t FLPA/Life Science Images, 167b Biofoto/Peter Funch; 168c BBC/Adrian Davies; 169t OSF/Wendy Shattick & Bob Rozinski, 169c Matthew R. Gilligan, 169 inset Matthew R. Gilligan; 170c FLPA/J. Watkins, 170 inset FLPA/Maurice Walker; 171t FLPA/John Watkins, 171b NHPA/Haroldo Palo Jr.; 172 NV/Jeremy Thomas, 172–173 OSF/Peter O'Toole, 173t OSF/J.A.L. Cooke, 174b NHPA/Stephen Dalton; 175t SF/Survival Anglia/Alan Root, 175b © J. Emmett Duffy, 1995; 176l BBC/Neil Bromhall, 176r FLPA/R. Austing; 177 NHPA/Stephen Dalton; 178–179 BBC/Peter Oxford; 180l NHPA/E.A. Janes; 181t FLPA/Terry Whittaker, 181b AL/Adrian Warren; 182 FLPA/Terry Whittaker; 183bl NHPA/E.A. Janes, 183br BCC/Hans Reinhard; 184t NHPA/E.A. Janes, 184b BCC/Jane Burton; 185l AL/D. Parer & E. Parer-Cook, 185r BCC/Hans Reinhard; 186bl NHPA/Steve Robinson, 186br AL/Adrian Warren; 187l OSF/Clive Bromhall, 187r AL/Adrian Warren; 188t AL/François Gohier, 188b Dr. Rachel Smolker; 189t OSF/Survival Anglia/Dr. F. Koster, 189c NV/J. M. Pearson, 189b AL/Hans & Judy Beste; 190t FLPA/W.B. Withers, 190bl BCC/Kim Taylor, 190br AL/M. Watson; 191t FLPA/B. Burrell Casals, 191b AL/Adrian Warren; 192b Phil Starling; 193 Popperfoto; 194t Phil Starling, 194b WP/Jane Burton; 195t Camera Press Ltd./Karsh, 195b Popperfoto; 196–197; NHPA/Andy Rouse; 198–199 AL/Jagdeep Rajput, 199t WP/Jane Burton; 200 WP/Jane Burton; 201b BBC/Rico & Ruiz; 202 WP; 203 OSF/Konrad Wothe; 204t WP/Jane Burton, 204 inset FLPA/Terry Whittaker, 204b WP; 205c AL/Doug Napier, 205b Axiom Photographic Agency/Paul Quayle; 206t RF/Chat, 206b OSF/Okapia/Joan Root; 207 Corbis; 208b AL/François Gohier, 208 inset OSF/Mark Jones; 209 AKG Photo, London/Erich Lessing; 210t BBC/Jeff Rotman, 210b PA Photos/EPA; 211 Martin Cavaney Photography Ltd.; 212–213 OSF/Konrad Wothe; 214c NHPA/Steve Robinson; 215 BBC/Anup Shah; 216t BBC/Dietmar Nill, 216–217 BCC/Gunter Ziesler, 217t NHPA/Daniel Heuclin; 218t AL/Chris Harvey, 218b WP/Jane Burton; 219c Natural Science Photos/Carol Farneti Foster, 219b BBC/Thomas D. Mangelsen; 220t OSF/Dieter & Mary Plage, 220b NASA; 221Nature Photographers Ltd./Colin Carver; 222b WP/Kim Taylor; 223l WP/Jane Burton, 223r WP/Jane Burton; 224t WP/Jane Burton, 224b FLPA/Jurgen & Christine Sohns; 225c PA Photos/Tony Harris, 225b PA Photos/Ben Curtis; 226 RF/Phil Coale; 227t Corbis/Tom Nebbia, 227b FSP/Gamma Liaison/David Creamer; 228t Corbis/Yann Arthus-Bernard, 228b Corbis/David A. Northcott; 229c FSP/Gamma/ Point de Vue/David Atlan, 229b FSP/Gamma/ Point de Vue/David Atlan; 230 BBC/Jeff Rotman; 231 RF/SIPA Press/Ilhami.

DISCLAIMER
The author and publishers have sought permission for the use of all illustrations and substantial quotations known by them to be still in copyright. Any omissions brought to their attention will be rectified in future editions of this work.